The Brothers Krimm

The bank robber and the hero

Cecile Wehrman (signature)

By Cecile Wehrman
with H. Rob Krimm and Charlene Krimm

H R Krimm (signature)
USAF/USMC
Ret.

PREFACE

Jimmy

September 14, 2009

More than anything, Jimmy liked to drive.

Just the feeling of being in control, being able to go wherever he wanted, the open road in front of him—that was freedom.

Freedom was a commodity Jimmy couldn't take for granted. He'd spent too much of his life locked up not to appreciate doing what he wanted, when he wanted, where and for how long he wanted.

He'd been guarding that freedom for three years. He wasn't about to give it up. At forty-two, he was a three-time loser, with thirteen of the past twenty-two years spent in prison.

Prison hadn't given him anything upon which to build a life as a free man; it only made him a better criminal.

The freedom to do as he pleased didn't come cheap—and that meant robbing banks.

It was an easy leap. He'd been doing armed holdups since he was a kid back in Michigan. Pointing a gun at a clerk in a party store at the age of seventeen wasn't much different than pulling a gun on a bank teller. The gun did all the talking. It was the easiest money he ever made.

"Cash-money-spew" was how he thought of it back then—and still did.

Man, what a rush!

You go into some place, pull a gun, grab the cash, get away, take the haul home, and buy whatever you want. Cash meant all the booze you could drink. Weed. Women.

When he used to hold up shops in Michigan, he'd come back to his mom's house and throw the bills on the carpet.

"Cash-money-spew," he'd say, as he let the bills fall to the floor. It might only amount to a hundred bucks or so. But back then, it seemed like a lot.

His only audience for these triumphs was his little brother, Harry. His mom was always at work. His dad hadn't been around for years. It was every man for himself. And Jimmy was good at taking what he wanted.

It started with candy bars. He discovered at the age of nine or ten that Heath bars were the best. They were slim and easy to conceal. It was a cakewalk.

Harry was such a wuss; he couldn't even steal a candy bar. It was easy to palm one and slip it up your sleeve. Harry tried it one time and choked.

Every man for himself. Harry could steal his own candy bars or go without.

Harry Robert. He went by "Rob" now, Jimmy reminded himself. *That's funny. I'm a robber, and my brother is a "Rob."*

That whole thing about Harry changing his name was just stupid, Jimmy thought. And to prove it, he stole his brother's identity and lived under it for a year. He'd even held a job. As a felon, and a felon on the lam at that, Jimmy couldn't get a job using his own name and Social Security number. If Harry wouldn't use his name, Jimmy could.

He would have liked to have been a fly on the wall when Harry found out. Hey, bro!

Harry turned out all right, though. *Joined the fucking Marines.* Jimmy tried to join the army, but they wouldn't take him. Fuck the army.

But Harry would always be Harry, not "Rob."

Growing up, Jimmy figured it wasn't his job to look out for anybody or teach anybody anything. Nobody looked out for him. Harry was just a tagalong nuisance most of the time. And Jimmy didn't need a tagalong. He didn't need anybody really. He was good at the solitary life. No ties. Just the open road.

At least, until lately. Lately, he'd begun to wonder again, about his dad. They'd even exchanged a few letters.

Jimmy hadn't seen or talked to his mother in sixteen years. It would have been nice to get the care packages when he was in prison in Canada, like he had back in Michigan. But he'd burned that bridge. Ma was not likely to help him out again.

Just to mess with her, one time, he'd mailed her a bunch of $2 bills. He addressed the envelope the same way he had when he used to write to her from the pen in Michigan—to "C. Krimm."

It had been more than a dozen years, but the address was etched in his memory. It was the only home he'd ever known. And she was still there.

He'd looked her up on the Internet. Sure enough, nothing had changed. She was probably still waitressing somewhere, still collecting things like silver dollars and $2 bills. It just seemed pointless to Jimmy. Money was for buying stuff, not collecting. That she would collect money when they had so little to begin with made Jimmy mad.

So he'd sent her those $2 bills to replace the ones he'd stolen before. She was pissed when she saw they were missing. Well, she could have her $2 bills. It wasn't like he was going to go around spending them. Who carried a wad of $2 bills? That would only draw attention.

He'd gotten the bills he sent her the same place he'd gotten all his cash: from a bank.

He'd learned a lot in his second prison stretch.

Armed holdups were easy; he'd learned that as a kid. When he graduated to robbing banks in Canada, he learned it was the getting away that really required some discipline, but he'd become sloppy. You had to be careful about where you robbed a bank and how often. He'd had seven years in a Canadian prison to figure all of those angles and learn from the fuckups of others, not to mention his own.

The fact was tellers were trained to give you what you wanted. Getting the money was the easiest part. But getting away, that was the finesse part. Just like the job he planned to do today. He'd scoped out a bank in Williston, North Dakota, a couple of years earlier on his way back from a job in Weyburn, Saskatchewan. Williston was the first big town in the States he came to after that. It was almost directly south, about 120 miles.

It was a sweet setup in Williston. It was tempting to do the job then, but that would break one of his rules. The reason bank robbers got caught was they got too greedy. Or they talked. Jimmy was greedy, but he wasn't stupid. And it wasn't like he had a lot of friends to blab to.

His number-one rule was "rob when you're hungry," not just because you can.

Most serial bank bandits he knew in prison told the same story. They'd hit five, six banks in a matter of days or just a few weeks, all in the same area. Stupid. Some of them even pulled more than one job the *same day*. These guys were whack jobs. You didn't have to be a rocket scientist to know you don't rob two banks in *one day*—well, unless the first one was a bust. It could happen.

If you were smart, you spread them out, let some time go by, put some miles on your car, and let things cool off a little.

But that also meant getting a big enough haul you could afford to be choosey. You didn't get enough money emptying one teller drawer. Jimmy could testify to that. He'd hauled in $39,000 robbing single-teller drawers over eighteen months in Canada, but it could easily have been five times that if he had controlled those banks, emptied all the drawers. That was how he did it these days. Same risk, same effort, many times the reward.

Too many of the bank robbers he knew were fueling a serious drug habit. That was what got them into trouble. The junkies robbed because they needed a fix, and besides that, the drugs made them stupid. Sure, he liked to smoke a little weed, and he was not above drinking his way into oblivion. But he wasn't stupid.

So, he'd seen this bank in Williston. He was always scouting future jobs wherever his travels took him.

Williston was just your typical Midwestern town, like so many others he'd seen. Being confronted by an armed robber was as foreign a notion to people in Williston as a flying saucer landing in their yard—not like in his old neighborhood south of Detroit. People *expected* to be robbed in Detroit.

But these prairie towns had virtually no crime. They actually bragged about it in the papers, like that was all they had to say to recommend the place? As if people were going to forget it got down to twenty below zero in the winter or that the only whores were black and shipped in from places like Milwaukee. Sheesh. He wasn't above getting some black ass, and he didn't really care if they were cute, but man, he got tired of the yakking—"Baby, this" and "Baby, that." *Just shut up and let me fuck you!*

Hell, he'd try to fuck anything once. One book he read had a name for that. They called it a "try-sexual." That was a good one! But it wasn't like he was gay or anything.

He'd had his fill of niggers in the joint. That fucking rap music! Niggers ruined prison. If not for niggers, prison was actually not that bad. They fed you. You got to spend most of your time just hanging out. You could even get weed.

But those niggers! It was just constant noise and commotion. Sometimes, he'd have to share a cell with one. But he had a remedy for that. It worked every time. If they put you in a cell with a nigger, all you had to do was make a shank—and not even a good one.

The first time he'd been moved to make a shank, he'd planned to kill a nigger. Then he'd gotten caught with the shank, which only added time to his own sentence. That was when he realized you didn't actually have to kill the nigger, just hide the shank under the nigger's bed and nark on him. That was how you got a nigger out of your cell.

Hurting a nigger was kind of like hurting a teller in a bank. It wasn't *necessary*. Why get your hands dirty? Why expend all that effort and time?

He had to admit, he liked North Dakota. Other than the whores, no niggers—no niggers anywhere.

Another rule about robbing banks was you had to be quick—two minutes, in and out. All the books said so. And he'd had time to read plenty in prison. That cracked him up too. How stupid were these people who stocked prison libraries? Prison libraries were full of books that told you stuff only cops—or criminals—would know. And they were giving these books to criminals? Now that was *stupid*.

Jimmy figured he had the equivalent of a college degree in crime, after reading all those books.

This Williston bank was sweet because of its location. It was on one of the busiest intersections on the outskirts of town. Plus, it would be easy to conceal his car where bank employees couldn't see it. You could walk in, do the job, and get back to your car in twenty, thirty seconds flat. You could drive away, and no one would have any idea which direction you went or what color your car was. Simple. That was the key.

"KISS—keep it simple, stupid." He'd read that in a book.

When he'd first started robbing banks, he'd made the mistake of making it too complicated, with different disguises and shit. Hell, none of that mattered. He'd had seven years to figure out simplicity was the key. He didn't even wear a mask most of the time. It was too dramatic. A mask tended to freak people out, and they'd just freeze.

All of his jobs went pretty much the same. He'd park the car in a concealed spot, walk into the bank from one direction, walk through the little swinging door to get behind the teller line, walk all the way to the end of the line, and make his demand from there, tapping the barrel of the gun on the counter to let 'em know he meant business. He'd collect the money as he walked back toward the door, walk out the door, walk back to the car, preferably making a big circle, so he wasn't coming and going the same way twice, and get in his car. Then, he'd drive away, but not out of town at first. He'd turn a few corners, and then drive out of town and not go back. Well, you could go back, and Jimmy had done that, robbing one bank a second time in Minnesota. But there were months in between those two jobs.

This Williston bank fit the scenario perfectly. He knew once he spotted it, it would only be a matter of time before he came back. He'd found plenty of easy pickings in between, but things were getting a little hot in his usual territory—down along the border between North and South Dakota.

He was actually on his way back from vacation—a camping trip with s'mores and Jack Daniels. Great combination. He'd spent a couple of weeks in Idaho. Aside from the asshole partiers who'd flipped him off and called him a faggot and the fact he'd chased them and wound up getting his second DUI in two years, it was a good trip. He'd also done a little business out there.

He'd stashed a car in a storage unit. He'd just bought it from a want ad in the paper. Naturally, he paid cash.

He had cars stashed in storage units all over. The cars were all legally registered and licensed, with an address he maintained almost solely for that purpose. There was no sense driving around in a stolen car, or in one with expired tags. That was just stupid.

And the beauty of having these cars stashed was, if he ever got in a tight spot, all he had to do was get to a storage unit—preferably across the state line from where he had robbed the bank—pull up to the unit, back out the "clean" car, place the "dirty" car inside, and drive away. Simple.

He liked doing jobs along the borders of states. It tended to fuck with the police. He had a scanner. He knew. Cops might put out a bulletin on their state radio, but different states had different systems. They couldn't always talk to each other. So a bank robbed in Williston, North Dakota, might as well be on the moon as far as a cop in Montana was concerned. The Montana cop probably wouldn't even find out about it until Jimmy was long gone in the clean car.

The clean car was just insurance. Most of the time, the color of the dirty car was not even reported. If it wasn't, it was good to use that car as the "clean" car the next time. He'd know whether or not the car was identified by watching the news. That was fun.

Sometimes, they'd broadcast the bank video. Sweet! *Look, Ma, I'm robbing a bank!* One time, he robbed a bank the day before his birthday, just to see himself on TV. Now *that* was a happy birthday. Cash-money-spew!

He'd been successful with this setup for years. He prided himself on the discipline it took to stretch out a spree that long. No reason he couldn't keep it going.

He'd been hearing on the news about some old duffer in San Diego, some senior citizen who was holding up banks. And he was getting away with it! Talk about a retirement plan!

For the first time in his life, Jimmy felt like a success. He had finally found something he was good at. And you didn't need some piece of paper to prove you could do the job. You didn't need a license. You didn't have to pass some test. That was freedom.

And the "cash-money-spew" was awesome. Walking around with a thousand bucks in your pocket, there was no feeling in the world like it.

Though he didn't think of it often—no sense setting yourself up for failure—Jimmy had given the possibility of capture enough thought over the years to know he was not going back to prison. Ever.

If the jig was up, it was up. No sense lollygagging around. He was forty-two fucking years old. Too old for prison bullshit.

He'd robbed so many banks now, capture meant life. Once they got you on one bank, they'd connect the dots and throw away the key.

Well, that wasn't really true. Capture didn't have to mean life. It could mean death. And if that's the way it went down, so be it. Just pull the trigger. Either shoot at the cops or shoot yourself.

The idea of shooting at someone, if it was him or them, didn't bother Jimmy. He'd never been faced with that choice, but he was pretty sure he could do it. Shit happens, ya know? Especially when you drink too much. But what was the sense in shooting at a bunch of cops when the end result was gonna be the same? You shoot at them; they shoot at you. Bam! You're dead.

You might as well keep the control. Die on your own terms. If it came to that, it came to that.

Every man for himself.

PART ONE

CHAPTER ONE

Cecile

September 14, 2009

You'd think I'd have some warning, some feeling something is amiss. But no.

I am just glad to be headed home to an evening alone, sans kids and husband, all of my stories filed and waiting to be assembled for the newspaper's weekly edition, hungry to vegetate in front of my computer and whatever movie I can watch on Netflix. Oblivion is what I seek, a chance to switch my brain to the "off" position.

I find an indie flick with a description that reads like a cheap novel, but it turns out to be surprisingly deep. I am absorbed by the story and hardly look away from the screen once in two hours, though I sit next to a window with a view of the road leading from the hill, half a mile from our house, to our driveway. Soon enough, the movie ends and the kids are home from the volleyball match they'd begged to attend.

It is time to huddle over who has what to do the next day and at what time. Does Mick work tomorrow? Is Cathleen's homework done? Does she need a shower? It is nearly 9:30 PM on a Monday, and my busiest day of the week, laying out the weekly newspaper, looms. I want to be in bed early.

The phone rings, and Cathleen hands it to me mouthing, "Grandma."

"I didn't want to tell Cathleen this; I know how she gets," my mother-in-law, Wanda, begins, "but there's an armed bank robber on the loose and they lost him somewhere between Alkabo and Westby."

Alkabo is two miles from our house, as the crow flies, and Westby, nine.

To understand the full impact of Wanda's news, you have to understand where we live. Elkhorn Township is about as sparsely populated as any place in our county of under two thousand people, in a state with fewer people than live in most medium-sized cities. North Dakota contains less than six hundred fifty thousand residents, and the nearest "town" to me has a population of seven. That would be Alkabo.

But we don't say we're from Alkabo. Our address is Fortuna, five miles west and fifteen people larger.

Our "neighborhood" stretches from the Canadian border seven miles north, to the Montana border nine miles west, to the county seat of Crosby twenty-six miles east, which is where our children go to school. Williston is the nearest "big" town. It's sixty miles to the south and has about fifteen thousand people. Nowhere in this landscape do the words *armed bank robber* belong.

"He stole a car from a farmyard south of Westby, and he's apparently headed this way. He's driving a black Nissan pickup," Wanda continues. "He's six foot three, 265 pounds, and may be carrying a case of Diet Mountain Dew."

Diet Mountain Dew? Is the green box camouflage for the money he stole? Is he dieting? But I skip over these inanities, quickly calculating how fast he could be on my doorstep.

Because my husband works in the booming Bakken oil field, overnights alone on our farmstead in the middle of nowhere have become routine for me and the kids. We never lock our doors. The last time we went on vacation, we had to lock our front door from the inside and leave through the side door, because the key for the main entry was lost at some point after 1991, when we moved in.

Our vehicles are never locked.

A huge gasoline tank sits in our yard full of $3-a-gallon fuel. No lock.

Our big four-wheel-drive pickup sits in the driveway with a handgun under the seat. My husband carries a concealed weapons permit, as do dozens of other members of our rural community, who are always prepared for danger, even though none ever comes. No lock on the pickup. No lock on the gun.

Every window in the house is unlocked. Several screens are missing. It is Indian summer, and we're still enjoying mild nights when the temperature stays above fifty-five degrees. A bank robber is on the loose a few miles from my home, and for once, I am glad for all the guns we have in our house.

Now, mind you, I have not fired a gun in years. I've always been a pretty good shot, but I've had little practice. The kids have spent the summer taking pot shots at the gopher colony that has taken hold in our yard lately. My son, Mick, looks for any excuse to take his dad's AR-15 out into the yard, even though he knows he's not supposed to touch it without his dad to supervise. Just the day before, Mick claimed to have spotted a mountain lion in our trees. The use of a semiautomatic weapon for personal protection seems perfectly logical in his sixteen-year-old mind. Lord knows, mountain lions are dangerous and have been the only kind of dangerous predator we've been frightened by until now.

There's a bank robber on the loose—between Alkabo and Westby. My nearest neighbor is my mother-in-law, up on the highway, a mile and a half away. A big green highway sign advertises a lake with an arrow pointing at the road we live on, and no one has any reason to drive on this gravel track at 9:30 PM on a school night, lake or no lake, unless it's one of us.

No matter how Cathleen "gets"—neurotic, overexcited, panicky—there's going to be no keeping this news quiet. It's not like turning down the TV to cover the tone for a tornado warning. At least with a weather alert, a parent can surreptitiously walk from window to window, eyeing the sky so an eleven-year-old doesn't have a conniption because she thinks our house is going to be sucked up into the clouds like Dorothy's in *The Wizard of Oz*.

No, this alert requires action—quick, sure, and overt.

"Mick, go out to the garage and take the keys out of the cars and lock them, and get the keys out of the pickup, too. There's a bank robber on the loose between Alkabo and Westby, and the police have lost him."

I don't add, "Grab the AR-15 on your way out," but of course, he does.

He disappears into the shadows between the house and the garage, not thirty steps away.

"Cathleen, I want you to lock all of the windows. And don't come back telling me they're stuck."

Faced with a real crisis, potentially as deadly as any natural disaster, she shows not a hint of fright.

Before Cathleen is finished with the windows, Mick is back, hunting up the .22, which is Cathleen's gopher-dispatching tool of choice. Only I am left unarmed, unless you count the telephone. I make a call to my publisher, but the line is busy. So I call our sometime photographer, Don, in Crosby. He has a scanner. He hasn't heard anything, so I dial Steve once again. I quickly advise him that no matter what happens from this point on, we're likely to have a very different newspaper to put together than the one we had half in the bag when we left the office at five o'clock.

I hang up, and the phone rings again. It is our oldest daughter, Catrina, newly off to college and a little homesick. I tell her what's going on and that I have to get off the phone. She is slightly miffed that the biggest thing ever to happen in her hometown is taking place when she is not there.

I call my husband, who is out on an oil rig, about one hundred miles from our house. That he answers is a miracle, considering cell service is poor in these parts. He reminds me of the handgun in the pickup but doesn't think of what dawns on all of us until later: that if a bank robber comes into our yard on the run and he finds a vehicle unlocked, he's going to be leaving very soon and very fast. But if he finds a vehicle locked, he's gonna come looking for the keys.

I send Mick, to whom all distasteful jobs fall when Dad is away, out to the pickup to get the handgun. He clutches the AR-15 in one hand and with the other takes the .22 from Cathleen.

He gives me the .22 and says, "Cover me."

It is at this moment I realize we are acting just a little silly. If there is a bank robber in our neighborhood, we're going to be able to spot him from a long way off. The headlights of any vehicle turning off the highway and heading down our road will be visible for three-quarters of a mile or more—assuming the headlights are on.

And what if a hulking figure, case of Diet Mountain Dew in hand, did lumber up the long driveway from the road. What are we going to do? Shoot him? Or be shot at?

Freeze? Hide, maybe?

And what were the odds, honestly, that out of the many farmyards dotting the neighborhood, he'd find his way to ours? Truly, it would be like finding a needle in a haystack—a very remote haystack, with the other needles in the package out of sight and earshot.

I call my mother-in-law, hoping for more news. There is nothing on the radio, and just a short blurb on the Williston newspaper's Web site about a bank robbery at gunpoint at 5:00 PM. This is when I realize I had been, literally, a sitting duck for most of the evening, home alone.

Wanda is getting scared. She suggests we come over to her house. I decline. The only thing that sounds worse to me than meeting the robber in my own home is running into him on a dark road or getting caught in some crossfire. If people are running around with guns, I decide, I'm staying put.

"I think we're better off staying where we are," I tell her and hang up.

So, we wait. For what? We are not sure.

I question Mick about whether our guns are on safety. I watch where the switches are, and he shows me how to pull back the slider thing on the top of my gun. I don't even know what kind of gun it is. I just know it looks cool, and it makes a savage sound when you cock it— *tck-tck*— steel on steel. The last thing we need is one of us shooting the other. I make the statement that if you have a gun, you're that much more likely to get shot, but we don't put the guns away.

We debate whether it is better to have the lights on or off. Will it scare a robber away if someone is obviously home? Or will it tempt him to take hostages?

Crazy thoughts run through my mind, like, *Can I talk my way out of a dangerous situation? Reason with him? Offer him the car keys and a map of back roads to Canada?*

We settle for lights off, the better to view the distant hill, from whence, we are sure, he will come.

Headlights! Oh my god! Oh my god! Oh my god!

Headlights coming over the hill! Sure enough!

Mick is at the side door. I am in the entryway. Cathleen is starting to get just a little freaked out.

I know just about exactly how long it takes the average lake camper on a late-night beer run to drive down that hill and past our house. Everyone, beer or no beer, drives fast on our road—too fast, fast enough you might think they were a robber fleeing police.

But this vehicle isn't going fast. It is taking its time. Hesitant, almost.

No one drives up our road that slowly, and this scares me. When the kids were little, we actually thought about putting up one of those signs that read, "Kids at Play," just to try to slow people down, but no one had slowed down, until now.

I see his lights flash as he makes the hairpin turn, not a quarter of a mile from our house. It seems like it is taking forever for him to get to us.

Again, I ask myself, *What am I going to do?*

I swear to myself if that vehicle so much as hesitates at the end of our driveway, the safety will be off the handgun, the window will be opened, and I will say something like, "Stop or I'll shoot." Or, I'll just shoot. I know I will.

I guess we'll see, I think. My heart is not even pounding, I realize. There is utter calm and composure. I am in limbo, like that moment before a lion springs toward its prey. But which am I?

The vehicle creeps toward the driveway slowly enough it could pull in, but it doesn't. It's a dark, full-size pickup. Is a Nissan full-size or medium-size? Or little, like the old Datsun pickups? I've never been good with such things.

I exhale as it goes by, noting no markings to indicate it belongs to a lawman, yet no proof it is a criminal's. What do I do? Am I supposed to call someone?

I call Wanda. She answers, in a whisper.

"I'm in the bathroom," she hisses. "There are five cop cars in my driveway. They're just sitting here."

I tell her about the truck that went by, but for some reason, intuition tells me, it's not the guy. If it was him, we speculate, he would have stopped, wouldn't he?

We hang up after agreeing to call back with any news.

That's when we see the lights in the sky. It looks like helicopters, circling, except one doesn't really move. They seem awfully close, in fact, at times, it seems they are between our place and Wanda's, in the hills, up by the abandoned radar base. We've always said it would be the perfect place for the next Waco-style standoff—with an eighty-foot-tall concrete bunker, the walls two feet thick.

We watch and speculate as the lights travel back and forth across the night sky. Mick offers, "This is actually kind of fun."

We are now camped out in the dining room, near the door that faces the road. Mick starts screwing around with the light switch for the porch, which has a blue light in it—don't ask me why. He flicks the switch on and off, on and off.

"Cut that out!" I say. "What if they see that and think it's some sort of a distress signal!"

Next, he wants to open the door, just to see if we can hear anything. We can't.

By now, it is nearly 11:00 PM, and still, we wait, watching.

The lights in the sky seem like they are in a holding pattern. We take that as a good sign.

I call Wanda again, and she reports the cops have just sped off from her driveway. A couple headed up the highway in one direction, the rest in the other, both away from us.

We take that as another good sign. They must know where he is now, and he does not appear to be in our backyard.

It is now 11:20, and I know tomorrow is going to be one of those days. No matter what else happens, I'll be calling the sheriff in the morning, trying, on deadline, to get as much information as possible for the weekly Wednesday edition. That's my job.

I give thanks to the news gods that this happened on a Monday night, rather than a Tuesday, so we can run the story at the same time as the dailies, instead of getting scooped. After twenty-four years in the news business, I can't help but look at it that way, even if I have spent the past two hours living the story.

The lights in the sky fade. The mood is suddenly different. I'm tired.

I let Wanda know we're going to bed. She promises to call if she hears for sure that it's over.

Mick takes the AR-15 to his room. I lean the .22 against the couch in the living room, and for the first time in my life, I lay my head on a pillow next to a handgun on my nightstand.

I am nearly asleep when the phone rings fifteen minutes later. It is Wanda. She has heard from the people at the bar in Fortuna.

"They got him."

I hang up the phone, not really knowing what that means. My imagination conjures the image of a man, hands up in a flood of light, surrounded by a bunch of police, guns drawn. For some reason, I assume it must be some local guy, some desperate farmer or some kid juiced on meth, someone familiar with the area. For how else, of all places, does a bank robber wind up in Fortuna, North Dakota?

There's no sense wondering. I know it will all be unraveled in the morning. All I really care about at this moment is sleep. Just sleep.

We are safe. It is over.

It isn't until a few days later I realize the story has only begun. It's a story that will test all of my skills as a researcher. I will have to examine my ethics as a journalist. I will have to open old wounds, personal wounds. My faith will be shaken. Inconsequential things, something as simple as finding a penny, will take on new meaning. My marriage of nineteen years will dissolve. And it won't be until many months into it that my research will uncover an inexplicable connection to this robber—this man who terrorized my neighborhood. It is a fact so startling it literally knocks me to the ground.

CHAPTER TWO

On Deadline

September 15–17, 2009

I feel just a little foolish when I hit the snooze button on my alarm clock and my hand grazes the gun I laid on my nightstand the night before. I still can't believe it. I sat with my children, all of us armed, watching for some bank robber on the loose. Crazy.

I'd been sitting there feeling like twenty-four years of journalism experience had brought me no closer to my story of a lifetime. I had stopped even believing anything like that awaited me. I just wanted to escape.

It was a pattern I'd fallen into over the previous year. I'd been disappointed months earlier when I'd lost a bid to be elected to the state legislature. I was bored with covering the same old stories I'd covered for ten years at *The Journal*. My husband was gone for days on end, working in the oil field, and I didn't really mind. His presence, when he was home, ruffled me. With one child recently off to college, the demands on my time eased, but instead of motivating me to give more attention to my other kids, it just made me wish they were independent too.

I was tired of trying to be a good wife and tired of feeling guilty for being a working mother. I was coming face-to-face with the reality that some long-held dreams might never come true—like finding my story of a lifetime or winning an election to effect real change.

But then the phone call from my mother-in-law, telling me there was a bank robber on the loose, went off like a bomb.

If that robber had come to my door, I would have opened it and offered a friendly greeting. It was chilling to realize how easily I could have been taken hostage. This life I'd lately been so "blah" about could have been over in a heartbeat.

I flip on the radio to hear the news from Williston, just like I do every morning, trying to get some information to give me a jump on the day while I get ready for work. I hope the station might have a few details to help me plot my course. *The Journal*, located a half hour distant in the county seat of Crosby, goes to press today.

Figures. If there is one coda to my work life, it is if something big does happen, I can count on writing the story on deadline. I have no clue who this robber is, where he came from, or whether he lived or died. The radio news is regurgitating facts known the night before. They don't even have as much as I gleaned from the neighborhood grapevine.

As we set out for our half-hour morning commute, my eleven-year-old daughter chatters about the night before, recounting from the time she and her older brother, Mick, came home from a volleyball game to the point when he'd gone outside and asked me to "cover him." That little snippet was destined for the family hall of fame, an anecdote we could trot out whenever the subject of the "bank robber" came up.

My gut tells me it had to be a local, and I already have a couple of characters in my mental lineup. How else does someone end up in the middle of nowhere, south of Fortuna, North Dakota, surrounded by police, with airplanes flying overhead? I still can't believe it. A bank robber! In Divide County!

The term *ghost town* doesn't really fit, but to anyone driving past Fortuna, the idea of obeying the reduced-speed sign on the edge of town would seem silly. I certainly never touch the brakes anymore. With barely twenty people still in residence, if there are such things as ghosts, it is easy to believe they can outnumber the living.

Looking at it these days, it is easy to assume Fortuna never amounted to a damn, but it had thrived for a time. Fifty years earlier, as many as 250 people called Fortuna home. Prosperity came from a U.S. Air Force radar post erected a few miles west of town. The base brought several Fortuna daughters a husband, including my mom. The base provided customers for the grocery store on Main Street, not that airmen were likely to need the buttonhooks still stocked in ceiling-high dry goods cases. The airmen brought cars that needed filling at the gas station and tires that needed replacing. There was even a six-unit motel, each room sitting like a separate little dollhouse in a neat row by the highway, for travelers who wouldn't think of expecting anything so lush as a continental breakfast or a pool.

Fortuna is the place I spent idyllic childhood summers with my grandparents, but now, each morning as I drive by on my way to work, seeing the town is just a little depressing. I think it was the grocery store that closed first, in the late 1970s, and not long after, the motel. On the south side of the highway, the gym in the old schoolhouse has been converted to a mechanic shop with cars parked every which way on the old playground, like a used car lot. The gas station burned down in the nineties, and the owners took it as a sign they should stay closed. All that remained on Main Street on the night a bank robber entered the neighborhood was a bar, a post office, a fire hall, and a senior citizens center—all four of which could easily fit within the footprint of the huge grain elevator on the north edge of town. Three old churches claimed space in the community, but only one of them still operated—with a handful of stalwart Christians whose number could barely throw a potluck supper together. The high steeple of the long-abandoned Catholic Church, rumor had it, had served the night before as a roost for a couple of locals with high-powered weapons, hoping to plug a bank bandit.

Normally, Fortuna is the kind of town where outsiders are welcomed for the chance to exercise little-used hospitality muscles. The people are almost hungry for the chance to look, however temporarily, at the face of someone whose family did not homestead in the vicinity one hundred years ago. Such a traveler might assume nothing has ever happened and nothing will ever happen in Fortuna, aside from the endless cycle of weather—winter, spring, summer, fall, but mostly, winter.

Until lately, they would have been right. In fact, virtually my whole lifetime, nothing much happened in Fortuna except for an endless cycle of decline, each generation returning fewer graduates. Hell, the average age of farmers in the county was nearing sixty! Even children with a tie to the land didn't stay because they'd seen how hard their parents struggled. Lately, however, young people have been returning, or moving in from other places to take oil-field jobs. Lately, there are lots of unfamiliar faces, and the oil boom is new enough people are still pretty welcoming, wanting to believe these are all nice young men, hardworking, even hard partying, but nice.

I'd come back to the land of my youth 19 years ago because I felt it would be a great place to raise a family, but the place I remembered from childhood didn't exist anymore. Lately, as the oil rigs sprouted like giant weeds in the middle of every wheat field, it was clear not all of the future changes in the environment would be positive.

Before the boom, one could at least appreciate the unbroken roll of grass stretching for miles. You could even laugh smugly at the thought of a thirty-mile commute in any other locale taking twice that amount of time on the road or revel in the knowledge you never had to stand in line for a movie or a meal. Now, even those few perks were disappearing.

After dropping Cathleen off at the elementary school in Crosby, I navigate the few blocks to *The Journal* office. I have already warned Steve, my publisher, that the front page will have to change. We have a new lead story set to run with a banner headline across the top. Somehow, I am going to have to collect the facts to write that story, quickly.

I know the sheriff isn't likely to say much, but I place the call. I have grown accustomed, over the years, to the deflection of virtually all inquiries about any but the most mundane of cases. Anytime he had real police news, it seemed like the sheriff called in the North Dakota Bureau of Criminal Investigation, and they never released any information. Chief Deputy Rob Melby answers the phone and tells me the robber is dead. I don't know why I am so shocked. Shit!

"How'd it happen?" I ask.

"You're gonna have to call Williston. But the guy shot himself."

"Wow. Crazy," is all I can muster.

"Thank God nobody got hurt except the 'bad' guy," Melby adds.

I know from my contact with Wanda the night before that people all over the community had armed themselves, lying in wait for the opportunity to defend their lives and property. I dial Spencer Legaard, whose home is located on the highway west of Fortuna, right near where the robber had to have left the roadway in the final chase.

A former deputy himself, Spencer probably didn't get too excited, but I know he's a talker.

"We're pretty well armed," he tells me, mischievously.

Fortuna resident Gary Rust tells me people in town kept themselves informed by passing tidbits heard on scanners.

"A person gets pretty darned nervous," he says, "with little information—only the knowledge that a potentially desperate criminal is on the loose." I could vouch for that.

Everyone had been on the lookout for a dark-colored Nissan pickup stolen from Cec and Jerry Raaum. I dial the Raaum's number, connecting with Jerry. Like me, they'd had no idea of a manhunt until quite late in the evening.

"We went outside and saw the pickup was gone," he says. "He just came right up in the farmyard and took it."

Next, I dial Detective Mark Hanson in Williston. He says the manhunt began after a gun-toting bandit approached tellers at the American State Bank in Williston, demanding money. A green sedan was seen leaving the area. About a half hour later, a Montana Highway Patrol trooper was shot at near Bainville, Montana, with the suspect's gunshots disabling his patrol vehicle.

I can't believe the story I am hearing! A dead bank robber? Troopers being shot at? Events like this may be an everyday occurrence in bigger cities, but in my corner of the world, they are unheard of. I scribble madly, wanting to be sure to catch every detail.

Though the suspect managed to elude police several times in the course of the evening, Hanson says, he got hung up in a rock pile in a durum wheat field near the Raaum place and had to hike about a quarter of a mile to get to their farmyard to steal their pickup. The robber left everything behind in his car except his gun, a scanner, and a backpack filled with cash.

Later, two police planes assisted officers from up to twelve different agencies, all converging on an area a few miles south of the Legaard place. They surrounded the stolen pickup, which got stuck in a slough about four miles south of town.

"The individual did exit the vehicle and took his own life with a handgun," Hanson says, quoting from a written release. He can't provide an ID on the robber.

"I'm not sure who he really is," he says. The robber carried various IDs, all of which needed to be checked out.

I am not called to do it very often in Crosby, but I know how to work a story on deadline. The fact I know or am a neighbor to just about every source I need to call certainly helps at a time like this. Talk about having a story handed to you on a silver platter! I have quotes and the basic story in less than thirty minutes.

I am pretty confident my angle about gun-toting vigilante farmers will best any color the *Williston Herald* can come up with. Besides,

I expect their story to focus more on the bank robbery itself. Only some-one who lived it would think of asking about people arming themselves. And only a neighbor could pick up the phone and get the quick quotes I did in a matter of minutes. For once, being from Fortuna is an asset instead of a liability.

It is late the next day and I am about to leave work when I get a call from Detective Hanson. He has the ID on the robber.

"We finally managed to find this man's parents," Hanson tells me. "We found the father in North Carolina and the mother in Michigan. That's apparently where he's from."

Michigan, hmmm.

Krimm, James Edward. The name means nothing to me. He was forty-two. Four years younger than me.

Hanson said Krimm's identification shows an address in Valley City, North Dakota, but he doubts Krimm lived there recently.

"I really can't give you any further information."

And I don't press. I mean, Krimm is a stranger to my readers. His identity will be old news by the time our paper comes out again in a week, just a name. And yeah, it all ended in Divide County, but so what? Wouldn't Williston be working this angle, the backstory, about who he was and why he was here?

It might seem crass, evaluating the news value of some guy's death, but it's second nature to me. I guess it's just a trait peculiar to newspeople that you can draw a wall around your heart and look at life and death in terms of reader interest. Is someone's demise deserving of a front-page story or relegated to a three- or four-inch blurb on an inside page?

It's easy to make those decisions when you don't know the family and you don't have to talk to them. Earlier in my career, when I'd worked in Wichita, Kansas, it seemed like I was making those calls every other week. I dreaded those calls. The stereotype of a hounding press, clamoring for information on a front lawn, is legend. It didn't come naturally to me. I was raised better than that.

The only way I'd ever been able to justify calling a bereaved family is that I would be giving them the chance to let the world know something of who that person was, beyond the crime that would forever be attached to his or her name in the newspaper.

Driving home from work, on the same road the robber last traveled, I can't help thinking about him—this criminal from Michigan. I was born in Port Huron, Michigan, but my parents divorced when I was a baby. I'd only twice visited there, and not until I was an adult. My uncle and aunts told me stories about how their parents remembered us at Christmas. My grandpa Otto and my grandma Mary prayed for me and my brother and sister all of our lives, though they never laid eyes on us after my mom filed for divorce. My father's parents knew nothing of what I looked like or what kind of a kid I was, and still, they prayed. It amazed me when I thought of it—strangers who loved me without even knowing me.

I can't help wondering about Krimm's family. What must his mother think now that her son is dead?

The next morning, the radio relays the details I already know: James Edward Krimm, forty-two, of Valley City. That's it.

But who was he? What was he doing here? Did he work in the area? Why was it so hard to find his family? Obviously, his parents were divorced. Was this robber truly a bad guy? Or was he just a lost guy? I wonder if the Williston paper will have anything more on him. They wouldn't have had much time if they got the ID when I did. But what if they didn't follow it up? Maybe I should be trying to locate the family. I had to have some kind of a follow-up in our next edition. With Steve's go-ahead, we decide I should spend some time looking for this guy's kin.

My first call is to my own sheriff again. He tells me the suspect's vehicle is impounded in town. He says it looks like Krimm lived out of his car. He had camping gear and firewood and stuff. There were prior arrests for DUIs, drugs, and no driver's license. He guesses Krimm was forced back into North Dakota because of the mobilization of so many officers in Montana. He may have been trying to get into Canada.

Sheriff Throntveit says the Bureau of Criminal Investigation (BCI) may learn more from photographs and letters found in the car. They also have more than one ID to investigate.

I am so intent on calling the sheriff I forget all about reading the Minot paper when I first get to the office. I grab for it, and suddenly... there he is: James Edward Krimm. The picture assaults my eyes. He looks so unpleasantly familiar in some way, like someone I know, but who? It's something about the eyes and the set of his mouth, very hard.

I flash on what would have happened if this face had turned up at my door that night, and that's when it hits me—a familiar, sick feeling of victimization. This guy looks like my stepfather, and that is not a similarity likely to create any sympathy in me. It does, however, cause me to wonder whether the robber, like me, was sexually abused as a child. There is no reason for my thoughts to go that direction, except this man looks like a predator.

I shake my head. No sense going there.

The *Minot Daily News*, I realize, must have gotten the mug shot from Hanson. I dial his number, glad to have an excuse to talk to the Williston detective again. Now that I know I am doing a follow-up story, I need more information from him.

"So it was pretty hard to figure out who this guy was, huh?" I ask, hoping to lead him to make a few comments.

"It's not very often you find someone who has no wife, no kids, no family," he says.

"But you found the parents?"

"His mother is in Michigan. She hadn't seen him in sixteen years. The first thing she asked me was whether she has any grandchildren."

What kind of guy doesn't call his own mother for *sixteen years?* And all she wants to know is if she has grandchildren. I have no trouble believing that, thinking of my own Michigan grandparents, praying all those years for their long-lost grandchildren.

"I can't even imagine," I say. "What about the father? North Carolina?"

"He claimed he hadn't seen him for thirty years."

That made two things I had in common with the robber: Michigan and an absent father.

In his thirty-two years as a police officer, Hanson says, he has never struggled so hard to identify someone.

"A very, very difficult guy to trace. I don't know what drew him to this state. Where he came from, what he might have done in any other locations, I don't know. He was kind of, pretty much, a loner."

In short, a mystery.

"This guy has quite an extensive criminal record," Hanson adds. "He's most likely involved in some other bank robberies. There's been quite a few in the state recently."

There'd even been a bank robbery in Weyburn, Canada, a straight shot sixty miles north of my house, up in Saskatchewan, a couple of years earlier. That one had given me the willies when I'd heard about it on the radio the morning after. A bank robber on the run from Weyburn could easily find his way past my house.

I don't ask Hanson for the mother's phone number. He can't give it out anyway.

Next, I talk to an FBI guy in Minneapolis. Of nine bank robberies since 2008 in North Dakota, he tells me, seven are unsolved.

Mr. Krimm is looking more fascinating by the minute.

I spend the next several hours searching the Internet. There is a James E. Krimm, born in 1967, with relatives listed as Charlene, sixty-six, in Taylor, Michigan; Rob, thirty-eight, with about a dozen addresses all over the country, and Julie,* thirty-seven, of North Carolina. Krimm is an unusual name. And the age of this Charlene adds up if her son was forty-two when he died.

I have her phone number. I just have to dial it.

---

* Not her real name.

CHAPTER THREE

Calling Charlene

I do not dial Charlene's number—not right away. Do I really want to bother this woman? Is it really appropriate?

I can tell her this will be a way to let people know her son was not just some name in the newspaper. But what business do I have calling Michigan? *The Journal* is a local paper. We cover local news. But that isn't the real reason I don't want to call.

I sit on the information for a couple of hours. Finally, it is nearly four o'clock. What if other news agencies have already tracked her down and I am the fifth to dial? She might get mad or be annoyed. Finally, I just have to do it.

I dial the number. Normally, when I cold-call someone, I don't leave a message. If they don't want to talk to me, it will be that much easier for them to avoid me once they've been alerted to my interest.

An answering machine picks up, and the woman's voice, high-pitched and so bubbly, jars me. Like the smiling pictures of people staring out at you from their obituaries, your average answering machine message is made with no thought of possible future tragedy. This woman, based on her phone message, is normally a pretty sunny personality. But learning her son is dead, and a bank robber, must be a tremendous blow.

I leave a message. Honestly, I just don't know if I can stand to hear this woman's pain. I can do a story about what a loner this guy was, without talking to her. I have plenty of new information from the police. Talking to Charlene Krimm is definitely not required. No one will miss that interview or think anything of it if it's not there.

I hang up the receiver, and I really hope she doesn't call back. That feeling, I realize, shows how far I've come. What difference could it possibly make to learn her story? It's just one more sack of sadness—and one more chance for someone to rail at me for intruding. The ball is in her court. It's her option now. I made the attempt. If she wants to talk, she can call me. If not, I am off the hook.

Arriving home after work, I walk in the door, and my husband tells me he just hung up from talking to Charlene Krimm.

"Oh my gosh!" I say, grabbing my notebook out of my bag.

"I told her you'd be home any minute."

"She's the bank robber's mother."

"Yeah, I know. I talked to her for about ten minutes."

What a relief! So I don't have to feel like a total heel for bothering her. You just never know. Despite my great reluctance in phoning, there were any number of times over the years when I called a family member of someone killed in a tragic or violent episode and they responded exactly this way. People either really want to talk or not at all. Now it is easy to dial Charlene's number.

"I'm more or less at peace right now," Charlene tells me, in her high-pitched voice, sounding a little less sunny than the version on her answering machine.

The news of her son's death, which she received the day before, has only begun to sink in. Having had no contact with him for nearly two decades, Charlene was resigned to the possibility he could be dead, but until the day before I called her, she had no way of knowing what had become of him.

At almost the exact time Jimmy was driving around the countryside with two airplanes spotting him, Charlene had been driving home from a Tupperware sales meeting in which she'd won a coveted prize. While police searched for the bank robber's parents the following day, Charlene had been volunteering at a Sylvia Browne lecture. Sylvia Browne, I would learn, was an important figure in Charlene's life. The renowned psychic is the founder of the Novus Spiritus church. This Gnostic belief system had given Charlene the peace that comes from knowing everything in life happens as an opportunity to perfect our souls for God.

Police had awakened her while she was napping the previous afternoon to give her the news about Jimmy. Neighbors gathered around outside her house until she came out to share the story.

It wasn't even every mother's nightmare, learning that her child had blown his brains out. It was worse than that, knowing you gave birth to a child who victimized innocent people and there is no chance for redemption—except that in Charlene's belief system, there is the possibility of being healed from the trauma of this life.

Less than five minutes into the conversation, Charlene shares the crux of what she believes went wrong with her son.

"I worked three jobs to keep my house, and while I was away, Jimmy molested his younger brother. Somewhere, he learned that. Someone had to have done that to him, too."

Charlene can't know, and I can't tell her right then, how this information affects me. Journalists are supposed to remain objective. But as a sexual abuse survivor myself, I can't hear information like this and not be touched. I've pondered the issue many times: what makes one abuse survivor turn out "good" and another turn out "bad"? What is that intangible thing that allowed me to overcome my abuse enough to get married and have a family and a relatively "normal" life, while so many other people turn to crime or drugs or alcohol—or worse yet, become abusers? I think, at that moment, I will never understand it.

"Somehow, whatever happened to him made him feel somebody owed him something," Charlene speculates, but that doesn't explain why his younger brother is okay. Charlene speaks with great pride of Harry Robert, who joined the Marines right out of high school and later transferred to the Air Force. He is set to retire from the Air Force in a little more than a year. He had been serving his country for almost the entire time his older brother was pursuing a career of crime.

"You do the best you can," Charlene tells me, "but in the end, it's up to each individual to make the right choices."

Charlene shares her belief we plan our lives before we get to Earth, and while the concept is interesting to me, it's pretty tough to swallow. Why would anyone plan to be abused as a child or to become an abuser? I know this is a little too deep to get into with *Journal* readers, who tend to be Lutheran and pretty traditional.

Yet Charlene's faith is unshakable, as firm as any fundamentalist Christian's. Here she is, finding out about her son's death, and her thoughts are centered as much on his victims.

"I am happy he didn't hurt anyone at the bank. I'm just very sad for those people," she says. "My prayers go out to them, and I pray they will have peace."

We talk for over an hour. I identify so closely with this mother. My own son, who is sixteen, has gotten into a little trouble. It was just kid stuff, but still.

"I know I did the best I could," Charlene says, but she also wonders where she went wrong. What parent hasn't felt that kind of guilt?

Charlene shares how, growing up, she had this picture of a "white picket fence kind of life." She grew up, got married, had two sons, and just when it seemed her dream was attainable, her marriage ended. Suddenly, everything she dreamed of was taken away. And her boys suffered. Coming home to an empty house she slaved to provide, Jimmy was able to dominate and abuse his little brother at will. It wasn't until Harry Robert was an adult, married, and suddenly having trouble in his relationships and job that the truth finally emerged. By then, Charlene was glad Jimmy was out of her life. Still, she mourns the loss of her firstborn child.

In an odd twist, Charlene is shocked to learn the name of the town my paper serves is Crosby. Her son's car at this very moment is sitting in an impound yard in the county seat that bears her maiden name. That he died a little more than twenty-five miles from a town that shares the name of his mother's family is a weird coincidence. I have to wonder if Jimmy ever traveled here before. Seeing that name on a map while roaming the highways aimlessly, how could he resist driving through that town?

Aside from feeling sympathy for Charlene and aside from my own memories of abuse being stirred, I get off the phone elated. This story is going to be amazing—a single mother, fighting to do the best for her children, the tragedy of abuse, the contrast of the two totally different directions her sons took in life, not to mention, finding peace in the belief everything happens as a chance for growth.

Before we hang up, Charlene gives me her e-mail address and also promises to send pictures of her family.

After my story runs, I gather up copies of all of the other articles I have found in different newspapers about Jimmy Krimm and I send them all to Charlene. I don't have to do it. But it is the *least* I can do. I want to help her any way I can, never mind that she could probably find these clips on the Internet. I am in a position to make a difference to her, and if I don't do it, maybe no one will.

Right or wrong, I am becoming involved. I've been in the news business long enough to realize the pitfalls of growing too close to an interview subject—not that I've ever been in a position quite like this before. What can it hurt to show this mother some kindness? It makes me feel good to help. And isn't that what drew me to journalism in the first place? The desire to make a difference? I ran for office out of a similar yearning to leave the world a better place. This is no different.

Plenty of times over the years, I'd met people I felt an affinity for, but only a few times in my career had I crossed the threshold into friendship with someone I'd met on a story. Too often, once a story was finished, I was on to the next thing. If there was an opportunity to make a real connection with another human, too often, I let it pass, unexplored.

Maybe it is the realization, after so many years of interviewing people, such connections are rare. And maybe it is because, beaten down as I am about the greater meaning of my own life, this is a chance to do something that feels important. Charlene's story calls to me. I can't leave that call unanswered.

Above all, she hopes that sharing her son's story will somehow get word to a girlfriend or child of Jimmy's that she would welcome his offspring into her life, if she could only find them.

"I would make such a good grandmother," she tells me, her yearning palpable.

In the days that follow, I continue working other angles of the story, like trying to nail down the locations of some of these other bank robberies the police mentioned.

I learn the medical examiner has completed the autopsy, confirming that Jimmy, indeed, had died of a single, self-inflicted gunshot wound to the head—never mind the fact some of the officers also fired on him. Charlene tells me she can't afford to claim her son's body. *The Journal* carries a story about how the county will pay for the robber's cremation.

About this time, the Williston newspaper asks for permission to carry my story about Charlene. Because of their concern about identifying victims, they cut out all references to abuse. I am furious! It's one thing to shield victims, but another to cover up what illuminates something so crucial to understanding this robber's mind-set, especially when the family wants the story told!

Any opportunity to shine a light on sexual abuse, if it can help one other survivor, is a story worth breaking rules for, as far as I am concerned.

I am heartened when several papers around the state run the article as written. There seems to be a great deal of curiosity about Jimmy Krimm.

I share with Charlene, in an e-mail, a bit about my past. She is so appreciative of receiving the clippings and the other bits of news I've sent her, I feel I owe some explanation—that I, too, have been touched by childhood sexual abuse. It is a "secret" I don't go around sharing with just anyone. I've never discussed it with most of the people I have worked with for years. But I have, on occasion, after court trials where victims testified, for instance, quietly let survivors know they are not alone.

Eleven days after Jimmy's death, I am seated at my desk at *The Journal* when a message pops up on my computer screen from a man with whom I already know I have a lot in common.

> FROM: Krimm, Harry R SSgt USAF ACC 4 CMS/MXMVS
> SENT: Friday, September 25, 2009 10:34 AM
> TO: Cecile Wehrman
> SUBJECT: Harry R. Krimm—Just saying hey...

It's the brother! I drop what I am working on, clicking immediately on the message to read its contents.

> Thanks for being so nice to my mother. Being military, I've come to realize dysfunctional is a word that describes about 90 percent of the population. Some of us join the Military to just get away, make a better life for ourselves. I too have made it my personal mission to do the right thing, as far as morals are concerned. I'm far from perfect. But, I've made a pretty good go of it in the military. I'm with my mom on breaking the chain of abuse. Let's hope there's more people like us in the world! I've always thought I should write a book about how a person survives and lives after abuse. Well, for me his death brings some closure to my life. I've noticed many coincidences, for example: Crosby is my mother's maiden name. Little things make you go "Hmmm..." Maybe after I retire, I will write that book, it would give me something to do. Only 1 yr and 4 months to go. Thanks for spreading the real story whatever it may be. Harry "Rob" Krimm

I respond immediately, sharing my frustration about the wrangling I am undergoing with the *Williston Herald* about revealing the identities of abuse survivors. I encourage him to write that book.

I address the message to "Harry" failing to notice the detail of "Rob" in his signature until later. Rob is the name he prefers, apparently, having grown up as Harry. I am just so glad to make the connection with someone seemingly as committed as I am to "breaking the chain of abuse."

Having heard so much about Harry Robert from Charlene, I feel I already know him. I feel immediately protective toward him. Even though he is writing from an address with such an official-looking title and even though I know he is a grown man practically ready to retire from twenty years of military service, I can't help picturing him as someone much younger—younger than me, certainly, by eight years—but younger emotionally too, for some reason.

Mine had been a coercive sort of abuse, punctuated by vague threats and virtually no violence of any kind—at least not until I got older and started resisting. No boy—no man—is going to take a raping without fighting it physically, which immediately puts Rob's abuse on a level of intensity I can extrapolate based on my own experience. The specter of male-on-male abuse just seems so much more violent than what I endured from my stepfather, who molested me repeatedly from the time I was six until I was nearly sixteen. Yet, Rob sounds so *open*. It amazes me that someone can come out whole from an environment as difficult as the one he was raised in with no adult present, no reprieve in sight, and only the promise of another beating or rape to replace the hurts of the day before.

Three weeks after the robbery, *The Journal* breaks the story Jimmy Krimm is connected to as many as eleven bank robberies in three states over the past five years.

Rob's reference to someday writing a book nags at me. If Jimmy Krimm really was a serial bank bandit, it would be one hell of a book. And if they could connect him to eleven bank robberies, there were probably many more to discover. This guy could turn out to be a modern-day Jesse James! The portrait of him that was emerging was very different than the romantic notion I had from Hollywood portrayals of figures like Bonnie and Clyde or Butch Cassidy and the Sundance Kid.

Robbing banks for a living is far from glamorous, if Jimmy's example is any indication. He was homeless, living out of his car! That didn't square with the romantic image.

And then there is the aspect of childhood sexual abuse. I know it is wrong to excuse Jimmy's crimes, but the element of possible victimization in his past goes a long way toward explaining for me how he wound up the way he did. His brother illustrates the other model—a victim who somehow rises above the abuse to try to make the world a better place.

Jimmy is such an enigma, and Rob is such a surprise! There is so much to learn about both of them. Can it be possible to trace Jimmy's footsteps? Contrast his choices with the choices his brother made?

And just what kind of a hero can be made out of Rob? He is a soldier, and while that conjures all sorts of patriotic notions, it is foolhardy to assume every man with a job in the armed forces is a hero. Charlene made Rob sound like he could do no wrong, but my own experience alerts me to the very real possibility Rob may not be everything he seems. I know what it means to put on a face in public, all the while dying inside. Had Rob ever felt like an imposter, the way I did when I was forced to play the various roles people expected of me?

Would Rob be capable of writing a book about his abuser? Is he emotionally stable? I have no way of knowing. Certainly, if he is going to write a book, he can't do it until after his retirement. By then, the story and any clues will be pretty cold. Not to mention, abuse stories are a dime a dozen. Another memoir by an adult survivor isn't going to set the world on fire. I call it the "Oprah effect." Ever since Oprah Winfrey came out on her talk show decades ago with the story of her own victimization as a child, it seems like such stories have grown mundane.

Oprah brought the ugly reality of childhood sexual abuse into acute public focus for the first time. But it seems like it also brought a backlash—not unlike the growing tedium of hearing celebrities recount their addiction battles—like drama fatigue.

Once the sexual abuse monkey was out of its cage, a lot of people looked at it and learned something, but then they wanted to lock that monkey up again. There is nothing unusual about these stories anymore—just a sickening one-upmanship in which today's "abuse of the week" is topped by next week's, and so on, ad nauseam.

It is no secret anymore that terrible, awful sexual abuse occurs in millions of American homes every year. But I can't ever recall anyone delving into the differences between those who survive, if not thrive, and those who become predators. It seems as if society has grown more understanding that such abuse occurs but never moves off center to try to understand what it means that one in four women and one in six men in the United States is a sexual abuse survivor.

What challenges do they have in forming healthy relationships? What coping skills have they developed? Is there some recipe common to those who take the higher road? Some insurance to prevent a new predator from emerging? It seems sometimes as if people are only titillated by the sob stories; they don't want to consider the aftermath. Yet, I know it is in the aftermath, as survivors grow up, that they either find the skills to rise above it or sink into behaviors that perpetuate the cycle.

Even with increased awareness and reporting, there is no shortage of new victims. A book written by a third party conscious of the dynamics, bringing in the elements of serial bank robbery and the contrast between two survivors, could break new ground.

Driving down the very highway that was the end of Jimmy's trail, I conceive the question of whether I can write a book about the Krimm family. Will they allow me to tell their story?

At home that night, I lay out in an e-mail for Rob and Charlene what the process would be.

I'd interview all of the law enforcement people involved and the tellers at the bank—anyone who could shine a light on Jimmy's actions. I'd look into his records. We'd have to mine every detail of their family's past. I'd want to do in-depth interviews with them and meet them in person. For Rob, especially, the process would be difficult, requiring him to delve into the darkest days of his childhood. Charlene would have to reveal personal details of her own and recall unflinchingly the ways she felt she let her boys down.

Much to my amazement, they are both game.

The motivation to cooperate, for Charlene, stems as much from wanting to locate any children Jimmy may have fathered as a desire that some good could come out of his life.

For me, the sheer curiosity of wanting to know what drove Jimmy is motivation enough, but added to my interest in exploring how abuse survivors cope, I know this is a story that can hold my interest through many months of research and writing.

For Rob, the project offers the possibility of further closure and healing, as well as the chance to help other people who have grown up in an abusive situation.

"I'm an open book," he says.

Lots of people say that. Few people actually are.

CHAPTER FOUR

Ashes

Suddenly, I am on my way to Michigan, the state of my birth. I haven't had the desire to fly anywhere in years, but now there is no stopping me.

It isn't easy convincing my husband I should go, but with his reluctant consent—and the excuse I am not just going to meet a bunch of strangers, I can see some of my own extended family, too—I start planning.

The first thing I need to know if I am really going to write a book is whether the FBI will cooperate. Will they provide the dates and places of Jimmy's suspected bank robberies once their investigation concludes? A press officer in Minneapolis tells me they will.

Next, I want to start getting to know Rob. I am embarking on writing a book largely on his life, and I have exactly two e-mails from him on which to base that decision. He is the best conduit to Jimmy. Charlene is an important piece of the puzzle, but Rob knows all the things only a younger sibling can know about a big brother, all the things only a victim can know about an abuser.

I send Rob a huge list of questions by e-mail, which he answers fairly quickly. I send follow-up questions and then—nothing. Days pass, and then a week, still no response.

Did my questions upset him? I have a knack for being like a bull in Pamplona, running headlong down a very narrow street, never mind what is in my way when I want information. Did my stampede put Rob off?

I reread my first e-mail. Then I reread his response. Then I read my follow-up e-mail, in which I also ask him for some reassurance I am not upsetting him.

Wasn't I supposed to be the perfect person to write this story because of my own abuse background? And what do I do? I just barge into this guy's life asking him to reveal details about the most humiliating times of his life.

I'm no psychologist, I scold myself. I have no way of knowing if Rob has ever been counseled for abuse, whether he is under a doctor's care, or even if he is emotionally stable. And now I haven't heard from him for a week after dredging up his most painful memories.

Given the fact his brother committed suicide just a few weeks earlier, the possibility of Rob harming himself begins to hang on me. I feel awful to think I may have caused him distress. I hate to alarm Charlene. She is still dealing with the reality one son is dead. How can I call her and tell her my questions may have sent her other son over the edge? And what if I am just overreacting? Sounding the alarm to Charlene would just destroy whatever tentative trust they'd both placed in me.

Next, real paranoia takes hold. I know absolutely nothing about Rob, really. I tell myself if he managed to survive a career in the military for nearly twenty years, he has to be pretty together. But what if he's only managed to hold that career together by a thread? What if his abusive past has scarred him so deeply his military career covers some heinous acting out of some kind? He could be an ax murderer for all I know, with a string of bodies strewn at every duty station from North Carolina all the way to my house!

I know I am being foolish, but I can't help it. I am home alone again with the kids, and my husband won't be home for days. Absent any response from Rob, I am working myself into a considerable dither. He is either hurting himself or about to hurt me for dredging up horrible memories.

With the feeling of vulnerability so fresh in my mind from the night Jimmy roamed the countryside, I feel scared I have gotten myself into something I have no business getting into. Am I putting myself and my children in danger by delving into so raw a past as Rob's?

Not caring how silly it is, I get out of bed and take the handgun off the shelf where it was placed after we learned Jimmy was dead. Tomorrow, I tell myself, I am calling Rob.

I have a phone number for Rob from the background search I did on Jimmy. Finally, I screw up the courage to dial the number; it is disconnected. Damn! I have no means of contacting Rob other than e-mail, which does not appear to be the best way to get his attention, based on the fact I haven't heard from him in well over a week. If he can't be prompted to answer me, how can I write a book about him?

There is nothing to do but write to him again, expressing my concern I have upset him and urging him to contact me immediately. I throw in a vague threat about telling his mom I am worried. The message is stern, scolding almost, but I get his attention.

"Don't be silly," he finally replies.

Oooo!

After days and days with not a word from him and very real concern for his welfare, this guy has the nerve to pooh-pooh me?

Sure, I overreacted. But his response is underwhelming to say the least! And his second round of answers only whet my appetite for more information. If we are going to write a book, we are going to have to *talk*—a lot.

After he supplies the correct number, I call him one night after work. I tell myself we won't even talk about the abuse right away. If my probing e-mails and Rob's sudden drop off the face of the Internet earth have taught me anything, it is to go at his pace and just have a conversation. Above all, I need to know where he is at emotionally—whether he is stable and whether delving into the past is something he truly wants to do.

"Hello?" he answers tentatively.

Despite the prior talking-to I give myself, I rattle off who is calling, how worried I have been, and how excited I am to finally get to talk to him in all of about fifteen seconds before I pause for a breath and ask if this is still a good time to talk.

"Yeah…yeah, this is good," he murmurs.

He is so soft-spoken!

"Wow. I'm going to have to learn to shut up around you; you seem a little shy," I say, hoping to break the ice. It works. After some awkward moments, there is almost no shutting Rob up for the next two hours.

"It all started with candy bars," Rob tells me.

Candy bars?

Heath bars were the easiest to steal, he explains, because they are thin and easily concealed. His brother stealing candy bars was just the first in a long series of criminal activities Rob witnessed as a kid.

We talk for some time about those activities, but what I really need out of this first conversation is a sense of where Rob's head is at. I scold him again for leaving me hanging for so long with the e-mails, leaving out the bit about actually becoming frightened he might turn out to be as screwed up as his brother.

"I really need to know the status of your mental health," I tell him.

"I've been seeing a therapist for about four years," Rob says, "for depression and attention deficit disorder." He also relays the belief there is an element of post-traumatic stress disorder in his makeup. The most difficult of the three conditions, in Rob's assessment, is ADD.

"It's made me look bad," he says. "I make mistakes. I'm not perfect."

Just the fact he is willing to reveal his warts goes a long way in assuaging my fears. I sometimes have trouble trusting my gut, but my bullshit detector is pretty healthy. I see none.

Despite the fact his brother has only recently committed suicide and despite the fact I am now asking him to dredge up a bunch of unpleasant memories, the very fact of his abuse, Rob says, gives him the ability to deal with drama.

"It's made me a stronger person. I've actually had to deal with loss, and I've made it through. My ability to cope with problems, that's helped me through the whole thing."

That he is under the care of a therapist and taking medication also makes me feel better. If our interviewing does upset him, at least there is a local safety net. And anyway, I survived some pretty traumatic episodes as a child myself. I'm not suicidal. I function every day. Why should Rob be any different? The words he said, in fact, about feeling strong and knowing how to cope are words I could easily speak myself.

At the same time, I keep reminding myself I must never lose sight of my objectivity. Our experiences and emotions in response to abuse may be similar, but Rob is not me. I have to be on guard not to project too much of my own experience onto the story he is telling me.

And yet, because of my own experiences, as we talk, I seem to be able to ask the right questions and pull out the greater details he glosses over in his first pass at a question.

Knowing Rob has ADD also clears up for me his lack of response to my follow-up e-mail. Expecting him to respond in detail promptly, and in writing, is not going to work. That presents some challenges to getting the information I need long distance, but I figure my tenacity can bridge that gap.

After hearing more of the details, one question I have to ponder is how Rob's somewhat troubled career in the military—lots of reprimands for minor infractions almost entirely related to issues like showing up late and failing to turn in paperwork on time—will square with anyone's notion of a hero? Is there enough contrast between Jimmy, the sexual abuser and bank robber, and Rob, the victim with a less-than-stellar military career?

Aside from the fact Rob is a functioning member of society and his brother clearly was not, I see Rob's very survival as heroic. His daily struggle, just getting to work every day, just staying on an even keel emotionally, when he so easily could have taken a path as destructive as his brother's—this is true heroism to me. Isn't it the very definition of heroism to have courage? It takes a lot of courage to look at your life and try to address the damage inflicted by others.

"I try to do the right thing," is how Rob puts it.

What more can we ask of our heroes than that?

It is after that first conversation in early October that I begin laying the groundwork for a meeting. I can continue to talk to Rob on the phone, but we need some serious face time to delve into the details of his childhood. I need to see the "scene of the crime"—the home Charlene slaved so hard to provide, the house she still occupies.

We agree Rob will take leave and drive up from North Carolina, while I fly in from North Dakota. Rob and Charlene will have a few days together before my arrival, and I will have a few days after our visit to see my family in the Detroit area.

The only person missing at this reunion is Jimmy.

I probe Charlene about her plans. Her son died weeks earlier, and still no words have been spoken, no service performed. Because she lacks the ability to take financial responsibility for his remains, she has also lost some say in the disposition of them. The county paid for the cremation, and while the cremains can be shipped to Charlene, the possibility of the ashes being lost disturbs me. Charlene is planning a small memorial service for when Rob comes home, coinciding with my visit. But will the ashes arrive in time?

The only practical solution I can see is to bring the ashes with me. I check my gut before making the offer. It's not that I am just trying to ingratiate myself. Sure, I want to be present for the memorial service—what writer wouldn't? But it is more that it simply doesn't bother me. Ashes are not human remains. They're what's left of human remains. Bringing Jimmy's ashes is something I can accomplish easily. And there is a certain satisfaction, a certain feeling of closure, for me, as well as for Charlene and Rob, that someone from the place where Jimmy died will bring Jimmy home.

By the same token, I realize it might seem just a little strange to some people—not only am I flying off to meet the family of a bank robber, I am, once again, approaching foreign territory when it comes to maintaining objectivity about people whose lives I want to chronicle. Aside from the Krimms, the local funeral director, and one or two people at work, I tell no one I am taking the bank robber's ashes home to his mother. I don't mention it at my house, knowing the kids will carry the story to school and knowing my husband will accuse me of "going deep end" over this story.

Besides, I tell myself, it's really no one's business. If you're doing something for someone, I figure, you do it without expectations. You don't seek recognition for it. I don't want recognition. I just want all of us—Charlene, Rob, Jimmy, and me—at the same place at the same time.

"'I've cheated undertakers, dam near met my maker, I'm tellin' ya all, I'm lucky to be here at all' —Montgomery Gentry" (written on the back of the photo, left)

Christmas 2008*

Well Dad,

How are ya! The last address I gave you was to Grand Rapids, Mi. And I didn't get any of your letters or money. Some bum from prison was living there and said I could have my mail sent there cause I was in a homeless shelter.

I fled to Iowa and tried to start new, but I got blamed for parking a hot Caddylac outside of the homeless shelter. I fought it in court—"Case dissmissed" after I was offered 2 plea bargan and turned them down.

The discription of the man who parked the car on street was Half my size with brown eyes. Go Figure.

I then went to Canada 9 months later. Cause of warrent in Michigan for yet another car theft.

—Merry Christmas, Jim

---

* Quotations from letters are reproduced exactly as written except when noted otherwise.

PART TWO

CHAPTER FIVE

Meet the Krimms

In the days leading up to my trip, I worry about a lot of silly things, like will I recognize Charlene and Rob in a crowd at the airport? Charlene has sent me photos of the boys as kids, and I have one later photo of her, but I have no idea what Rob looks like now.

Charlene's picture, the one we ran with the story about her boy, the bank robber, shows her with short hair, but she's also lately sent me a more recent photo, in which her long graying hair is piled in a bun almost on the top of her head. She is a good-looking lady, a little on the heavy side, and quite obviously a jovial sort, based on the sparkle in her blue eyes.

Looking at pictures of Rob as a ten-year-old, I try, like a forensic artist, to imagine the face grown older. I can't do it.

I can make no sense at all of the pictures of Jimmy as a fourteen-year-old compared to the mug shot police provided after his death. As a forty-two-year-old bank robber, he looks nothing like the mischievous teen with the deep dimple in his cheek.

What happened? What turned that good-looking youngster into a man who reminds me of my own abuser? And isn't that really, if I am honest with myself, the reason I want to know what Rob looks like before I meet him? Aren't I just a little worried he might look more like his grown brother, even though they looked nothing alike as kids? If Rob does look like the grown-up Jimmy, I need to be prepared, because, as much as I try to shake it, every time I look at a picture of Jimmy Krimm, it strikes something inside of me that is just a little disturbing.

Feeling like a lonely heart in a singles chat room, I ask Rob to e-mail me a photo, ostensibly so I can recognize him when we meet. I provide one of myself for him, as a gesture of my good intentions.

Shortly before he takes off to make the long drive from North Carolina to Michigan and just a few days before I leave on an airplane to fly there, two photos of Rob arrive in my inbox. I cringe as I click open the first file, almost afraid to see what it will reveal.

Whew! What a relief! I see no hint of the menace I feel looking into his brother's eyes. The face that looks back at me from my computer screen is kind, not at all threatening. This photo was taken while Rob was in work clothes, I surmise, based on the khaki T-shirt. His arms are folded across his chest in what I imagine he might consider a "tough guy" pose, and there is no smile. But even with graying hair at his temples and eyes that look tired, there is no way of getting around it. Rob doesn't look all that different as a grown-up than he had as a baby-faced youth. His is a solid face, I decide, an apple-pie face. He looks a lot like his mother, which makes sense, because he's already told me he takes more after his mother than his brother did.

As much as I have already talked with him on the phone, I still can't quite imagine his soft voice coming out of this big man's body.

The second picture is of Rob in civilian clothes, with silver-rimmed eyeglasses. It is taken at sort of an odd angle, making his face look longer and his expression, quizzical. One eyebrow is slightly cocked, creating wrinkles in his forehead. His mouth looks like it suppresses a chuckle. If the first photo reveals Rob's inner tough guy, this photo reveals the inner goofball. I'd already gotten a taste of his humor on the phone. I have an easier time matching the voice, and the personality, with this photo.

If the first photo is Superman, the second reveals the mild-mannered Clark Kent. Something tells me the second image is closer to the persona Rob presents to the world most of the time, but the steely resolve of the first photo hints at a man who has seen hell and doesn't want to go back.

Traveling with someone's ashes in a carry-on bag is not as easy as I imagined. By the time I lug Jimmy through two airports, I am looking forward to relieving myself of the burden. Did Jimmy ever fly on a plane before? It is the kind of crazy question I find myself asking a lot lately and just the latest one for which there will probably never be an answer.

I have chosen comfortable travel clothes anyway, ones I imagine allow me to look professional and—just as important—unwrinkled by the time my plane touches down in Detroit. No sooner than I turn on my cell phone, there is a text from Rob, informing me I will find him and Charlene at the baggage carousel. I am not good at this texting stuff, much as my kids try to suck me into it. I manage to eke out a brief reply.

I spy Rob and Charlene as I ride down the escalator, pointing and waving at them before they recognize me. Soon, I am through the glass doors that separate the secure area from the baggage claim. Charlene is already crying. These disturbances, I will learn, blow up suddenly and tend to clear just as quickly. I am enveloped in her ample embrace, and for some reason, I am crying, too.

Hugging Charlene is like hugging Mrs. Santa Claus. Her spirit, I know from multiple phone conversations and exchanges of e-mail over the weeks previous, is so giving, so devoid of ego, it is hard to square with her own self-assessment that she used to be combative or obnoxious where her boys were concerned. If anything, I can imagine her as a mama bear—so intent on protecting her young she could rip your arm off and have it for breakfast—but in a nice way!

The sheer improbability of the situation and the events that bring us together overwhelm me, but Charlene's tears probably have as much to do with welcoming me as the fact I carry the ashes of her firstborn child.

I turn next to Rob; our hug is awkward and quick. I already know so much about him, but we are strangers nonetheless, and I sense he is not nearly the spontaneous hugger his mom is.

He is so tall!

I suggest Rob come with me to get my rental car. Charlene will meet us back at her house. Right there, in the parking garage, I hand Charlene the bag that holds the container of Jimmy's ashes. As usual, when something delicate just needs doing, I just do it, figuring people will at least appreciate my straightforwardness. There is no good way, no good time, to hand someone a package like this. At least Charlene will have a few moments alone with him, to collect herself, before I start asking her a bunch of questions about her life.

As Rob and I get into an elevator, I tell him he looks much younger than his photos. Only the creases at the corners of his eyes reveal his true age—that, and the gray hair, which is more noticeable in person. Feeling like an older sister, I make a crack about how he has more gray hair than I do, and he dishes it right back, explaining it is the military that prematurely ages people.

We fall into a fairly easy banter after that. I feel absolutely comfortable—and that includes slapping Rob's knee when he flips a guy off for nearly broad siding us at an intersection.

"Don't do that!" I exclaim, so accustomed as I am to scolding my son for similarly macho behavior. I am not above deploying the random road bird myself, but it is an urge I've learned to squelch after twenty years in a locale where anonymity is nonexistent. I have to laugh for having taken such a liberty. I have never slapped the knee of an interview subject before. Oh well! We are going to be getting to know each other pretty well in the next few days, no sense putting on any kind of a show. I am about to conduct the most in-depth interviews of my career. Instinct tells me the best thing I can do, the best way I can act to put Charlene and Rob at ease, is not to act at all.

This is the first time in my life I've met people who already know the hardest thing about me and vice versa. It is a relief to leave off the mask I wear, most days, just for the benefit of appearing "normal."

What you see is what you get, I tell myself. And I hope my demeanor will engender the same behavior in my hosts.

Upon our arrival at Charlene's house, which is on an orderly street that curves a little to the right just past her place, I find the door is open. This is a settled, working-class neighborhood. The term "tract housing" came to mind, but the modest bungalows have settled into a mostly well-kept middle age, with mature trees lining the boulevard and mostly well-maintained, if not ornate, lawns. The small ranch-style one-story is abuzz with the sound of a vacuum cleaner. Charlene's good friend Estella; her husband, Wayne; and their granddaughter, Mallory, are visiting from Virginia—and helping Charlene get her house in order.

Charlene's living room, not particularly large to begin with, is nearly bursting with so many people and things occupying it at one time. *Cluttered* is the word that leaps to mind, but not overly so. Hers is the sort of space I find myself immediately at ease in because it is so homey. Row upon row of framed pictures line the top of an entertainment center on one side of the room. A recliner, quilt-covered loveseat, and a rocking chair line the other. The walls are just on the edge of busy, with quite a few knickknacks, and as I enter further into the house, I can see the hallway sports more photos, including a large framed portrait of Rob in uniform.

A plant stand by the front door is the resting place for Jimmy's ashes, which Charlene has already draped with a piece of fancy fabric. Before I can apologize for so unceremoniously springing the ashes on her at the airport, she shares how glad she is to have had a few moments alone to collect her thoughts.

"I carried him for nine months. I can carry you a few steps more," she told him, as she made her way to the car, tears streaming down her cheeks. Passersby, she surmised, would have assumed she was upset from saying good-bye to a loved one embarking on a trip.

I exchange pleasantries with Wayne and Estella, but having gotten up at 2:00 AM to be at the airport by 4:00 AM, and with only one meal since, I confess I am famished. I know Rob has a special meal in mind for lunch—one that can only be gotten at a place called Senate Coney Island. It is a favorite haunt from high school days when band members used to stop there following a Saturday-morning parade. He claims the place has the best Coney dogs and cheese fries in the world. That sounds absolutely perfect to me.

Once at the restaurant, I am struck for probably the hundredth time in just a few hours by how crazy it is that I am really in Michigan, really face-to-face with Jimmy's mother and brother. I am growing anxious to learn more about the Krimms, but in the meantime, I show pictures of my corner of the world. I'd taken several snaps of my house and some sites around Fortuna, just to give them a better sense of the sparseness of the population and the isolation of the landscape. Rob says something about maybe liking wide open spaces but not a place so devoid of any trees. I show Rob and Charlene pictures of my children, and before we know it, our food is in front of us. Charlene and I share an order of cheese fries, in addition to our dogs, and we just about conquer the whole plate.

Arriving back at Charlene's, it is time to get down to talking, never mind this trip is already feeling more like a reunion than an introduction. Not one to assemble questions in advance, I am leaving nothing to chance on this trip, knowing we have such limited time. I want to move chronologically through their family story, as much to help me organize details as to try to keep all of us on track. But keeping Charlene and Rob on track is no easy task—first, because Charlene is capable of imbuing the most mundane of events with a mystical aura rich in detail. Second, because each paragraph they utter generates a whole new list of questions.

We spend quite a lot of time covering family history. Charlene's mother passed away when she was ten, and she'd lived with her grandparents for several years until her father remarried. We covered the family's heritage: Pennsylvania Dutch, which I learn is closer to German, with some Scottish and English mixed in.

Charlene is more than willing to delve into the reasons her marriage to "Big Jim" didn't work, and it is fascinating to catch a glimpse of the dynamics at work in the family when the boys were younger. But, absent Jim's consent to participate in the project—I had yet to even contact him and Rob has not spoken with his dad in about fifteen years—I don't know how much of this material can be used. Private citizens have a right to their privacy.

Besides, it wasn't until Jim was out of the picture and Charlene managed to buy her house—on a waitress's salary of $1.65 an hour plus tips—that all hell broke loose in their lives.

Prior to my arrival, my aunt, who lived in Taylor when her husband pastored a church there for a short time, told me the less-than-gracious label people in northern suburbs applied to the area: "Taylor-tucky." It was a reflection of the many imports from other states, attracted by the chance to work in an auto plant. Over the decades, rural Taylor lost its identity.

"You knock down a farm of sixty acres and you put up 150 houses," local historian George Gouth told me, dissolving any sense of community and creating a social vacuum. That wasn't the aim, but it most definitely was the result.

For all that Charlene wanted to provide her boys with a proper home, the only one she could afford was in a rootless community with no tradition. There were no grandparents to help out in case of illness or lack of employment, no neighbors to mind your kids the same as they would mind their own, and huge blocks of HUD housing full of young, economically and socially vulnerable people.

That first day in Michigan, Charlene shows me a chore notebook she established to try to run her household in absentia, leaving two boys, ages twelve and eight at the time they moved into the Taylor house, to get themselves up each morning and come home every night after school to make their own supper. Charlene worked the 3:00 PM to 11:00 PM shift at a truck stop, filling in several more hours each week with two more jobs, including a couple of shifts a week at an all-night store.

That Charlene still has the notebook, filled with her own handwritten instructions and the scrawls of the two boys indicating which chores had been done, astounds me. There are even scoldings from Charlene for things left undone and back talk, mostly from Jimmy, illustrating his lack of respect for his mother's authority. Reading the notebook is like traveling through time—not just hearing the echoes of everyday family life as recalled, but having the luxury of actually witnessing disputes unfold as the pages turn.

Charlene calls herself a "pack rat" and also confesses to having a bit of the hoarder's obsession with stockpiling food. The stockpile of family moments captured in that chore notebook are so valuable, I thank the heavens for Charlene's compulsions, without which, it would be impossible to reconstruct the minutia of their daily lives.

As we continue talking, Charlene prepares a supper for the three of us. As she cooks, I bring up the subject of Jimmy's prison stint in Michigan. He entered the prison system for the first time when he was about twenty and wasn't released until he was nearly twenty-six years old, in December 1993.

"How often did you visit him in jail?" I ask, expecting Charlene to answer because it doesn't dawn on me that Rob would have visited his abuser.

"Once," Rob says. He has a memory of seeing Jimmy at Christmas in 1989. He remembers wearing new clothes he'd opened as a gift that morning. New clothes were not a frequent luxury, so the attire stood out.

"No," Charlene says, "You had your uniform on. I remember seeing a picture, you and Julie."

Rob claims no recollection of such a visit, but Charlene skips over his confusion to get at a point I too find much more curious at the moment.

"Why did you even want to go or care about seeing him in prison?" she asks him.

"You wanted to go, and I just went with you to see him," Rob says.

"That took a lot of courage for you to do that," Charlene says thoughtfully.

"I don't know why you sent him care packages or anything like that. I was just like…I just went. In my mind, I was just numb to that whole situation and that was in the past. I was more there for you."

"That just took a lot of courage for you to do that," Charlene marvels. "To face him again and try to be, like, try to smile at him. That did take a lot of courage. And I had no idea, no idea. But I appreciate that."

The love in Charlene's voice is obvious to me, and I know I have just witnessed a unique moment in the history of this mother and son. In just a few sentences, Charlene both acknowledges what Rob endured and what that visit to his abuser must have cost him.

Charlene visited Jimmy maybe every other month. He was moved around frequently, she says, and she wasn't really sure why. Rob felt it was just a function of Jimmy's security level or what programs he may have been enrolled in.

"And I guess he had proved to them he was mild mannered and not a real threat, then he would get to these halfway houses…It looked like a fuckin' day camp to me, more like a psych ward or something, converted into a jail."

The talk of Jimmy being in jail reminds Charlene of something she mentioned earlier—some letters Jimmy wrote to her from prison.

"I brought them out," she says. "I don't know what all is in there."

She goes to a stack of folders stuffed full with papers and cancelled envelopes and passes them to me. These aren't *some* letters, I quickly realize. This is more like a running diary documenting Jimmy's five years of incarceration. I am stunned at the depth of what she is handing me. There are dozens upon dozens of sheets covered with Jimmy's block-style printing. I open one of the folders randomly, pulling out the first letter I see.

"Hello, Charlie? Not Mom?" I ask.

Charlie is Charlene's nickname. She even has a little plaque with the title "Charlie's Angels" written on it—her angels being Jimmy and Rob.

Charlene considers my question, that it is kind of odd for a son to address his mother by name.

"I guess…" she answers, with a tight little laugh that becomes almost a cry. "I don't remember," she says, shaking her head and going back to tending the food she is preparing.

Rob is seated in the recliner next to where I sit on the sofa. As Charlene bangs pots and pans in the kitchen, Rob leans over, rather conspiratorially, to remark, "That says a lot…that he didn't write 'Mom.' He wrote 'Charlie.' He's just pissed off at the world."

In the meantime, I'm continuing to read, and the words in front of my eyes at that very moment seem to conflict with what Rob reads into the greeting.

"I love you, exclamation point, X-O-X-O," I read aloud.

I am absolutely enthralled. *Thousands* of Jimmy's thoughts, literally, dropped into my lap. I could not have dreamed when I proposed writing a story about his family, that there could be an opportunity to actually read his thoughts, examine his words. It is almost overwhelming.

"How am I going to go through all of this?" I say aloud. "Wow. Wow."

Coming back to where Rob and I sit, Charlene announces it is time to eat. The aroma is tantalizing. I can understand why Rob raves about his mother's cooking and why, even in his bachelorhood, it seems he is continually concocting some homey treat for himself—something he's either learned from his mom or evolved on his own, through trial and error. His smoked ribs, he claims, are to die for, and Charlene confirms it.

"How much weight do you figure you're going to gain while you're here?" I ask Rob.

"I'm going to try to make all of his favorites," Charlene says, thrilled by this rare opportunity to cook for her youngest son. It is an event made all the more poignant by the realization she will never share a meal with her oldest again.

One thing we haven't talked about yet is Jimmy's relationships with women. I'd heard mention of various girlfriends.

"Was he charming to girls?" I ask, putting a forkful of potatoes into my mouth.

"Those potatoes might need a little salt," Charlene interjects. "What do you think? I put a little seasoning on them, but no salt."

"They're good," I answer.

"Those are Virginia potatoes from Estella's garden," Charlene announces.

"He had the van," Rob answers, picking up the thread of my dangling question. "Back then, having a car was a big deal. You could go places, do things."

Our whole supper conversation goes this way, ranging from serious topics to the mundane, but all piling up, building, brick by brick, to the rich portrait I am gaining from being in the house where the serial bank robber grew up.

Following supper, Charlene hauls out photo albums and boxes of pictures. There is Rob in the drum major's uniform Charlene assembled for him when he was in the high school band. There is Charlene, pictured among the Tupperware "Constellation of Stars," and later, Charlene and Jim, bound for Hawaii after Charlene won a drawing in a recruitment drive for the company. I see pictures of the boys as little tykes, each picture producing another story, from Rob's earliest memory, holding up his fingers to declare, "I four years old," to memories of a family dog they called "Runt."

There is an awkward moment between Charlene and Rob in relation to the dog, and I am confused by the exchange taking place between them.

"I know what happened to him," Charlene says softly. "That's his sick brother."

Rob told me a story on the phone about how Jimmy tortured a dog, but this doesn't seem to be the episode Charlene is referring to.

"Uh…" Rob stammers. Clearly, they both know something I do not, but it is also clear Rob is unsure what he should reveal.

"See, because, I've known…" Charlene says leadingly, looking at Rob. "I thought it happened outside."

I am lost and say so.

"I don't know what you guys are talking about," I tell Charlene. "I don't know what's going on."

"Do you want to tell her?" Charlene asks Rob.

"No. Go ahead," he murmurs.

"Jimmy raped the dog. He raped him," Charlene says, matter-of-fact as you please.

Such a shocking statement seems all the more incomprehensible, relayed as it is, in her high-pitched, Mrs. Santa Claus voice.

I know from discussing other events with Rob over the phone that he has never had an open conversation with his mother about the abuse Jimmy inflicted upon him or about many of the other illicit activities Rob was aware his brother engaged in. In fact, it wasn't until Rob was twenty-six years old that anyone learned Jimmy abused him. When the story finally tumbled out, it was Rob's wife at the time, Julie, who shared some of the details with Charlene. It wasn't that Rob wanted to continue hiding the facts from his mother, only that he was uncomfortable discussing the details with her. It was a difficulty, I'd learned, that was unique to their relationship. He could relay to me, with very little emotion, pretty specifically, the ways Jimmy demeaned and used him, but not to Charlene. He just couldn't go there.

"I thought it happened outside," Charlene continues, "but Julie told me that he took him in the room. He'd had him inside. And Runt was such a nice dog…and after a while, I did kind of notice that he would, like, growl, and I'm thinking, *Why are you growling with me?* Because I didn't know what happened to him…but…there's things that I know," she says. "Nothing you can do anything about; it just happened…"

Rob, I worry, is going to get overloaded. We've covered so much ground in this first afternoon and evening, and I have already established with Rob and Charlene that some of my interviewing will be done with both of them, jointly, while other parts will need to be done one-on-one. Rob has agreed the two of us will delve more deeply into the specifics of his abuse the next morning, in advance of Jimmy's memorial service in the afternoon. Our plan, by default, is cramming a lot of emotion into these three days, and I need his reassurance I am not asking too much of him.

He assures me he is fine. No big deal. But the question of where to conduct the interview still hasn't been settled. I can't expect Charlene to leave her home open to us all morning because she has preparations to make for the service. And I don't feel comfortable inviting Rob to my motel room. That has less to do with the obvious objections I can hear coming out of my husband's mouth and more to do with my own desire to try to retain some semblance of professionalism.

We make a plan that Rob will come to my motel first thing in the morning, and if I haven't come up with an appropriate space by then, we'll just wing it, somehow.

By this time, I think I am going on about nineteen hours awake, on about four hours of sleep the night before. Before I leave for the night, I want to formulate some sort of a plan for reviewing Jimmy's letters. There must be a couple hundred of them. With the limited time we have over the next few days, I can't spend hours and hours reading them—let alone transcribing words that could become absolutely critical. I know how much these letters must mean to Charlene, never mind what they can mean for the book.

"Is there a copy shop around here somewhere where I could maybe get them copied…?" I begin, trying to find some opening that will lead me exactly to the solution I seek—taking them home with me.

Charlene flat out offers to let me take them home when I fly back to North Dakota.

"This is so huge," I tell her. Does she even realize how big this is? I can't believe her willingness to trust me like this. For me, this is much bigger than carrying Jimmy's ashes; this is entrusting me with his life!

"I will carry them on the plane. I will not let them out of my sight for a second," I tell her. I promise to keep them in my possession until some point in the future when I can return them in person.

I am going on and on about how fascinating I am finding the information in the few letters I have already looked over as we chat on other subjects. Rob excuses himself, as Charlene and I yammer on and on. I'm sure we must sound to him like a couple of hens clucking and clucking. After awhile, it seems Rob must have fallen in.

I whisper to Charlene, "Where did Rob go?"

Jumping to conclusions, as usual, I worry something I said upset him. I hope that isn't the case.

"I think he just went to the bathroom. Rob?" Charlene calls. "Where did you go?"

"I'm just laying down," he calls from the bedroom.

He hadn't said a word! He'd just slipped away. Charlene and I exchange a look. *Does he do this a lot?* Apparently, he is done for the night.

"We thought you fell in," I call from the living room, a little sheepishly.

Now I really feel bad. I wish I could take back whatever insensitive prattling of mine propelled him from the room.

"I'm just a little worn out," he replies.

"You and me both," I say.

I file away in my brain the intention of apologizing to him the next day if I said anything to upset him. I try to go back over in my mind how much I may have fawned over Jimmy's letters or gone on and on about how important they were.

He has to know his story is just as important—more so, in fact. I need to be sure he knows that. I can imagine how odd it must be to have some stranger ask you a bunch of personal questions, sit there while your mother talks about your dog being raped and the disintegration of her own marriage—details I'm sure Rob would have been just as happy to forego hearing—and then, to top it all off, have some writer go on and on about how fascinating she finds the brother who abused you. I could kick myself for being such an insensitive boor sometimes.

I can't worry about it, though. We just have to press on. I can't get so caught up in worrying about Rob's feelings or in feeling so much sympathy I can't pull out of him the story we have agreed we want to tell. Somehow, it just has to work, in this limited span of time, no holds barred.

Besides the fact I have never before spent eight solid hours interviewing two people, I am sure I have never found two people more open and dedicated to revealing the truth, no matter how it reflects on them. We three are on a shared mission, but Rob preferred to take the next leg of this journey without Charlene.

Tomorrow morning, Rob and I would walk through some of the land mines in his childhood. But first, I have to find the right space to make that process as comfortable as possible, not that any place really could.

CHAPTER SIX

Brothers

After getting up early at the motel, I go down to the lobby to ask if there is a room where I can conduct an interview. I am staying in a big, older place a few miles down Eureka Road—one of the main drags in Taylor—from Charlene's house. It isn't really set up for meetings the way newer hotels are.

The manager shows me a cavernous banquet hall. There doesn't appear to be anything like a VIP or hospitality room—a motel room without a bed. That's what I really need, just a room with no sexual overtones. That's not how I put it, but I get my point across.

On the same floor as my room, he shows me a suite with a living room on one side and a bedroom on the other, separated by doors. When we walk into the suite, all I see is the sitting area. There is a big comfy couch and a coffee table. There is a big window to let lots of light in. It is perfect.

I tell Rob to come to the side door by a set of elevators, and I am at that door to greet him when he pulls up in his fortieth-anniversary-edition Mustang. It is a hot car. And he cuts quite a figure in his mirrored sunglasses, leather jacket, and jeans. Rob is a good-looking man and well built, but his demeanor makes it clear he doesn't see himself that way. I know from past discussions he's pretty much given up on women and isn't sure he is "relationship material." He is content just to pursue his own interests. It seems a shame. He has a lot to offer someone.

I am pretty sure he likes being the center of attention, though. He likes having someone listen to him and, more important, understand the emotions he expresses. If I can be that person, I am happy. I am getting the chance to tell a complex story, and he is getting the recognition, finally, of how much he has endured just to be considered an average Joe.

I quickly explain the setup I've found, and the conversation flows so naturally as we walk to the room, I don't even catch the first bit of the actual interview on my tape recorder. Settled in the comfy suite, on opposite ends of the long couch, we start out talking about "normal" childhood stuff.

Rob watched the borning of a serial bank robber. I am curious what clues might be apparent now, in hindsight.

Left to their own devices at the ages of ten and six, Jimmy and Harry Robert did what all kids do when there are no adults around: they pushed the limits. As long as the house didn't burn down and the police didn't knock on her door, Charlene believed her kids were okay while she worked.

Jimmy, Rob says, never seemed to have a filter between impulse and action. Though Charlene left the boys a few dollars every day to pick up groceries, they also had money of their own from mowing lawns, but that enterprise was short-lived.

"It turned from mowing lawns to why work for it when you can just take it?" Rob says.

Mostly, Rob remembers being an annoyance to Jimmy.

"I was kind of like the cat that you try to shoo off your foot and try to run out the door and close it that reattaches itself to your leg."

Any interaction that took place between them, even in legitimate "play," usually devolved into aggression.

"We'd play 'crash 'em up derby'…and he would always win because my car would just crumble into little bits. So I guess he was competitive in that sense; he wasn't one to go into something and fail. But I thought he was just an asshole because he broke my car."

They both enjoyed blowing things up.

"We would take tennis balls, and we would take the tennis ball case, bore a hole in the bottom of it, shoot lighter fluid down in there, put the tennis ball in there, and light the lighter fluid, and it'd shoot straight up."

The boys had a few board games, but Jimmy was more likely to make up his own games in which he set the rules.

"His favorite was either a screwdriver or a pocket knife, and we would stand there, with our legs shoulder width apart, and he would throw the knife in the ground. Wherever the knife stuck, you had to put your foot," even if it meant doing the splits.

Playing with fire was one of the few activities that left some evidence behind to cause Charlene to go ballistic, like the time the brothers burned cones of incense, leaving little round marks on the coffee table.

"She'd get pissed and tell us we were gonna burn the house down."

Charlene had an answer for the damage to her table: she took something that belonged to each of them, destroyed it, and then placed the item on their beds to drive home how frustrating it was to lose something of value.

Rob learned the one thing he never wanted to hear was his full name, "Harry Robert Krimm," spoken by his mother.

"That was like, 'Oh shit! Hide!' But before you heard that, you would hear, 'Goddamnsonuvabitch!' That was her favorite word, all said together with an upward inflection. She would never run out of the house screaming. She'd run *through* the house screaming. She had a time where she was taking diet pills, which was glorified speed, and she'd come home to find we did nothing to clean up the house. She'd get home round 11:30 at night, wake us up, turn the radio on loudly, and make us do something... I still remember cleaning the wall till the paint came off. I'm thinking, *This is stupid. Can we sleep now?* Eventually, she bottomed out, and we all slept."

Charlene was just as likely to come home overflowing with affection.

"I remember she'd tuck the blanket around my body like a little cocoon. I'd feel so safe, and I'd nod off into la-la land.

"All things considered, she did an amazing job," Rob says. Their father, Jim, was still in the area but saw the boys infrequently. One time, he took them off-roading.

"He had bought a new four-by-four pickup truck. I remember it was white. I sat in the middle because I was smallest. We went down to the mud hole and just had a good ol' time. It was dangerous, and I think we almost hit another four-by-four down there. It was me, my brother, and Dad. It was the best day I'd ever had as a family."

But even that memory is marred for Rob by the realization he may have put a damper on things.

"I think I kind of spoiled the moment because I probably got scared and started screaming," he says.

Other visits were less spectacular. Rob remembers feeling like his dad was just going through the motions.

"Visits with him were just kind of 'blah'—just hanging out."

Rob feels his father saw them out of obligation.

"It was like 'What can I do to get away with the bare minimum?' We just ran around the apartment and annoyed him for a couple of hours."

The presence of his father is less a memory than his absence. This is just one of many similarities we share. My own parents divorced when I was a baby, and other than one time when I was three, I never saw my biological father until I was an adult.

"I don't remember that presence of him, like teaching us things, and whenever we didn't know how to tie our shoe, there was none of that presence where he should have been there," Rob says.

Jim visited the kids at the house a few times.

"Whenever he would leave, we'd give him a kiss good-bye. Nothing weird, but he had a scratchy face, and I remember it almost tore my lips off...And that's about the only real memory I have of him."

Once Jim was laid off from Ford's, he disappeared. Rob didn't understand it at the time, but Charlene was left with no child support, which put even more pressure on her to work as much as possible outside the home.

"As hard as Mom tried," Rob says, "I remember that she called Jimmy an 'asshole' frequently. She had limited time, so, as kids, we never got the luxury of having a patient mom."

Charlene used a wooden board to paddle Jimmy when he misbehaved.

"Back then, a paddling was acceptable, and that's the way she did it to make him realize something is important—she beat it into his brain, so to speak," Rob says. "And he would get, like, ten...It wasn't like she was just whacking him upside the head."

Jimmy expressed his resentment by rejecting Charlene's efforts to do anything nice for him, like buying each son a chest of drawers. Jimmy refused to put his in his room.

"I just remember him and her fighting over it and him just being resentful towards her, saying he didn't want anything from her and stuff like that, yet at the same time, here he is stealing her coin collection," says Rob.

Charlene began saving silver coins when she and Jim were first married. She also saved half dollars from tips in a big old elephant-shaped bank.

"He would turn the thing upside down and take a butter knife and get out whatever it was he wanted," says Rob.

It was the same when Charlene's grandpa gave each of the boys an old silver dollar from the 1920s.

"Jimmy, of course, hocked his, like, immediately," Rob says. "My mom bought me a belt buckle that the silver dollar went in, and I put the belt buckle together with the silver dollar. And I stuffed it in a cotton glove, and I threw it in the bottom of my toy box, so I would still have it...I hid it, 'cause that's the only way I could have it."

Jimmy searched in vain for his brother's silver dollar many times, growing angry when he couldn't find it.

When Charlene discovered infractions like Jimmy stealing from her or from his little brother, it was time for the paddle. Though Charlene tried other punishments, like grounding Jimmy, she couldn't enforce them because she wasn't home. And she never had the luxury of saying, "You just wait until your father comes home."

In the winter, what the boys called "the creek," which was actually a drainage diversion canal ringing the neighborhood, would freeze up, and they'd ride their bikes there.

"And because you're in that valley sort of thing, it was just like quiet, and you couldn't hear any cars...and it was just like, peaceful," Rob recalls.

On Friday and Saturday nights, the boys shared a late-night ritual, brewing coffee and laying in a supply of snacks so they could stay up and watch comedy shows. Their favorite was *Fridays*.

"It was on Fridays, and it was just like *Saturday Night Live*," Rob says, except instead of "Live from New York," it was "Dead from Detroit."

A favorite skit involved a young Michael Richards (later, he played "Kramer" on *Seinfeld*) playing with little green plastic army men.

"He's got the tank, and he's making the tank noise...and then he'll act like he's shooting a missile on them, and demolish the entire scene, and he'd have this look on his face like, 'crazy kid'...We lived to watch that scene. It was like, 'C'mon on, *be* there!'"

Rob suspects Jimmy bullied other kids in the neighborhood.

"One time, these kids were picking on me, and I said, 'My brother's going to kick your ass.' And they said, 'Who's your brother?' I said, 'Jim Krimm.' And they said, 'Yeah, we better not mess with him,' because they knew who he was...They didn't want the likes of Jim Krimm after them, so they left me alone."

Charlene might call home once during an evening to see if the boys were okay. Charlene couldn't know, and Rob couldn't tell her about the threat that was inside the home.

The abuse began more like a game. It was one young Harry Robert soon grew tired of, but one he had no option of sitting out. Rob explained to me on the phone, before we got to Michigan, that as a youngster, he went by his first name, Harry. When he looks back at the abuse today, it is Harry he describes as being harmed.

It is upsetting for Rob to realize, initially, there was some fascination with what was going on. At the age of ten, Harry was not mature enough to ejaculate.

"I wasn't developed enough to understand that's what happens. I guess that's why it's so disturbing, like, 'Oh, that's kind of neat,' and it was just kind of something new...It all got worse after that."

There is shame in the remembering—shame for feelings of curiosity, shame for not fighting back, shame for not telling someone. But it seems to me as I listen to Rob talk factually and with little emotion about what happened, the shame has diminished with time and with a greater understanding he is not to blame for what happened.

If there is any emotion left in Rob about the actual abuse, it appears to be rage. That rage is expressed, on this morning before a ceremony called in memory of his brother, in a total disdain for the event he is about to attend.

"This is just a day he gets. He gets *this* day, and you know, I support it because my ma feels strongly about it, and I'm just like, 'All right!' I'm doing it for her."

Clearly, Rob does not expect to shed any tears at the memorial service, which is just a few hours away. As strange as the timing seems, we need to get into the nitty-gritty of what happened, and I ask Rob to tell me more about the first instance of abuse. It is an episode he's already written about, at length, taking place at their grandparents' home in Pennsylvania, when Jimmy was fourteen and Harry, ten. Something as innocent as expecting the two boys to share a bed turned young Harry's world upside down, opening a door for Jimmy to violently and repeatedly rape his brother over a period of five years. The activity finally culminated in the transfer of abuse to the family dog—a development Rob looks back on with horror, but also, with a sense of relief.

"I feel bad for the dog, but now the dog knows how I feel," Rob says.

I can sympathize, and I am also amazed, seated there in a comfortable, peaceful setting, that Rob can so easily admit a feeling that would probably be foreign to someone who has not been abused. I understand, having been powerless as a six-year-old to stop my stepfather from molesting me. I know that any deliverance, any reprieve, so long as it took the assault away from me, would have been welcome.

"Whatever made him leave me alone was just fine with me," Rob says.

Anything to avoid waking up, as he had in Pennsylvania that summer he was ten, to find his brother fondling him.

"And I was like, 'What the hell are you doing?' Like, 'What the fuck are you doing?' And I think that was the start of it. And what compelled him, to like, put those two pieces together, I don't know. I mean, there was no penetration at that time, but I think he just did a dry hump or put it between my legs or something. He was just demented, and so from that point, it was, you know, accelerated or amplified."

Harry's life changed for the worse that summer.

"Nothing was ever the same after that. This was about the same time that my mom and dad lost contact with each other too."

Rob wonders if the loss of his dad is what caused Jimmy to act out so inappropriately.

"He would blame Mom for it that she was chasing Dad away," Rob says. "The fact is they were young and not mature enough to give each other the respect that the other required. I have a lot of respect for my mom in that regard. She was able to give us the security of a house. She was always thinking about taking care of us. Right down to getting our teeth filled."

Or making sure the boys had some contact with the extended family in Pennsylvania.

"She would just drive the van down to Pennsylvania," sometimes staying with them as a family vacation. They would do things as a family, like visit an amusement park.

But even as a kid, Harry could also see why his mother was so detached from her own family.

"You want to be the opposite of your parents," Rob says, and that seemed to be the case with Charlene. In Pennsylvania, the boys found strict rules with Charlene's father and stepmother.

"I never remember calling them Grandma or Grandpa," Rob says.

Yet, up until that fateful visit, "These summers were filled with happy memories," including riding bikes down a track they dubbed "the thirty-five-mile-per-hour hill."

Riding to the hill, "I'd slam on the brakes on the blacktop, and it would make the tires squeal. Then the people in the houses would come out and yell obscenities to us like, 'You damn fucking kids'—typical old people curses 'cause they don't really know how to swear."

It is one of the few memories Rob has of Jimmy acting like a "normal" older brother.

"Jimmy would always go faster for some reason. But I would just let the momentum go until my bike was going so fast that I thought my front wheel would rattle off…I'd start screaming, 'Out of control!' I thought for sure I was gonna crash and go splat.

"Jimmy said, 'Just slam on the brakes!' So, I did, and the back wheel locks up making that cool squealing noise that I like so much."

The boys would return to their grandparents' place, flying down another hill into the yard and skidding.

"I once broke a pedal doing that. But it was always fun as hell! Whew, next up was Kool-Aid and baloney sandwiches, TV, and walk around aimlessly like kids do."

It is the closest thing to an idyllic childhood memory Rob possesses. If not for Jimmy's advances in the bedroom they shared, these would have been some of the happiest days of Harry's young life.

"I just wanted to sleep, but Jimmy kept acting stupid. He kept doing gay things. I'm not sure of the details because I've blocked it out of my memories. I just would want to get up and eat some cereal. Be left alone."

When Jimmy wouldn't stop, Rob would start to make a fuss.

"It's just moments that are difficult to talk about…He just sort of got himself off, and that was the start of it. He kept trying to push it," until Harry got upset, and as Rob puts it, "acted like a crybaby."

That worked, at first, and Jimmy would stop.

When the boys returned home after that trip, there were no adults around to notice if Harry made a fuss.

"The beatings and abuse continued until I was about fourteen or fifteen."

Jimmy had a hundred pounds on Harry, and he was a foot taller. Harry had little choice but to comply.

"At first, I was resistant, and I was, like, 'No!' and then I got my ass beat."

Jimmy developed a code word for the act. Rob has no idea where it came from. It is a word Rob never wants to hear spoken, *humpyegg*.

"That's what he'd say," Rob tells me.

I am embarrassed for him, sorry he has to reveal something so disgusting to him, but glad he is willing to trust me with the information. Though the words I am hearing are taking me back to episodes in my own life that echo the twisted logic an abuser employs to gain compliance, I try to keep my face blank.

"It's like one minute we're sitting there watching TV, then he'd say 'humpyegg.' That was the first word he called it before he started numbering 'it.' Number one and number two were already taken by the general population...So, he started with three, four..."

The numbers referred to different positions—a small consolation that developed when Harry complained of the pain and Jimmy would attempt to find a less uncomfortable method of penetration. If Harry still said no, Jimmy would insist.

"He'd just say, 'Humpyegg,' as if to make it less of a disgusting thing."

"And I would instantly become frightened and start saying, 'No, I don't wanna.'

"He'd be like, 'C'mon humpyegg,' telling me to go to my room and get ready. Then, if I didn't, he'd go to his room, get a belt, and start popping it to make that loud noise like it does.

"I'd start screaming, 'No!' But he would just snap the belt. I used to have imprints on my stomach of the design that was on the belt itself. So, I had my choices, and I would force myself to go through with it."

These episodes left lasting trauma on Rob's mind and body.

"The ass was not designed for this type of thing. What if something happened, and I had to be rushed to the hospital because of internal bleeding? Like, I'm thinking about this as an adult now, but that was never a concern for him."

It wasn't until Jimmy was in prison, when Harry was about sixteen, that he awoke one day, bleeding from his anus. Harry woke his mom to take him to the doctor. The doctor told Harry not to push so hard when he had a bowel movement. No one questioned that there could be any other explanation.

Someone who has not been abused might think it would have been easy to tell a doctor what was really going on. But I know the dynamic of abuse, the power abusers wield over their victims, even behind bars. There was no way young Harry could tell a doctor, or anyone, what really caused the damage. The shame alone prevented him, never mind the fear.

During the time when the abuse was ongoing, "I tried to tell people and cry out for help to the neighbors or whatever. They saw me and my brother outside and me obviously smaller and not able to defend myself. All the neighbors wanted was for us to stop making noise."

He remembers one neighbor in particular, who should have realized something was amiss.

"He could have helped," but he did nothing.

How well I know that feeling of helplessness. Being threatened not to tell on the abuser is always a part of the equation, as is putting on an act that everything is okay.

Whether robbing someone, stealing a car, or sexually abusing his own brother, Rob believes Jimmy knew right from wrong, "but he would do it if he thought he could get away with it. He always knew it was wrong. He just didn't care."

I need a break, and I sense Rob does too. The story Rob is sharing is bringing up so many feelings for me. But hearing his tale of abuse, I am not only forced to recall moments that echo his, but also to see some silver lining in the fact that I *can* understand, that I *can* sympathize. It is so crazy. If I'd known at the age of six or eleven, or even fourteen that the ways my stepfather was harming me would one day allow me to sit and listen to a man share his own painful abuse episodes, would it have helped me endure it? How can I possibly look back now on the loss of my own innocence and see some benefit to it having been stolen?

"Some guy with no neck took a picture of hisself at the Jack D. Grave stie [site] (then broke camera)"*

January 10, 2009

Hello Dad, Thank you for writing & pictures.

I drove down Christmas to see ya! Where the heck is (Street name)?

I called an internet phone number that was suppost to be yours, got a womans voice twice & left my number to call back to no avail.

"Google earth" showed no (Street name). I went to (town name) Sunday morning church by the highway & asked the usher if he knew where (Street name) was. He said Connley Creek Road some where.

So off I went, past the neibourhood watch signs, all the way up to top, then back up fork in road to dead end.

Then someone followed me half way back down till I pulled overe in a drive way. They looked at the buffalo on my plate & made a phone call. So I left & went on to Lynchberg, T.N. to Jack Daniel Distillery Tour (sent card).

Caught poltergiste (ghostly) picture there in "04" at the Hollow where water comes out of mountain. Showed a few people & They agreed.

(OVER)

A few said wow! Whats that? Im back in N.D. Now, where the snow is plowed 10-15 feet high and more—at malls etc…

Last night Minot N.D. got 14" of snow—They don't know where to put it! That's what the news said & I believe them!

So much snow this year!

---

* Written by Jimmy on the back of this photo.

Just before I came to visit we had the worst snowstorm in 10 yrs! When I left to go south before Christmas it was -21F. Temp. not wind chill.

Glad to see you are alive & well! I though the camels and Budwieser would have got ya by now. You must have quit?

I quit smoking in 1991. Took me 5 tries—cold turkey.

(Next Page)

The only drug I do is whiskey, and yes that's a drug.

I quit drinking for 2 months then started up for a month. Then quit for a month then something would piss me off, and to get even I'd go drink.

I've kicked coke—last I did it was 1996. I smoked it. Not needle fan.

Pot once in while doesn't always do me good. When I was in Canada 2 summers ago I smoke pot with some campers. I got so sick I puked! 3 times!

So that's not a habit for me. I'm on asprin reginmen—4 yrs ago had blood clot in leg while in Canada visiting. Leg swelled up like ball bat & almost died "again." "Deep vien thrombouses" it was called.

(Next page)

Must get this in mail today!

In 2 days or more will have Fresh Pictures to send you.

You have to email—or send directions so I can visit.

Where is (Street name)?

The people down there are Rude drivers (I now know the meaning of road rage.) Now wonder theres crosses everywhere!

IF you'd like to come here you are welcome.

Bring "thermal clothes" boots, glove, hat, shovel, salt, too.

Worst winter in 10+ years.

Love Ya, Jim

(Flip over)

For Shits & Giggles I play with 70 mph radio controlled cars & 4 wheel drive trucks in the snow.

I also fly radio controlled (electric)-(Lithuim Polymer) Batt planes. Lost 3 planes—they just flew away...

"Song of Day"
Trace Adkins
"Muddy water"

Have 3 "Montgomery Gentry" C.D.s

Drove Blue Ridge Parkway. No snow—Had a spiritual moment—like in Canada.

Very nice.

CHAPTER SEVEN

Abuse

I excuse myself for a moment, leaving Rob in the living room of the suite.

I understand everything Rob is telling me. It is almost like that song, "Killing Me Softly." Our stories are interchangeable in so many ways—not the actual acts of abuse, but the emotions in response to it.

I understand the coercion, the twisted logic that allows an abuser to wheedle his way into ever more compromising episodes of violation. My own abuse had begun as I sat on the couch in our living room, coloring a picture of Santa Claus, at the age of six. I made a mistake on the page and let out a little sigh. That was his opening, allowing my stepfather to sidle up beside me on the pretense of feigning interest in what I was doing. That alone alarmed me. The next thing I knew, he was asking me how my culotte pajamas came off.

Rob's words, "He always knew it was wrong. He just didn't care," summed it up nicely. Implied in Rob's words and confirmed in my memory is that *we* always knew it was wrong, too. We just didn't know how to stop it.

Rob takes a break too and then our talk continues. If innocence lost is a theme with which I can easily identify, the next part of his story is one I know so well from my own experience, our stories are virtually identical.

At the age of ten, the simple act of walking home from school, for Harry, felt like walking to the executioner—not knowing what torture Jimmy might have in store.

"That was a fear of mine, always, when I would come home," Rob says. "I remember a rainy day—it was just like a happy sprinkle rain, and I was just like, skipping, just being a kid and skipping and walking home from school and, you know, not knowing that when I get to the house he's going to be pissed off and beat my ass for something."

Only the element of physical violence is missing from my own story, though my stepdad once threatened to throw battery acid on my face if I told anyone. I think I was thirteen at the time. But I know so well the terror of rounding the bend in my street to see my stepfather's car in the driveway. It took all the courage I possessed to walk up and open that door, knowing what was likely to happen when I got inside the house.

On this particular rainy day, Rob recalls, Jimmy's rationale for "punishing" him was that he'd seen his little brother doing something "stupid" at school.

"It was just an excuse, but as a kid, I didn't know that so I was like, putting everything out there…'So, I can't take a fake microphone and fake like I'm singing into it?'

"And he's like, 'No you can't do that.' And so I would go through all the things I might have done during recess. And he would just say, 'No you can't do that, can't do that, can't do that,'" Rob says, counting off each action on his fingers.

That particular day, walking home in the rain, perhaps, was the genesis of a coping mechanism, allowing Harry to trade his awful reality for a world where there was beauty and serenity—a place his future wife would label "Krimmland."

"That day skipping home in the rain, it was really just a mist of tender tiny droplets, almost fog-like. I still love the rain, and for some reason, I can find pleasure in the tiniest details, or even find a positive; where most only see a cloudy day, I see a beautiful overcast that colors the earth in overtones of grey—sometimes, making reds redder, and shiny stuff this perfect white that gives you a feeling of living inside of a fairy tale," Rob says.

These images are like poetry to me. I was a "rain kid" too, finding magic in the mundane, wondering at the possibility of fairies, seeing beauty in the most ordinary of natural objects.

In Krimmland, Harry could escape, soaring in an environment of his own imagination, where no monsters—or older brothers—could harm him.

"Where else am I going to go really, you know? And that was just like, that was the beginnings," Rob says. Prior to that, "I hadn't really developed a method of escaping. I was just sort of blindsided."

With no outward defense against the molestation, Harry created a mental shield Jimmy could not penetrate.

"I would daydream to the extent that I could block out the entire world around me and go into my own little world."

It is uncanny, the descriptions Rob is sharing. I am trying to remain objective, trying to be professional, trying not to insert too much of my own experience into the interview, trying to share only enough so Rob will know I am following him, when in fact, we are walking, practically in lockstep. He can't know, and I can't tell him that I did exactly the same thing, built up the same sorts of mental defenses.

I can't explain, and perhaps he wouldn't even believe that as an adult, the powers of my concentration are so developed, I once gave my kids a code word to try to snap me to attention when they couldn't get my attention any other way. They could literally be standing right next to me, but lost in my own thoughts, nothing short of a slap in the face would lure me back to the present.

As I listen to Rob, I have to keep reminding myself Rob is not me. If I don't pay close attention, I might project too much of myself onto his story and miss the ways his experience was unique. Thank goodness for my tape recorder. If there is any confusion later, I can go back and listen again.

All I can tell him at the time is that I am feeling that confusion. I ask him to forgive me if I misunderstand something he says or inject a dynamic that wasn't present. But it seems, as we continue the interview, that my own experience serves as a catalyst instead, allowing me to ask the questions that bring his experience into sharper focus for both of us.

Only when Rob talks about the violence of his encounters with Jimmy can I see the difference between what was done to us as children.

"He would get the same board my ma would beat his ass with and start hitting me over the head and over the back and over the chest. I had a big welt on my head and stuff like that. Here I was, happy, skipping home, and I'm getting my ass beat for no reason. And then he'd tell me to go to my room, and I'd just go lay there and cry because I didn't know if he was going to come to my room...and I just laid there in tears and just not knowing what to do...You know, what did I do to deserve that?"

Charlene's discipline with the board had some structure, but Jimmy took paddling his little brother to the extreme.

"She was frustrated, and she was taking her frustrations out, but she only hit on the ass," Rob says. "I got the board everywhere."

Rob sees today how the aggression could have been a way for Jimmy to cope with the rage he had toward their mother.

On that rainy day, "Did ma beat his ass for something he did and then he's going to take out his frustrations on me?"

Perhaps.

"Because we both burned holes in the table, but she just got so used to blaming Jimmy," he says. "It really was about shit rolling downhill."

If Jimmy couldn't get back at Charlene, he would take it out on someone who seemed to curry more favor. The beatings and rape continued until Harry was about fifteen years old.

"I was supposed to go to my room and await his majesty to administer the royal pain in the ass, i.e., get naked, lay there, and willingly take it," Rob says.

And it wasn't as if, after these episodes, Harry might earn some "normal" treatment from Jimmy or even feel like doing "normal" things on his own.

"This left me feeling depressed and used. Like, now that I did it, was I going to get to play, like, be myself, run around the backyard?" or do something with his brother that was fun or instructive or in any way positive?

"Abso-fuckin-lutely, nothin'. He got what he wanted, and then sometimes he'd just take off…every man for himself sorta' thing."

After each rape, he says, "It was just like, go clean myself up, you know, take a shower and take a crap. Try and wash the bad feeling off. And thinking about it today just makes me wonder what I did to deserve that? Nobody should have to go through that, nobody should. And I don't know why I went through it. It was torture, you know; it was just pure torture."

Just as I can sit, as an adult, and feel sympathy for the little girl I once was, my desire to embrace the little boy, Harry, hidden inside of the man, Rob, is so strong I hardly know how to contain it. My admiration for Rob, for enduring what he went through, for his strength in surviving the hell he describes, is as strong—stronger—than the credit I give myself for surviving my own abuse.

There is another stark difference, though, in our aftermaths, and I sense it stems from the element of violence. Rob's abuse, because of the penetration and the beatings, seems to have created an anger beyond my experience. It is in this way, I sense, I might be further along in the process of dealing with what happened to me as a child. Forgiveness is a concept completely foreign to Rob.

"Gee whiz, do I feel bad he blew his brains out, what little he had?"

No.

"The best thing he ever did was blow his brains out. Worthless piece of shit."

There were times, early on, when Harry tried to avoid Jimmy's advances by making a fuss to Charlene about going to work with her. If the purpose of putting up a fuss was to avoid a beating, it was ineffective.

"She had no idea. But you'd think that would have been a flag as to why am I in tears? I realized, begging her to take me to work with her, it wasn't going to happen. It merely would increase my ass beating."

Rob has lasting physical damage from Jimmy's repeated assaults. Again, it is a difference in us I can only sympathize with. As damaging as my own abuse was, my scars are all emotional. I have no physical reminders.

"To this day," Rob says, "something I have to live with is that tissue down there does not heal…and the doctors go, 'How is this possible?'"

Though he eventually had minor surgery to repair some of the damage, prior to that, "The doctor looked at it and said, 'This is not possible.'…It's a vein that is sort of pinched by the sphincter, and it's supposed to be inside but sometimes it's outside. And in order to avoid getting a painful hemorrhoid, I know the symptoms of it…if I notice it starting again, I just jump in the shower and fix it."

This physical damage is a lasting insult on top of the original injury.

"I guess it brings up all that emotion from my past, and I knew the right thing to do, but I didn't have a choice. Being four years younger, you know, I'm a foot shorter or more and I was just helpless. I get part of an ass beating, and then he's like, 'All right, you gonna do it now?'

"And I'm like, 'All right. Whatever will make you stop kicking my ass.' And that's the way it went. And you know, from then on, it was just kind of like—fuck it. I either get an ass beating or I just do it and get it over with."

Like choosing to have your finger chopped off with an ax or a chainsaw, there is no good choice. Yet, Harry never fantasized about getting even. That surprised me. I had.

"That thought never crossed my mind," he says. "Not once."

Even at a time when Rob knew Jimmy had a gun in the house, he never thought of shooting him with it.

"Never an evil thought. I simply would avoid sticking my hand into fire in the future," he says. Or he would fantasize about Jimmy winding up in a hell especially designed for him.

"...one where he'll be butt-fucked by a spiky sword till the end of eternity."

Five long years.

"Five years, yeah, I couldn't imagine going any longer than five years. It was at least once a week," Rob says, and the anticipation of what would be expected of him in the next episode only added to the torture.

"We could be walking at the store and in public, and instead of saying something that sounded gay, he could say, 'Number three, number four,'" and Harry would know what Jimmy planned when they got home.

The numbering of different sexual positions wasn't Jimmy's only "concession" to the pain Harry complained of. Even the idea of a "concession" or "consideration," in Rob's estimation, gives a false impression.

"It was more just whether he was going to be able to get his rocks off and me switching positions didn't make it hurt any less...so his solution was to tape some batteries together and coat it with wax so that he could try to stretch it out so it wouldn't hurt anymore. Yeah...implements of torture in my life...I guess, you know, that was his solution...the lotion on it...and the lotion and shit smell just, like, permeated the whole room, and it just...it was nasty. And anytime I smell that lotion, it just reminds me of lotion and shit."

These words, the degradation they contain, slap me harder, perhaps, than any others Rob has spoken. They take me back to the aftermath of an episode in which, for the first time ever, my stepfather ejaculated on me, the cum landing on my neck, cold and fishy. I was maybe eleven or twelve at the time. Afterward, I lay on my own frilly bedspread in the unsafe haven that was my childhood room. I worried, somehow, it would make me pregnant.

As horrible as the memory is for me, the abuse Rob describes goes far beyond my experience. As an adult, Rob wonders how his brother, a teenager at the time, could have been familiar with the concept of anal dilation. It begs the question whether Jimmy was ever sexually abused and if so by whom and at what age? Rob has his theories.

One theory, based on the premise that pedophiles often fixate on children who are the age they were when they were first abused, would place

Jimmy around the age of ten when someone, at some time or place, could have done the same things to him.

"It could have been anybody in the apartments," Rob says, referring to where they lived before they moved to the house in Taylor. "When we were kids at the apartment complex, we would run around, and I was too young to hang with his crowd for any length of time."

Rob remembers an instance in which he narrowly missed being molested by someone in the complex.

"I was bored and talking to this guy working on his car or something. Then I was like, 'Okay, gotta go; my mom is calling me.' I remember he started saying, 'You don't have to go. Just stay here.' I think that was probably a good thing my mom started calling my name at that time."

Once installed at the house in Taylor, the boys were in close proximity to what became, over the years, a notorious haven for illegal activity. The Pine Ridge Apartments were full of single mothers and their children, and later, crackheads. The complex could have been a magnet for any predator bent on victimizing children.

"There was a veritable oasis of kids," Rob says.

It isn't a stretch to imagine Jimmy, with his desire for comforts in short supply at home, being lured into sexual activity. Jimmy was a child at risk no less than Harry.

Rob believes it is plausible that Jimmy's code word, *humpyegg*, is a clue pointing toward his brother's own victimization.

"It was like he already knew the name and just started referring to it that way," Rob says.

Humpyegg, a silly word for a horrible, tortuous penetration. It sounded like a word out of a nursery rhyme, like the name of a game a young child could be coerced into playing. And what of the batteries? Was Jimmy's application of batteries as a tool for anal dilation a method someone used on him? Were the batteries, once inserted, like "eggs" that were later laid, in advance of penetration by an abuser?

Though Jimmy's abuse of Harry became violent, a more coercive approach to abuse, especially with younger children, is more common. I am intimately familiar with that approach. By introducing the abuse as a form of "play" or as a secret "game" to be shared, the abuser obtains cooperation without violence or aggression. Jimmy's approach to Harry too began in a coercive fashion. It was only as Harry aged and grew less compliant that Jimmy's aggression escalated.

A piece of information Rob sees as supportive of the theory of his brother being abused comes out of Jimmy's autopsy. Rob notices the mention of a physical detail that might indicate anal trauma. Such a detail suggests to Rob that Jimmy was raped at some point, too.

"Even though he was pretty strong...he worked out, he was big... there's always somebody bigger," Rob says.

Even at the age of fourteen or fifteen, Rob says, Jimmy seemed to have a prison mentality.

"You know, 'I got my bitch.' And I was his bitch."

Even as a young teen, Jimmy seemed to have a sense of entitlement and an absence of scruples.

"Just bulldozer over anybody else's personal feelings. He was always take, take, take, take, take, and he never gave back," Rob says.

Though he was developing mental techniques of escaping, young Harry also began to seek out physical escape. He would roam the neighborhood after school, waiting until his now high-school-aged brother would leave for work at a fast-food restaurant.

"I'd know he would have to go to work at Taco Bell or somewhere else, so I'd go hang out on my way home from school," Rob says. "I'd go to the house, and the van would be gone, and I'd be like, okay, good he's gone...uh...conflict avoided. But it was just this constant thing that I had to worry about."

As the years went by, Harry grew more adept at staying out of his brother's reach.

"I recognized the pattern, and the pattern was, if I'm at home, it's going to happen, regardless."

It was while avoiding Jimmy that Harry found himself walking through the parking lot of the Pine Ridge Apartments one day, and heard someone with some talent, playing on a drum set.

The boys already had a drum set of their own, though Harry was the only one who used it. The drums were a Christmas present. Jimmy found the set before Christmas.

"And I was like, 'I don't know; I didn't ask for drums. Maybe she got them for you.'

"And he was just like, 'I don't want 'em.'"

Charlene's idea was that whoever wanted to play drums could play drums, but only Harry played.

"I just started out crashing and bashing, beating on drums," but then Harry heard a real drummer.

"He could whale," Rob says.

Or as the drummer himself put it, "fuck holes in other worlds."

Harry was blown away, hearing someone that gifted.

"He'd turn on the radio and just jam to the radio, and that was sort of my first introduction to what the drums could do. And you know, the first thing I bought for the drum set is another floor tom...for $60. And I made it with the money I accumulated by selling joints."

Harry's foray into the world of "crime" was short-lived—and it also served a greater purpose.

"I'd buy the dime bags, roll it up, sell it, buy another one. Pretty soon, I worked my way up to an O-Z, an ounce, and I'd roll the ounce up, and I'd get like, $70 or something out of it, and I came back and bought the floor tom for sixty bucks."

At that time, in that neighborhood, marijuana was an ever-present part of the culture.

"You could walk up to any party store or liquor store around here, and there'd be people walking around," offering to sell joints. Harry sold pinners—really skinny joints—for a buck apiece.

This information fascinates me—that Rob actually participated in illegal behavior he didn't recognize at the time as "wrong." Rob acknowledges what he calls today a "skewed sense of right and wrong" on his own part. Compared to the crimes committed against him at home, selling pinners was nothing. This is like a window into how Jimmy degenerated into someone who committed crimes every day. But how is it that Jimmy became a serial criminal and Rob did not?

One difference I notice is the budding entrepreneurship. Rob's illegal activity seemed to stem purely from wanting to make some money to buy a floor tom. Rob is sure *that* is one concept that did not come from Jimmy. It is a concept nothing Jimmy's record suggests he ever considered.

Along with the sexual abuse and beatings Jimmy inflicted, he also stole from Harry. The combination of making his own money and wanting to protect it from Jimmy caused Harry to take some pretty grown-up steps at a young age.

"He had raided my piggy bank of fifty bucks. So I got smarter; I got a bank account. By the time I was fifteen, I had a job, a car that I bought by myself, and a bank account."

Today, Rob considers how he went one direction—getting a bank account, saving for a car, and getting involved in the school band—while

Jimmy went another. While his younger brother was taking the steps toward becoming a contributing member of society, Jimmy was honing "skills" good for nothing but landing in prison.

Somehow, by the grace of God or with the help of some guardian angel, Rob's choices propelled him toward an ever more productive future, while Jimmy propelled himself to a dead end.

It is time for us to head to Charlene's. Having spent the morning delving into all of the ways Jimmy abused his brother, I am not feeling at all sympathetic to Jimmy, even with the very real possibility he too was a victim. I understand why Rob's only motivation for participating in the service is to benefit Charlene.

My own abuser passed away years earlier, and I hadn't even learned of it until a couple of years after the fact. I wouldn't have felt the need to attend a service in his honor either. But I also know, the ability to forgive is, perhaps, the last step in coming to terms with what happens to us as victims. I can only hope attending this memorial service might lead Rob in that direction. Seeing the anger he still carries, I can't help but believe forgiveness would give him some peace, even though I haven't been able to forgive my abuser either.

CHAPTER EIGHT

Service

Rob and I leave the hotel and drive in separate vehicles to Charlene's. Soon after we arrive, I learn Charlene has arranged for Rob to pick up an old girlfriend of Jimmy's. Paula Almas, who dated Jimmy on and off in the years before he left Michigan, still lives in the area.

With Rob out of the house, there is time before the guests arrive for Charlene to fill in some of the gaps in Rob's narrative.

A few years after the divorce, she says, in 1979, Jim left Michigan because he was laid off. When he left, Charlene had to pay for everything. He just disappeared. The boys were twelve and eight, and Charlene had no choice but to work as many hours as she could—almost every night, in fact.

"There were times I would just cry all the way home, because I was just sad," Charlene says. "I was sad that I couldn't be home with my kids. I missed my husband. I just missed the fact I couldn't talk to him about things, and then one night, after I came home from work, I was just sniffing, like down the hallway. Jimmy could hear me sniff, and he said, 'Are you okay?'

"And I said, 'Yeah, I'm just a little sad.'

"And he said, 'Are you sad about Daddy?' And he said, 'Yeah, me too.'"

Charlene mourned the loss of Jim's presence in the home as much as the loss of the kind of life she'd always dreamed of. Just when Jim had a good job at the Ford plant and just as they were becoming more financially comfortable, the chance for "the perfect little life," as she puts it, went away.

The boys lost their mother as well as their father, because Charlene had to work all the time.

"I did try to go on welfare," Charlene says, "but when I went to the welfare office and they asked me everything in blue blazes, I had to be so dirt poor. I couldn't own a house and be on welfare. And I'm thinking, I have to be almost with no place to live before these people will help me."

Charlene felt there was no one to whom she could turn for help. All of her relatives were in Pennsylvania. They claimed later they would have helped her if she had come home after the divorce, "but I don't think they said that to me out loud."

Values picked up from her parents, about work coming first, were deeply ingrained. Even if one of the boys was sick or she was needed at home for some reason, Charlene rarely missed a day of work. It meant more than just losing $1.65 an hour in wages. It meant losing a whole day of tips.

"I would work, regardless. I would feel so responsible, regardless. I would make sure I would stay there."

The hand-to-mouth existence, Charlene says, is what she thinks is responsible for her tendency today to hoard food.

"I was just always afraid I was not going to have enough food to feed them, you know? Because I only had myself to take care of them."

Charlene was raised to believe you didn't ask anyone for a handout.

"I never asked anybody for money ever. It was just one of those things I kept from Pennsylvania. We took care of ourselves. You didn't ask people for things. People didn't want to be bothered with you."

That was the type of attitude Charlene tried to instill in her sons, too. Work hard. Make an honest living. Don't expect something for nothing.

Charlene never needed to discipline Harry.

"He was such a sweet little boy. I don't even remember ever yelling at him. I would say, 'You can't do that.' I would just talk to him. He would do what I asked him to do."

Jimmy would not. As he grew older, larger, and more out of control, Charlene was at a loss.

"When his dad left, there was no regular person around that could actually, I don't want to say take control of him, but...guide him. He didn't have anybody to compare himself with that would support him...I know he missed his dad."

A paddle with the board acted as a stand-in.

There were lessons in Jimmy's youth, Charlene says, that should have laid the foundation for doing the right thing—like the time she was cleaning out his room when they were getting ready to move into the house. She found a man's wallet.

"And I said, 'Whose is this? Where does this belong?'"

It came out that Jimmy had found the wallet outside on the ground at the apartment building where they lived.

"Somehow, he thought he could keep it."

The wallet contained only about $10, but Charlene explained to Jimmy, who would have been nine or ten years old at the time, that the man would have to go and cancel all the credit cards and replace his driver's license.

Not to mention, the man lived right in the next building.

"I said, 'You know, it doesn't belong to us; it's not ours,' so we went over, and Jimmy handed it to him.

"My wallet!" The man exclaimed.

He was so thankful to get the wallet back, he gave Jimmy the $10 as a reward.

"And you would have thought that would have had an impact to do the right thing—but, um, apparently not," Charlene says.

Put into the role of enforcer as well as sole breadwinner, Charlene found the paddle was the only effective punishment, continuing until Jimmy was past the age of twelve.

"One thing I did, I put the fear of God into these kids...I had to be both mother and father to them. I had to think of all the things guys would have to think about and be that to them, too."

One time at the dinner table, Jimmy flipped Charlene the bird when her back was turned.

"I reached over that table, and I grabbed him by the scruff of the neck and his shoulder. And I pulled him up to me, and I said, 'You ever, ever, ever do that again and I will fucking kill you,' and I slammed him back down there. I said, 'I am your mother, and I demand your respect...I work hard to provide you with everything you need, and you will not ever, ever disrespect me again.'"

Charlene was exhausted, not only physically, but emotionally.

"I'm working all these jobs...I'm doing all this, and you have the nerve to flip me the bird?"

Charlene regrets using corporal punishment, but at the time, she didn't know what else to do.

"I could not get his attention. There was nothing I could say or do to him that would get his attention."

When all else failed, Charlene reverted to what she had been taught as a child.

"My father beat me until my butt was black and blue," she says, for infractions as small as failing to do the dishes when she got home from school.

By the time Jimmy was ten, Charlene believed he was capable of watching over his little brother. Better that than some teenaged sitter smoking pot in her house or stealing from her, as had happened in the past. Besides, "Those days, our kids just went out and played. We didn't have to worry if someone was going to come out and take them or anything."

She rarely worried about fire or any catastrophe striking.

"When I bought the house, I just thought this would be such a great thing. They're safe in the house. There isn't anyone who could hurt them. There was food here, so I guess I kind of just took it for granted that they would be okay."

One person who saw a different side of Jimmy was his childhood crush, Paula.

When Rob arrives with Paula, I am stunned to see she is riding in a wheelchair. She doesn't share a lot of information about her illness, only that it is debilitating—even life threatening at times. She has been in and out of hospitals frequently in recent years.

I can't help wondering what would have happened if Jimmy and Paula had somehow stayed together over the years. Knowing Rob's assessment that all his brother did was take, how could he have given Paula the kind of support she needed?

They'd met in the sixth grade.

"He used to ride his bike to my house and sit across the street, and he wouldn't talk to me," Paula tells us.

This went on for several weeks, perhaps months.

"He'd just wait there until dark."

If she left the house, he would follow.

"He would be behind us on his bike, never saying anything to us. Just stood there and stared."

Finally, the stalemate was broken when a neighbor invited him to come into Paula's house.

"He was great. In fact, I locked the door; I wouldn't let him leave. He was a great guy," she says.

They started "going steady."

Even now, knowing that Jimmy became a bank robber and also abused his younger brother, Paula says, "He was not a bad person at all."

The statement seems a little trite to me, like the kind of thing you're supposed to say when you're invited to the memorial service of a long-lost boyfriend, the kind of thing you say for the benefit of the mother. And indeed, Charlene seems to be eating Paula's words up.

I steal a glance at Rob, who seems just as interested to be viewing his brother through someone else's eyes.

Jimmy, she tells us, had a goofy sense of humor.

"He definitely was fun-loving. He was always kind of happy."

Jimmy liked to tease her.

"I was furious, and he would just laugh at me. I just wanted to strangle him!"

These are sides of his brother Harry never saw.

Later, Rob tells me, "I don't know the Jim Krimm that Paula did. He never let me into his life."

Paula is not the only old girlfriend Charlene invited to the service, but it is unlikely, she tells us, the other one will show up.

Annie*, Charlene says, is something of a psychic. Though I am skeptical of such claims, I am open to them. I want to meet Annie, perhaps even more than I wanted to meet Paula, and Paula is an important conduit herself, having lived briefly with Jimmy when he escaped a halfway house before he disappeared from Michigan forever.

The only reason Charlene has even been in contact with Annie is because she works at the same fabric store as Annie's aunt. They realized Annie had dated Jimmy as a teen.

One day, about three years before Charlene was notified of Jimmy's suicide, Annie called her. She asked Charlene if she knew how Jimmy died. It was an odd question, because Jimmy was very much alive at the time, although, with no contact from him, Charlene often wondered if he might be dead.

Annie believed Jimmy had passed away. She told Charlene she had had a vision in which Jimmy came to her.

"She says even her daughter saw the shadow in her house when Jimmy came to visit her—this is what she's telling me; I'm not saying whether it's true or not," Charlene says.

---

*   Not her real name.

Annie told Charlene Jimmy wanted her to mention a conversation they once had. Annie said when she and Jimmy were fourteen years old, he told her the name of someone who molested him. It was someone known to Charlene but to accuse someone, based on someone else's "vision" years after the fact and with no concrete evidence, was impossible. There was no way to corroborate Annie's story, but Charlene believes Annie was sincere. If nothing else, the confession of a teenaged boyfriend must have weighed on Annie over the years, until she felt compelled to tell someone. And now, it didn't look like Annie was going to show for the service.

Estella and Wayne arrive and shortly after, the minister and her husband. Charlene's little living room is once again packed to bursting. Because I am not personally connected to Jimmy—and after hearing of so many of his assaults on Rob, I am not feeling any sadness at his passing—it is natural for me to take care of some of the more mundane tasks. It will be my job to run a couple of songs, one Charlene wants played and one Rob chose. I am also in charge of running Charlene's video recorder. I'll be running my own tape recorder as well, and I am tickled to have a role that relieves me of having to act like anything but a detached observer. Because I want to observe—Rob's reactions most of all.

Charlene starts out the service by sharing a poem she wrote for Jimmy when he was in prison as a young man.

"My baby boy, my firstborn son, how happy you were with games you won…" she begins. "Where did I go wrong? Was I blind all along? Where did I lose you? How did I make you blue? Was it me, my son? 'Cause surely you were gone—lost to me for many years."

The words are poignant, considering Charlene wrote them well before Jimmy disappeared for good. She sobs through the delivery of the lines, which is certainly understandable, never mind it has already been nearly two months since Jimmy's death. If the service had been held any sooner, she probably wouldn't have been able to speak at all.

She continues, through her tears, "I see you now through a window glass, and I wonder how long it will last. Not for me, oh no, not for me, but for you. I have my greatest plea, for you see, my firstborn son, the time for realization has come—the time to think and meditate about the things that were mistakes. For you, the hours are long but always you must be strong. Think of a better life ahead and how to use your head. How I wish I could see my boy as happy as could be, but other things keep coming into view and set your life into a stew. Now we quietly ponder ahead while I see your empty bed and wonder if I will ever have a part of my son back."

The fact Charlene now, indeed, has a part of her son back, is lost on no one.

When Charlene concludes her reading, it is my cue to start the song Rob chose. He wanted to play a Johnny Cash song I shared with him, called "Hurt."* The story it tells, of a man reaching the end of his life with many regrets, seems to us also to tell something of what Jimmy's thoughts may have been at the end.

As the song plays, silent tears roll down Rob's cheeks. I am surprised, frankly, given his assertions that Jimmy is not forgiven—can never be forgiven. The tears tell me Rob is not immune to feeling some compassion for his brother—for what they both lost and for what will never be regained.

Next, Estella speaks a few words.

"Jimmy reminds me of that little spider I told Charlie about, who was building a web. At a very young age, someone came and tore it down. He built it back up again, and it got torn down. And each time he built it, it was a little more irregular, a little more beat down, a little more broken. So I think everybody should remember the next time they say a harsh word or do a mean thing, you might be tearing down someone's spiderweb. And it might never quite be the same."

The chance to speak is moving down the line, and now it is Rob's turn. I know, based on our earlier interview, there are many harsh things Rob could share, but instead, he chooses to build on Estella's theme.

"Hopefully, the webs get rebuilt stronger," he says.

A eulogy, with details Charlene has provided to the pastor, gives the vital statistics: In McKeesport, Pennsylvania, James Edward Krimm was born, March 10, 1967, named for his father; the family moved to Michigan, and Charlene and Jim divorced.

"It is at those times that life seems so unfair," Reverend Anita Mahon intones.

"Their mother tried so hard to provide a good and happy home for them, taking them camping at Bay City State Park...roasting hot dogs and eating s'mores. The boys both enjoyed riding dirt bikes with their mother."

---

* http://www.youtube.com/watch?v=clq01TXQR0s&feature=related

Reverend Mahon makes the point the adult Jimmy seemed quite different than the image his mother has of him as a child.

"But really was he?" she asks. "We know his actions, but are we in a position to know his soul? Only our loving Mother and Father God would know that, and they love him unconditionally. Something that can be very hard for us is not hard for them. Their understanding is eternal. We are not God and should not put limits on their love, and because we are not God, sometimes it is best to let them forgive, to let them understand, to let their love be pure, while ours can be left to be simple."

The Gnostic concepts the reverend shares are not entirely foreign to me, but they differ from my own Lutheran background. The concept of letting God forgive is the same, but I feel, too, the responsibility I've been taught to forgive others. Her point about none of us being in a position to judge Jimmy is one I vow to keep in mind throughout this project. It is a reminder that no matter how many bad things he may have done, none of us can know what may have driven him.

Rob is fond of pointing out it is all based on decisions. He sees Jimmy's abusiveness as a choice Jimmy made, but I am not completely convinced. I am not a bank robber or an abuser, but I know there are excuses I make for myself, in my life, because of the abuse I suffered. Perhaps I am just as guilty, in my own way, for making choices that hurt other people. My choices are not illegal, but just like Jimmy's, they tend to hurt me as much as they hurt others.

Another point Reverend Mahon makes is that Jimmy's life tells its own story, and his family, the good in them, tells something about the quality of his life.

Somehow, throughout the service, I hold out hope Annie might decide to turn up, but she doesn't. If she chooses not to go on the record about Jimmy's admission of being molested, the chance of gaining more information will be lost forever.

Charlene has a spread of food prepared for everyone to graze on at the conclusion of the service. Rob sits enthralled as Paula shares more stories with him—of a big brother so unlike the abuser he knew at home.

After an hour or so, Paula is growing tired, so Rob wheels her out of the house. Knowing now how he must have struggled to bring her in, I follow them outside, wanting to offer some kind of help, but there is nothing I can do. Rob must lift Paula out of the chair and into his low car. It isn't an easy process, and I can only imagine it in reverse, picturing him going through the same task at Paula's place.

The pastor doesn't stay long, and Wayne and Estella are leaving too. That leaves Charlene and me with more time to talk about Jimmy. As I come back into the house, I notice again the ersatz shrine Charlene has set up just inside her front door—a plant stand upon which she's placed Jimmy's ashes, the utilitarian plastic container draped in a cloth. Added today is another little stand by the door, with a book the funeral home sent from Crosby. Charlene points out to me the names of all of the local businesses that sponsored the memorial book—the same businesses, in her mind, that had been terrorized by Jimmy's last bank robbery. I know the geography makes it unlikely these particular businesses felt threatened, and I don't have the heart to tell Charlene it is something they probably send to every family, regardless of the circumstances. She is so touched by it she plans to write a thank-you note.

One thing I am curious about is why Charlene never remarried. She is a good-looking, intelligent lady. She's fun to be around and very sociable.

Charlene brought men home through the years, she says, but there were no stable male influences in her boys' lives.

"The guys I'd hang around with, they weren't always father material," she tells me. "They might come over, but it wasn't any length of time...If it wasn't going to be somebody I was going to pick to stay here, then I'd rather the boys didn't even get attached."

Charlene saw the lack of a healthy male influence as a possible cause for Jimmy's aggression and troublemaking but made no progress in trying to provide a role model for him.

When Jimmy was about fifteen, Charlene noticed a change she attributed to that lack. He was growing more defiant, getting into trouble at school, not paying attention, or just not showing up. Charlene tried to locate Jim and ask for his help.

"I said, 'He just needs to talk to you,' because I could just see, and I felt for him, because he didn't have a dad."

Jim, I learn later, has no knowledge of any such appeal, recalling only that he was being hounded by the court for child support, which forced him "underground" for a period, until he had to pay catch-up support of about $17,000.

"Mostly, by being a truck-stop waitress, I dated truck drivers," Charlene says. "So that's why today, if I see truck drivers, I will try to run them off the road. I would like to say, 'There, you fucker! Are you one of those ones who came and broke my heart? Are you one of his kids?' You know, get him off the road." She laughs.

She is so funny! Charlene has a knack for finding the humor in even the most heartbreaking of memories, and her laugh is low and deep, much lower than her high-pitched, grandmotherly speaking voice.

"Asshole truck drivers," Charlene continues, shaking her head at the thought of her wilder days. "Of course I thought sex was love. If I liked them well enough, I might go to bed with them. I've climbed in trucks. I went to parties. There was a bar, and they loved to see me coming because I'd bring all the truck drivers with me. 'Oh, Charlie's coming!' because I was head waitress, so I'd bring all the waitresses and the truck drivers, and we'd all have a good old time!"

There was one man, Charlene says, who might have made a good model for her boys, but he already had a wife.

"He treated me nice, and he took me places, when he could. It ended up that he might have left her," but Charlene felt it was too much to ask to expect him to leave his own children to be with hers.

"I said, 'I tell you what, if you go back and you really can't make it and you're going to get a divorce, whenever you move out and you start, like, going through these procedures, then call me. Then I'll know.'"

He never called.

Even as Harry was taking the steps to form a conventional, law-abiding life, he was witness to or had knowledge of most of the crimes Jimmy committed while he was still at home in Taylor. Though Charlene knew nothing of the crimes he was committing against his brother, she started becoming aware of Jimmy's bent for theft.

"I discovered the $2 bills were missing, and I also discovered there was a roll of silver...he got $10 for them, and if he would have taken them to a coin shop, silver quarters, he would have gotten a lot more than $10."

It was the same with the antique Lionel train set that was his dad's.

"And this Lionel train set had everything—you put the little pebbles in it, and it smoked, and it had the little 'choo choo' sound. And it was just like brand new. It was still in the same case it was bought in," Charlene recalls.

Rob has returned, sharing what he remembers of the set.

"This was solid steel…It was nice, and it was, like, older than both of us," Rob says. "Jimmy hocked the whole set for, like, 80 bucks."

"And when I found that out, I went looking for it and tried so hard to buy it back," Charlene says.

At that time, Charlene was storing some things in the family's Econoline van—to which Jimmy had access.

"And that's when he hocked it because it was in the van," Rob says.

The van was a sore subject for Jimmy, who thought his mom should have given it to him. He didn't understand why Charlene couldn't afford to give it to him.

"Money was always something to spend; he didn't understand the working part of it. Well, he understood it better when he went to work at the Taco Bell, but he still didn't really have to work for it, you know, because he could just hang out there," Charlene says.

Jimmy repeatedly raided Charlene's big elephant bank for the half dollars she managed to squirrel away out of tips.

"Jimmy took the $2 bills and the train set; he took the record player that I bought him…a stereo system…And I noticed that he hocked it, so I went down there in enough time to get it and buy it back."

By the time Jimmy was seventeen, he had advanced to driving off in the van without paying for gas and got caught for it. Charlene tried to help.

"I went to court, and I think it just ended up that I had to pay money… It was just a slap on the wrist to Jimmy, but I'm the one that suffered for it. Because I paid for the lawyer, and I think I paid a $500 fine."

"That's an expensive tank of gas," Rob interjects, considering how short for money the family usually was.

Jimmy was also pulling armed robberies.

"I know of three times that he did this," Rob says. "Who knows at what rate and speed it really was."

The gun was loaded.

Rob relates a story, which occurred in the very room in which we are sitting, of Jimmy practicing with the gun.

"He would actually practice if he was going to hold it in his coat pocket…then if they doubted him, he might take it out and prove that it's real or something," Rob says.

Rob has no idea where the gun came from.

"It's Detroit." Rob laughs. "I don't know if it was a hot gun or what. He just had it, and he put bullets in it. He was afraid he was going to shoot his toe off because he cocked the hammer back on the gun, and we're like, 'Oh shit! We can't get the bullets out with the hammer back,' so it's like, 'Oh shit! How're we going to do this?' And so, he held the hammer while he pulled the trigger and let the hammer back nice and easy, and the whole time, we're worried the gun is going to go off. So we're pointing it at the floor...and I'm like, freaking out, like, 'The gun's going to go off!'"

As Rob tells the story, the smile on his face reveals what his words do not. Fiddling with a loaded 9 mm in their mother's kitchen as teenagers is one of the few times Jimmy let Rob in on his life. Rob knew what Jimmy was doing was wrong, not that he dared challenge him.

"He was going to put a mask on...I didn't really think of the whole 'it's illegal' part of it." Again, Rob believes it is because of his own skewed sense of right and wrong, given the crimes he was victimized by every day.

Jimmy always had to push the limits, Rob says.

"And I was like, 'Let me know how it goes.'"

Witnessing Jimmy's elation upon returning with, at best, a couple hundred bucks, today gives Rob a sense of what the future bank robber must have experienced when he walked out of a bank in LeMars, Iowa, with $47,500.

"He would take the money and just, like, whip it on the living room floor, and he would say, 'Cash, money, spew!'

"And I would be like, 'What's this for?'"

Now when Rob thinks back, "the tone of his voice, it was just kind of happy, you know? He was proud of it."

It was like a nonevent to little brother Harry.

"I was like, 'Well, thank God you didn't get caught.' He would never slip me a twenty or a five or nothing. It wasn't benefiting me...So fine, go rob your fucking gas stations and stay the fuck out of my way."

The idea of following in his brother's footsteps to rob people was never a consideration.

"That was his thing. The thought of stealing a candy bar crossed my mind, but I couldn't bring myself to actually do it. I went in there, and I just couldn't actually walk out of the store with it. I just felt so guilty, even thinking about it. I just put it back. That knot in my stomach and the butterflies stopped me from doing anything wrong. I couldn't do that. I couldn't physically bring myself to do it. He'd come home with hordes of Heath bars."

Or a fistful of cash. Or a tank full of gas. Or someone else's car.

"He didn't think there was anything wrong with it. He didn't worry about getting caught, obviously."

Harry once witnessed Jimmy fondling a girl who was, perhaps, eleven. Rob's recollection is that Jimmy reached down her pants, "but that was as far as he got."

The girl got up and ran away, and the play returned to a more age-appropriate activity. Rob is incredulous that Jimmy had the nerve.

"Aren't you worried about getting in trouble? Doing the wrong thing? And he never—it never even crossed his mind."

Charlene remembers the girl and also remembers asking Estella, later, if her girls were ever harmed by Jimmy. Even knowing that Jimmy managed, with intimidation, to keep Harry silent, Charlene can't believe she didn't see the signs.

"Jimmy threatened him to not say or not tell, and Jimmy acted like things were just fine when they were home," says Charlene. "And why didn't I see any bruises or why didn't I see any—you know? I don't know what I would have done. I might have killed Jimmy. I might have actually killed him. Because when I found out, I just, I just collapsed."

But that would come much, much later. In the meantime, there was growing evidence of other illegal activity.

"One day, I found a key," Charlene says, "like a car key that was somebody's car key, and I'm thinking, *What is this?*"

She confronted Jimmy, telling him the keys needed to be put back where they came from.

"I don't know who they belong to or where they belong, I says, but if there's a car involved, you need to take these keys back, put them in the car, and walk away."

Harry knew what Jimmy was doing. But, long accustomed to keeping Jimmy's secrets, he never thought of telling.

"He bragged about the cars, just like he bragged about the money from the party store," Rob says. "He had a big long list of twelve of them."

Many of the cars were taken right off of car lots at dealerships.

"He just liked driving nice cars. He didn't have one, and he wanted one. He told me about the one he almost got arrested for. He got into a car at the dealership. Back in those days, they kept the keys in the ignition. Jimmy gets in the car in broad daylight and drives off the lot."

By this time, a paddling from Charlene was out of the question. Jimmy was now well over six feet tall and two hundred pounds. He dropped out of school and did little to help around the house, despite the chore notebook.

Like a remote control on a television set, Charlene hoped the notebook would push the necessary buttons on the boys to make things happen in her absence.

The notebook fascinates me.

"Gas money?" is the first entry, in Jimmy's handwriting.

"You get paid today," is Charlene's answer.

An accounting of bills Charlene already paid for Jimmy, followed by the question, "Would you like to pay some bills?" is the next entry in the book.

Jimmy's answer reveals frustration.

"I work so much, and nothing seems to come of it."

Charlene replies his problem is too much partying. Jimmy crosses out "too much" and scribbles "not enough."

"When you get your money, you think you're rich," Charlene admonishes.

Beside this, Jimmy comments, "Only for one day."

Charlene makes reference to having asked Jimmy to pay room and board. He was over eighteen at the time, and if he wasn't going to go to school, she expected him to help out. If Jimmy didn't always contribute financially, he was a good handyman. Any mechanical breakdown in vehicles, washing machines, or lawn mowers became his chore. If there was a problem with the toilet, it was his job to fix it.

"The blue round thing needs to be pushed down and stay down for water to stop," Charlene writes, or they would wind up with a big water bill.

"I fixed it," in Jimmy's handwriting, appears below Charlene's line.

Another entry reads, "Jim, car runs good. Thanks."

Even holidays were acknowledged in the notebook.

"BOYS, HAPPY EASTER...Love, Mom," is just one example. In another, Charlene directs that they can open one present before she gets home, presumably, for Christmas.

Charlene had plenty of communication with Harry in the notebook, too—mostly relating to work he should do around the house. Often, the chores had squares drawn next to them, and more often than not, X's would be filled in to show the jobs were completed. There is even evidence Harry did work assigned to Jimmy. Mixed in with the running dialogue are Charlene's notes from a computer class, but no matter the other uses for the notebook, the communication between family members continued.

"Where's my iron skillet?" Charlene asks on one page. "Please put it back. Whose bike is in the side yard?"

On another day, the size and speed of Charlene's writing shows her mood. "Jim, That $10 was for supper and for you and Harry to split. I want it back if you are that greedy. If you need money for something, you can ask for it. Don't take my money for what you want."

"I'm not greedy," Jimmy replies. "The van is."

Instructions for food preparation are frequent.

"Strawberry juice in the blue glass—mix with milk and make milkshake" or "put chicken in foil and put in oven for one hour—good baked chicken."

Nearly every message from Charlene ends with "Love, Mom" or "Have a nice day."

Humor is evident in the exchanges too.

"Hi Harry," reads one with a list of boxes for him to check off: "Sit and watch TV; have some coffee; eat some breakfast; have a nice day; feed dog and cats—Love, Mom."

Dutifully, Harry filled in each box.

Jimmy, too, often signed his messages, "Love, Jim," like the one that reads, "Mom, went camping and boating. Be back Sunday."

The van popped up in communication again and again.

"Jim, you can take the van to work today. We'll start payments on it next pay," Charlene writes.

Two pages later, Charlene has changed her mind.

"You can't drive the van anymore. It isn't yours, and you took advantage of the convenience. It was only your transportation to and from work."

"Thanks, Mom!!!!!" came Jimmy's reply. "This is what I get because of a camping trip? I even went canoeing in Bruin Lake. I had a good time. You will ride me to work when it rains! P.S. You're a very Rude person."

It was around the time Jimmy was eighteen or nineteen that he decided he would join the army.

"Jimmy actually shaved his head and everything." Rob laughs.

I can tell from Charlene's reactions that many of the stories Rob is relating are events she had been completely unaware of previously.

Knowing how Jimmy operated, Rob suspects he didn't give the idea of enlisting much thought beyond getting a haircut. That is, if Jimmy actually made it to the recruiter's office.

"He told me, 'I couldn't pass the test,'" Rob says. "He had a record and all sorts of stuff, but I think that if he really tried and really wanted to, he could have made it."

Jimmy had some aptitude for mechanics, Charlene and Rob agree, but no training beyond his high school shop class or the oil change place where he worked briefly.

"He was good at mechanics. He could get a lawnmower running after a long winter, but as far as pursuing it, he would get only so far...There was just, like, a disconnect when it came to getting certified for stuff. It was just too complicated for him," Rob says.

Though Jimmy was never diagnosed with ADD, his school records— once again, saved by the self-described "pack rat" Charlene—show an inability to test well. The records certainly point to the possibility Jimmy could have had ADD too. Rob did not learn he had the disorder until well into adulthood, so it isn't something the school system in Taylor was likely to have noticed in Jimmy either.

Knowing what he knows now about ADD and his own drive to achieve, Rob has little sympathy for his older brother's lack of legitimate accomplishment. Whatever ambition or drive Rob possesses, he believes he got from Charlene's example, but it never rubbed off on Jimmy.

"It was just something that was instinctual to me—get a bank account, get a car, make money, support yourself, and you know, I was in the band...It was instinctual to me just to do it, and I got up and did it," Rob says.

It has been another long day, an exhausting day for all of us. We agree Rob and I will meet again in the morning, and then I will spend some time with Charlene while Rob runs some errands for me.

I leave Charlene's house that night wishing we had more than three days. Tomorrow will be my last day of interviewing before I drive north to Port Huron to visit my own relatives. As drama-filled and tragedy-filled as the Krimm family story is, I feel completely at home—and I am honored to have been able to share such an intimate time as Jimmy's memorial service with Rob and Charlene.

Rob and I still have many difficult moments to go over—moments he is comfortable sharing for a book that could be read by strangers but doesn't relish having to recall in front of his mother. I am curious about how the abuse came to an end, because I know it dissipated even before Jimmy went to prison.

CHAPTER NINE

"It's Not Gay"

I am outside the side door of the hotel, waiting for Rob when he pulls up. I can't wait to get back to our discussion of the day before, mining his memories for clues about the genesis of a serial bank robber and insight into how Rob coped with his abuse.

I have been drawn to this story from the beginning by the dual pulls of curiosity about the bank robber and the desire to explore what makes one victim into a predator while the other struggles every day just to maintain normality. How could I have thought this would remain an intellectual enterprise only with no cost to my own emotions? As I listened to Rob's story the day before, I was drawing on my own experience as an abuse survivor to pull details out of him, but at the same time, I was reliving episodes from my own past.

My conception, at the outset, I suppose because of my age and gender, that I was "further along" in the process of dealing with my abusive past, could not have been further from the truth. Just because Rob is eight years younger, just because he is a man—and I have it in my head that men tend to be less in touch with their emotions—and just because he has continued, throughout much of his adult life, having issues maintaining his emotional equilibrium, it doesn't mean he is higher or lower, further or closer to healing than I am. What was foolish was ever putting it into those terms. Given the severity of his abuse, I am amazed Rob is even sane.

We walk, a little nervously, to the end of the hall to what has become his confession chamber.

"I feel like this door should be painted red," I remark, as I swipe the key card letting us in.

"Yeah, really," he says, and I know he understands red is the color for all of the scorching moments of shame we covered in our talk the day before.

We start out talking about Paula's revelations after the memorial service. I had been engaged in talk with Charlene and Estella, so I hadn't heard everything Paula told him. I exchanged e-mail addresses with Paula so I could get more information from her later, but I am curious to hear what Rob has already gleaned from her.

"Hearing Paula say he was proud of me, that...kind of put a smile on my face. It's a side that I never really thought of. He actually is a person—it's a side he never let me into because I was always the tagalong," Rob says.

"Is there some deep, dark corner—some shred in your heart—that still wants to be able to love your brother?" I ask.

"Ah, maybe," he says, pausing to consider. "Maybe about a tenth of a percent. But it's—it would have required him to do the right thing from the beginning. And he's just...he never did right by me, and I knew that would never happen between us."

"Is there any regret that now it never will?"

"No. No. I mean, nah. I'm not regretful. It's still a relief. I'm relieved that he is just out of the picture."

"I suppose there's no way that you could ever have trusted him?"

"I know!"

"Even if he came to you and said he was a born-again Christian and he had a good job and was stable and came to you and said, 'I'm so sorry for what I did to you. I was sick, and I was hurt, so I hurt you'?"

"If that were at all possible for him to accomplish, I would have different feelings about it, but I—but I never saw his personality, as you know, becoming spiritual and finding himself born-again Christian. But like, you know, like you see on the movies, if it did happen, I would be stunned. My jaw would just hit the floor, and I'd be like, I'd have to think about it, but eventually, you know, I could probably bring myself to forgive him if that were the case."

"But you'd always be waiting for the other shoe to drop?"

"Yeah, like, 'Can I borrow your car?'" Rob says, making a buzzer sound, like someone has just given a wrong answer on a game show. "What do you want to borrow my car for? You want to go see the world?"

We laugh. Rob is right. Any notions I have about trying to put Humpty Dumpty back together again are about as sophisticated as a nursery rhyme. When pigs fly is how Rob looked at it. The possibility of Jimmy ever redeeming himself would have been the longest of odds.

It was when he was about fifteen and Jimmy, nineteen, that Harry's protest of his brother's abuse finally had an impact.

With his own job and his own car, Harry was more successful at avoiding situations where he could be victimized. And he also had a new tactic. The protest that finally made some headway also went a long way toward preventing Harry from telling anyone else about what was going on: the fear of being labeled homosexual. Scarier still was the fear that somehow, Jimmy's attacks would actually affect Harry's sexual orientation.

"I'm like, what if I don't like girls because of this?" It was a very real concern for Harry as a teen. "I'm thinking this in my head...*Is this how gay people start?*"

When Harry spoke his concern out loud, he got a reaction.

"I really started objecting, like, 'No! I don't want to be gay!' That was like my new excuse, to try and make him realize this is gay—I don't want to grow up to be gay, and you're teaching me how to *be* gay. And in a kid's eyes, that's all I could think of. I'm like, 'No, this is gay, and I don't want to be gay,' and that's what I told him, and I meant it," Rob says.

"It's not gay," Jimmy answered.

But Harry could see the seed of doubt in his older brother's eyes.

"I think he was sort of saying it in a questioning tone, like, 'It's not GAY-ay?'...You know? Kind of questioning, is it?"

Then, Jimmy grew angry.

"He chased me out of the house, and I took off...I realized I was starting to get bigger and a little bit stronger, smarter—and you know, that was a real issue with me. I was really saying that I don't want to become gay," Rob says, never mind that, "I've always found girls attractive. There is nothing about a man's hairy ass that is attractive."

"So, was Jimmy gay?" I ask.

Rob doesn't really think so. It was only that Jimmy's sex drive and his lack of scruples made Harry a convenient receptacle.

"That's what I felt like, too." Rob laughs ruefully. "A receptacle."

By this time, Jimmy knew girls he could have sex with.

"He'd call 'em up and say, 'What are you doing? Can I come over?'...
And they weren't real pretty or nothing."

One time, Jimmy offered to let Harry have sex with one of these girls.

"It was just his 'fuck buddy.' Him and her were in the living room.
I don't know if they were joking, but basically, offering you know...do
I want to fuck her, and I was like, 'Uh-uh.' I couldn't. I was like...I was
afraid of her, like 'wildebeest.'"

"He was like, 'I don't want to fuck her; you fuck her.'"

"And I was, like, 'No, I don't want to.'"

Looking back on the incident, Rob sees the measure of control Jimmy
had, not only in trying to order his little brother to have sex with the girl,
but putting the girl in the position of being offered up for the taking.

"I think they went in the bedroom and did it anyways. But you know,
why don't you go find more of these wildebeests and go fuck them? You
know? Like, leave me alone."

Once the issue of homosexuality was raised, Jimmy turned his aggression in a new direction. The first incident, which Jimmy made his brother
watch, was with the neighbor's dog.

"He's showing me, 'See, I'm showing sympathy to you. I'm going to
fuck the dog instead.'"

Harry watched as Jimmy hung the small dog from the light fixture in
his room, trying to kill it, so it wouldn't bite him during the act.

"He tried to kill it, but the light fixture broke...He wanted to butt
fuck the dog."

Later, the family pet, "Runt," became the target of Jimmy's assaults.
Rob believes Jimmy raped Runt on a number of occasions.

"He wasn't really, like, secretive about it. And I mean, just like,
bringing the dog in and you know, he just had this smirk on his face that
you knew...nah...you're not really? And it's just like, why can't you just
be like everybody else and take care of yourself? And it's just like...like
he had to take...take whatever he wanted."

Jimmy had to dominate.

"There was just no other reason for it. Other than he wanted to take.
And that's like...kids torturing small animals is like a sign of a murderer
in the makes."

Only, Jimmy was no longer a child.

"He was nineteen then...He wasn't a kid anymore."

Only as an adult did Rob begin to wonder from where these aberrant behaviors stemmed. Was there a mental defect or psychological disorder? Was Jimmy acting out things he'd seen?

Even when Jimmy was finally arrested for stealing a car, Harry told no one about Jimmy's crimes at home. Even locked behind bars, with a sentence of up to five years, Jimmy retained an awful power over Harry, more controlling than any threat of retribution.

"I felt ashamed that I let it happen," Rob says. "So now that I'm a part of this thing, it's like I'm telling on myself, too, and I have to reveal something that's a part of myself that I'm ashamed of."

Rob never planned to tell anyone what Jimmy did to him.

"I didn't think logically about it. I didn't think that anybody would take action on it. I just thought it would further victimize *me*."

Rob looked at Jimmy's incarceration as a gift—a reprieve from further abuse.

"I just wanted to move on with my life," Rob says. "And since he was out of the picture, being bitter and holding a grudge against him would just take too much energy—energy I could be using to get stuff done."

Harry threw himself into a frenzy of activity during high school, centered around work and playing in the band.

"I was working delivering pizza and making a life for myself. My mom was low on cash so I'd bring home $25 for her, and I'd keep the rest…I'd go to band parades on Saturday mornings…half-time shows Friday night. Then while everybody was ready to play and hang out and party, I barely had time to rush off to Hungry Howies, work till about 2 AM…I really worked my ass off," Rob says. It would be years before he realized all that activity was merely a way to avoid dealing with what had happened to him.

"You're just so happy that the unpleasant environment is gone now… It's like, 'All right, I won!' That's the way I felt. I felt like I triumphed over it, and if I'd have had my wits about me, I would have told on him… Because that would have really cooked his wagon."

Harry met Julie as a high school freshman. It was a couple of years before Jimmy went to prison and around the time Jimmy's abuse of Harry waned.

Getting involved in the Tri-Union band, made up of students from three schools, exposed Harry to new possibilities. Instead of the druggies in his neighborhood, the band made up his new social set.

Julie recalls, on the phone, a few weeks after my interviews in Michigan, "We started to become better friends right before we went to band camp the summer after our freshman year. He got into a lot of trouble that band camp for being caught out past curfew with a girl that was in another band."

Often as not, Harry and Julie were in competition with each other for the various trophies awarded at camp.

Charlene finally had a work schedule that allowed her to be involved; she was managing a Denny's restaurant. She threw herself into boosting for the band.

"I was a force to be reckoned with when Harry was in the band," Charlene tells me. "I ran everything—even if they didn't want me to."

Charlene marched both ways in Harry's parades, providing hot chocolate or Kool-Aid and snacks at the end of each march. She served as a cabin mother at camps and even went so far as to help buy an instrument for a student. It frustrated Harry that Charlene seemed to want to take care of the whole world.

"I just wanted her to take care of me," he says.

At the same time, her hovering and what he saw as her meddling in his life was hard to deal with.

"She was resistant toward people in my life," Rob says.

But according to Charlene, there was more to it than that. She didn't trust Julie to stand up for Rob because of an incident when someone accused him of smoking pot. Julie didn't come to his defense—but with good reason. Julie knew about Rob's past marijuana use; Charlene did not.

When it came to advocating for her son and the rewards she felt he deserved, says Julie, Charlene "was off the chain...She was just controlling, obnoxious."

That freshmen year at band camp, Julie says, "It was a tie for a trophy, from what I understand, and since he got into trouble, that broke the tie. Charlene wasn't happy and said some ugly things to me like I didn't deserve the trophy, her Harry did."

Though Charlene was difficult to deal with, Julie didn't let that stop her from being a friend to Harry.

"We would go out for breakfast at Denny's and do the movies and stuff with other band kids—call each other and talk about our relationships we were in with different people."

It was during this stage Julie began to have some contact with Jimmy, over the telephone.

"I would hang up on him," Julie says, because she found him creepy and strange. Sometimes, he would refuse to tell Harry she was on the phone, or he would make inappropriate comments to her.

Jimmy Krimm went to jail for car theft in the fall of 1988 and didn't walk out a free man until a little more than five years later. It takes me weeks to piece together the timeline, poring over his letters and prison documents.

"He could have killed someone and gotten out quicker," Paula says.

Jimmy's sentence didn't start out that long. In fact, it was deferred, and he was put into a diversion program after the first arrest—for stealing two vehicles in a single weekend. When he stole a third car less than a year later, he was sentenced concurrently for all of his offenses, including a fourth stolen car charge he'd incurred while awaiting sentencing on the other three. The real issue was drug and alcohol abuse.

Jimmy reflected, once in prison, "Only two or three times, I remember stealing a car sober. But the other fifteen or twenty times I stole a car I was drunk or had been drinking."

However many thefts he actually did the time for, he deserved a much longer sentence—not to mention the sentence he would have gotten if his crimes against his brother had come to light.

In his own description of his first arrest, at 1:30 AM, he walked up to a 1977 Thunderbird parked in front of a convenience store on Eureka Road in Taylor. The keys were in it. He got in and drove off. The following day, still driving the Thunderbird, he found a Ford Escort with the keys in the ignition at a gas station. He ditched the Thunderbird and drove off in the Escort. He continued to drive the car for the next two weeks, parking it in a space at the neighboring Pine Ridge Apartments when he wasn't using it.

Jimmy was arrested for the theft at 2:00 AM one morning when he passed out in the car, motor running, in front of what Michiganders call a "party store"—a convenience store that also sells liquor.

The diversion program sentenced Jimmy in the spring of 1988 to three years probation with the first year to be served in a county jail. While in jail, he was referred to a residential drug treatment facility, Hope House. According to a presentence report, he walked away from the place the same day on which he entered it in June, but he stole a fourth car four days after entering Hope House—from another resident of the facility—so if he did walk out the first day, he didn't get very far.

"The night of the offence, I was drinking," Jimmy told the investigator. "I overheard a conversation stating that the key was left in the ignition of the '78 Chevy Luv pickup, so I took it without permission to visit my girlfriend in Taylor, Michigan."

Officers spotted the vehicle the morning after it was reported stolen and pulled the driver over.

"At that point, the driver stated he didn't have his driver's license with him and began going through the glove box. He pulled out a number of papers."

When asked his name, Jimmy looked down at the papers and read the name on the registration.

Once in custody, Jimmy couldn't hide his true identity.

He was released on bond.

An evaluation conducted by the state in advance of his sentencing outlined the positive factors Jimmy had going for him upon entry into the prison system: a mother who supported him and gainful employment. But the "weaknesses" in his background were many. According to the summary, Jimmy claimed a history of substance abuse dating back to the age of fifteen, experimenting with marijuana, LSD, PCP, and cocaine.

"The defendant states that he last used crack cocaine in October of 1988," just in advance of his incarceration.

Jimmy told the interviewer he smoked marijuana three or four times per week and first took LSD in 1985, using it about once per month until the summer of 1988. Jimmy claims to have used PCP about ten times between the ages of seventeen and eighteen.

All of this substance abuse occurred during the period when Jimmy was abusing his brother, but with no confession and Harry bound by the shame of what was done to him, Jimmy's aberrant sexual behaviors could not be addressed by the court.

"The defendant states that when he was eighteen years old that he would consume either a fifth of wine or liquor per day. He states that he continued to abuse alcohol in this manner until August of 1987 when he was introduced to cocaine (crack)."

Though he had five warrants pending, Jimmy didn't go to prison until November 5, 1988. He was finally taken into custody when he was involved in an accident he blamed on being upset with his girlfriend at the time.

> I think Shelly helped me have my car accident. The night of the crash when I had a few drinks in me I drove by her house to SPY on her and see If she was home. She wasn't. IT was Fri. night I figured she went out with her husband because only one car was gone. Being drunk and jelous, I threw a fit of anger. I got another 5th of wiskey with my friend. What does a drunk do when he gets depressed? Drink more? I could have died that night, or worse yet killed someone...Each time I look in the mirror I am reminded (because of scars)...I guess love can heal & it can destroy a person...I asked Shelly what she did Fri. Night when I wreacked my car. She said she had to pick up her divorce papers. At 8:30 at night? Bullshit.

Jimmy's explanation of the accident in a letter to his mom shows a failure to take responsibility for his own actions. In Jimmy's mind, it was Shelly's fault he was upset, Shelly's fault he was drinking, and by extension, her fault he had the accident.

Fighting, failed drug tests, and generally poor behavior stretched his sentence. It was pure stubbornness that sealed the term at the maximum of five years.

During the roughly 1,825 days he was inside, Jimmy wrote nearly two hundred letters to his mother. Every nine or ten days, on average, Jimmy recorded his thoughts, telling Charlene what he saw, felt, ate, listened to, and learned behind bars. Many of his statements seem to me to stem from racism and ignorance. But the letters also show me a young man in turmoil—frustrated with his drug and alcohol addictions, claiming to make an effort to better himself, and sometimes doing so. He quit smoking repeatedly and started again. He tried to curb an eight-cup-a-day coffee habit. He was forever hatching plans about what he would do once he was free. He used weightlifting to sculpt his already powerful build. He was by turns hopeful about the future and what he might accomplish with hard work and hardened in the belief the world owed him something.

As I pore over his letters, I have to remind myself Jimmy may have been a victim once, too. As harshly as I view the abuse he inflicted on

Rob, I also have to try to keep an open mind. The point, I tell myself, is not to judge Jimmy but to try to walk in his shoes and see if there are clues to tell me why he was so destructive to himself and all of the people around him.

The first letter from prison arrived in a plain white, business-sized envelope, addressed on the outside, as most of Jimmy's letters were, to "C. Krimm," in neat printing. Capital and lowercase letters and punctuation are used with little rhyme or reason. There are frequent spelling errors.

> Hi Mom, Thought I'D write a line & Tell you how I've beeN. EveryThing here Is going O.K. But It's very Boring. I Think About The PasT & Future, moreso, oN The Future. IT's Never to late to make something of myself. I have the skills & Ability, aNd a Family that cares About me…When I Finally get out of This mess I Am going to Be somebody. For The last 2 yrs. I've Been Nobody. IT's high Time things take a change For the Better. Drugs Put me Here, ~~Honset~~ Honesty, love, & Reality will Keep me out. I've got my mind very set on staying ouT of here. This is No waY to live my life. Will Right again soon. Love Jim.

Jimmy spent the first couple of months in the Wayne County Jail in Detroit. Almost immediately, he began a running discourse on the racial tension he felt.

"There are so MANY Blacks here, iTs like Living with The Plant planet of The Apes."

In an early letter, he shared that he had been doing a lot of reading.

"The Book I'm reading Now is called 'Getting Control oF your life.'"

He copies out the blurb from the back cover, including the line, "You will see the Amazing truth Behind what makes you do the Things you don't want to do. You will discover you can only start Getting Control of your life as you are learning to give control of your life to God."

Another book he mentions reading in prison, called *What Cops Know*, is like an encyclopedia of criminal methods in all types of crimes.

His letters jump from subject to subject, from getting control of his life to worrying about a lawn mower sitting in the backyard at home, which he would be unable to fix.

"…remembered about Tom's Lawnmower sitting out there. Could you have harry take it over to him?"

Of all of the misplaced capital letters in Jimmy's writing, his brother's name rarely rated one.

The friendship between Harry and Julie turned into something more at the band camp held the summer before their junior year of high school.

Julie tells me, "Charlene was watching Harry like a hawk, because he was gonna get that award at band camp this year. She was pushing him, which was stressing him out, and he was riding his section hard."

Harry was the drum section leader, while Julie headed the flute section.

"We were all tired, hot, and stressed out. We started just messing up the whole routine—everyone was. The band director stopped us, made us sit down, and tore us a new one. Then, out of nowhere, my friend, John, starts tearing Harry a new one, going at him about how he is riding them all the time, how he isn't that great of a drummer."

Julie could see the criticism was getting to Harry.

"So I got up and started yelling at John and went to Harry and hugged him so no one would see him crying."

She told John being a section leader wasn't easy, and the other section leaders jumped on the bandwagon to back her up.

"Then one of the band directors gave us an hour to get it together and come back to practice. That is when I started becoming his 'mom,' so to speak," Julie remembers, not that she recognized it at the time. "We were friends for a long time, and over time, we got comfortable, and then it just moved into a relationship…He was nice. He had a job. He was cute and a good friend."

They kept their romantic relationship secret for more than three months.

"We didn't tell his mom, and we didn't tell the other band kids," Julie says. She says it was because neither of them wanted to deal with the inevitable gossip or with Charlene's reaction.

Being with Julie exposed Harry to the kind of family he'd always dreamed of.

"I was their adopted son almost," Rob says. "They were mom and dad and were together, and they made their home…I just got a warm feeling from it."

The extended family of a grandmother, uncles, and aunts also made him feel welcome. His experience with them included going to church, where he was moved to tears because everyone was so nice to him.

"It was just that missing part I was searching for," Rob tells me. Not just a home, but the kind of family relationships he'd always longed for. With Jimmy in jail, it finally felt to Harry that life could be good—that as long as he worked hard, there was no reason he couldn't have that kind of home and family for himself one day.

Having Jimmy in prison also served to make Charlene hypervigilant where Harry was concerned.

"I think she was trying to make sure my life went straight," Rob says, but it was sometimes too much.

Charlene was determined to see her younger son succeed.

"I was driven to make sure that Harry had everything he needed to do the best he could in school and in the band. I lost one son, and I sure wasn't going to lose another," says Charlene.

She got Harry moved from the class of a teacher who seemed to be treating him unfairly. This scenario played itself out several times, with Harry complaining a teacher was picking on him and Charlene intervening on his behalf. Eventually, Harry was in danger of not graduating because he'd dropped so many classes with Charlene's help.

As his relationship with Julie came into the open, the relationship between mother and son grew strained.

"The more obnoxious she got, the more he would just shut her out," says Julie.

Though Charlene was motivated by wanting to help Harry, her assistance served just as often to cause him stress. And he was already stressing about his future.

"Harry had no clue. He just knew that one day, he wanted to work a job and wear a shirt and tie to work," says Julie. "I was sending things off to colleges, trying to figure out what I was gonna do."

Midway through their senior year, Harry called Julie and told her he was thinking of joining the Marines. He wanted to get paid to be a drummer in the Marine Corps Band.

"He was all excited," she says, talking a mile a minute, but there was one catch: he said he wouldn't go if Julie wouldn't wait for him while he went through boot camp. Julie began to rant that it was a crazy idea, that she didn't want him to go.

"Then something in me said, 'Who are you to stop him? He needs this,' and I stopped and then told him it was a great idea and that I would wait for him and that I definitely thought that was exactly what he needed to do…I could have totally changed his and my life if I had told him no, I wouldn't wait."

For Harry, the Marines represented not just an opportunity to get paid for playing the drums but an opportunity to learn how to live right.

"I wanted to be certain that I stick myself in a position where I'd be sure to get myself on the straight and narrow. Military was the key. That was my guide for me to set me straight. So, I never needed to develop any rules," because the Marine Corps had a set that had been working since 1775!

A psychological profile assembled early in Jimmy's incarceration is a gold mine of information. But it contains some glaring flaws. Absent any knowledge of Jimmy's long-term abuse of his brother, the evaluator misread a high score on tests given to classify criminals into a particular personality type. The character typing conducted in January 1989, known as a Welsh code, contains a score the evaluator said must be viewed with caution.

"His MMPI profile is considered invalid due to an F score of 98," the evaluator stated. It is a reading that would indicate a seriously flawed personality—so flawed, given the limitations of his known criminal history, the evaluator distrusted it, concluding Jimmy's answers were "baked" to produce the score.

Further, Jimmy is mislabeled in the Megargee classification, which is used to lump prisoners into one of eight offender personality types.

Looking at the scores after his death, an independent psychologist familiar with both Welsh codes and the Megargee system said, beyond the failure to take seriously the elevated F scores, the prison psychologist misclassified Jimmy as a "Charlie"—one of the character types least likely to be rehabilitated—when he should have been characterized as a "Foxtrot"—*the least* likely personality type to respond to rehabilitation and *the most* likely to reoffend.

Even as a "Charlie," Jimmy's character description by the prison evaluator paints a picture of an individual with serious challenges.

"This profile usually typifies an individual who is antisocial, bitter, hostile, and come (sic) from inadequate family backgrounds, characterized by poor parenting. They often have poor interpersonal relationships and tend to get involved in illegal behavior," the evaluator stated. Alcohol and drug abuse, anxiety and immature behavior, a lack of goal direction and low self-esteem, deep feelings of insecurity, and a tendency toward superficial interpersonal relationships all are mentioned as applicable to Jimmy.

He was screened as a "middle" property risk and as a low risk for assault of other prisoners. He was recommended for classes to complete his high school education, vocational counseling, and a work assignment.

Further, his evaluator concluded Jimmy was depressed and prescribed the drug Sinequan, a medication never mentioned in Jimmy's letters to Charlene. But he did write home frequently during the few months he was on the drug, expressing that he was a "changed man."

"I feel like a totally different person now that I'm away from drugs and alcohol," he wrote in May 1989, about a month after starting the drug.

Sinequan or doxepin is a tricyclic antidepressant often prescribed to alleviate the symptoms of withdrawal from drugs and alcohol. It may also be prescribed for insomnia, among other indications. In June 1989, Jimmy continued to report a pretty positive state of mind.

"I think the time in here has helped me, #1) By not being able to get drunk, I have no craving for booze. #2) By showing I have a mother who still cares—that means the most to me.#3 no erge to do drugs."

He made frequent references elsewhere during this period that he intended to stay sober. He stopped taking Sinequan late in June 1989, probably because taking an antidepressant made it impossible for him to pursue the rehabilitative programs within the prison system. It seems counterintuitive, but the system did not allow for placement into vocational programs while medicated.

"We do not place people until they have been off psychotropic medication for a calendar year," stated a letter from the community programs administrator for the Department of Corrections dated August 23, 1989.

Jimmy wrote prison authorities repeatedly asking to have this policy rescinded in his case, since he was only on the drug a short time and only, he claimed, for insomnia.

While Jimmy was in prison, in the spring of 1989, Shelly, the girlfriend Jimmy blamed for his car accident, gave birth to a baby boy she initially claimed was his. Charlene either never knew or doesn't remember Shelly's last name, nor does Paula. The length of Jimmy's acquaintance with Shelly, how their relationship evolved, or exactly what led to their breakup are details Jimmy's letters hint at but don't clearly define. Jimmy wrote of her often that first year.

"She is the Best Friend I ever had & makes life worth living," was how he put it.

About two months into his sentence he confessed to Charlene, "I've been thinking about Shelly a lot...I call her once or twice a week. I wish I would have met a girl woman like her 2 years ago. She's a one of a kind! I know with a friend like her I can stay strait."

Around this same time, it is obvious Shelly's pregnancy was causing Jimmy to consider deeper issues about himself.

"Sometimes I wonder what if I have a son? I won't know how to teach him to hunt or skin a fish. But the things I will be able to teach may better him for the future."

In an undated letter written in the spring of 1989, Jimmy tacks on a postscript, letting Charlene know she is a grandmother.

"I am the Proud Father of a 9 pound Baby Boy! (Shelly wrote!)"

Around this time, Jimmy related, "There are good things to live for in life. Being in here is not one. Dope put me here. Things will only get better if I never do dope again."

The next indication that Jimmy and Shelly continued to be in touch is mentioned in a letter to Charlene dated May 14, 1989.

> Oh, By the way, I got a letter from Shelly. She said she tried to forget about me (nice girl hun?) But she couldn't. I don't know if I should write her back ever again, or talk to her or think about seeing her when I get out. It really hurt my feelings when I found that out. What do you think?

Jimmy repeatedly asked his mother if she had heard from Shelly and inquired whether Shelly had ever brought the baby over for her to see. He began to doubt the child was his.

"...if she was knocked up with my kid why would she try to forget me? Must not be my kid, Right?"

The possibility that Shelly might have been torn about raising the child as the son of a felon seems not to have occurred to Jimmy. By December 1989, Charlene was advising Jimmy not to put "all your eggs in one basket."

He never had. Jimmy was in touch with Paula, or wanted to be, throughout 1989, based on references he made to her in letters from that time. In a letter postmarked May 24, 1989, at a time when he believed he was the father of Shelly's baby, he wrote about his frustration with Paula and the fact she appeared to be moving on without him.

"Paula never came to visit me yet. She wrote me a letter and said she was sick, that's why she couldn't come."

Charlene said there was nothing much Jimmy could do until he got out of prison. Much as she did with the married man in her own past, she suggested Jimmy set Shelly free. Charlene continued to be in contact with Paula, and she urged Jimmy to call Paula. Late in 1990, he made contact with Paula's family.

> Yesterday I got a letter from her mom. She said Paula moved back home because she was pregnant. Then she went on to say the Father is Dead. We both know mom—the Father is not dead. (smile) The Father dumped her. They (Paula & whoever) were suppose to get married. So now Paula is preg. Without a father to see his son born. (They know it's a boy because ultrasound scan said so). Mom what do you think I should do or say? Nothing?

Though the letter at once seems to suggest Jimmy could be the father of Paula's baby, Charlene and Paula both say, regardless of what Jimmy wrote, that is not the case.

As for Shelly, Jimmy wrote early in 1990, "I really loved her and she'll always have a place in my heart, but, shes still married, and I wouldn't like to break up a family that I can't (yet) take care of."

At the time Jimmy wrote the letter, he believed he still had about ten months to serve, but in reality, it would be three more years before his release. Shelly responded to Jimmy's letter, calling him a "boy" and her husband a "man."

"Well," Jimmy wrote to Charlene, "I could shave some hair off my ass & Chest and mail it to her, But I'm not. I know Im a man—Just Because Im in here does'nt turn me into a BOY. Any woman or girl that thinks Im a boy is very wrong! Um, Shelly also let me off the hook! Trever isn't my son! Praise God!"

He went on to express gratitude to Charlene for standing by him, using his mother's nickname.

> I'm sorry if my letters sometimes sound insane, but some times I go through mood swings, especially since I quit smoking. You

know Charlie, you're the "only" person who stayed with me through "This," without your being with me through this thing, I surely would have went insane.

Around this same time, though perhaps prior to being let "off the hook," Jimmy lamented in a letter to Harry that "Shelly never did send me pictures of my kid."

To Charlene he wrote, in February 1990, "I wish Shelley would write. I would like to hear from her. I don't suppose you know what happened with Paula do ya? I told her goodbye because she was making this time I'm doing harder than it really is."

At a mass band concert, in the spring of 1990, Harry's senior year of high school, Harry was forced to choose between his mother and his girlfriend.

"She called Julie a hussy," Rob says.

Julie had come to the stadium to support Harry, and they were open about their relationship for one of the first times in public. Julie gave him a hug and a kiss, which sent Charlene into a tizzy.

"My mom was at the band function, supportive and helping," Rob says. Or she was at least until she saw Julie's greeting.

Charlene came up to him just as he was sitting down at his bass drum.

"She was just infuriated," Rob says, which is when the "H" word flew.

"She was cursing about me bringing that hussy here. She's like, 'It's either me or her,'" Rob recalls. There was also the hint of a threat from Charlene about whether he wanted to continue living in her house.

"That was that," says Rob. "I put my arm around Julie…She didn't deserve to be treated that way. I'll be damned if the one moment I get to stick up for Julie, I bail."

But beyond the insult to Julie was the fact the episode had played out in front of the entire band, embarrassing Rob.

"That she even said that but then to say that in front of all the kids she cares about?"

That night, Harry went to stay with Julie's family, and he remained there until he left for boot camp at the end of the summer. He felt, at the time, he had no other choice.

Charlene looks back at that time and sees herself as a different person.

"I was running his life, and he told me in no uncertain terms, 'You don't like Julie, and I love her.' I knew that I'd gone too far, but I didn't think I went too far," because she believed Julie would let him down.

Cut off from his mother, with his abuser in prison, Harry wanted a completely fresh start in the Marines.

"He said he didn't want to be Harry anymore," Julie remembers, so she suggested he go by his middle name. "I said, 'I'll just start calling you, 'Rob.'"

As hard a habit as it was for Harry to learn to call himself by a different name outwardly, there was some harder work going on internally.

"I think he was trying to shed 'Harry' and all the problems that came with Harry. 'Rob' was this new person and would get a new start," Julie says. Even though, at the time, she didn't know the extent of the problems Harry was dealing with, she supported him wholeheartedly.

"She was always supporting me, supporting my ideas, everything down to the very last," Rob says.

For Rob, the new name was almost like a mask.

"At the very least, shed the masks or baggage of the past and create — this new life."

And that new life was centered on a future with Julie.

"Rob graduated boot camp November 10, 1990, in California," Julie remembers. They spent the holidays in Michigan.

"He didn't want to go to see Jimmy at the jail," Julie says, but Charlene insisted. "Jackson State Penitentiary. That was my most memorable Christmas ever."

After spending an idyllic Christmas Eve with Julie's family, Julie and Rob, in his dress uniform, went with Charlene to see Jimmy at the prison. Charlene brought him a big box. "And, of course, being Charlene, she brought ten thousand items, dispersing it amongst all of the inmates."

Julie felt the hour-long visit stretched interminably.

"Jimmy was trying to finagle for us to send him money and writing to him and did I have any friends who wanted to be pen pals?" Julie remembers. "The Christmas tree was ready to fall over," and the topic of conversation was manipulated by Jimmy, who wanted sympathy for his plight.

"He was icky and creepy at the jail," Julie says. "I remember when we went to leave the jail, he went to hug me and I'm like, 'Unh-unh.'" She offered him a handshake instead.

A photograph of Charlene and her two boys—one in dress blues, the other in prison blues—is the only proof Rob has that he was really there. He has no memory of the visit.

"Makin faces at the camera. I didn't realize how I could scare women and children with this picture (shits & giggles)"

January 17, 2009

Hello Dad!

Here are pictures! Made doubles so please keep them.

Today bought new film & will send more pictures.

I am single—forgot to answer that question on last letter. Smell my own farts & no others.

It is impossible to put my last 20 yrs+ on paper! Life story!

I got a kid or two out there—tring to find them on internet like I did with you. Old girlfriends & such.

I was hoping you would call my cell phone (701-219-XXX). Had that number 3 yrs.+.

Not on parole, probation, etc.—Have money & Good Guy, also spare kidney. So Call & Just say Hi—Please? We can talk about Canada Be hind there back.

Glad to see you are doing okay! $ & Health. I have been through struggles with women & I under stand what you went through with mom. I lived with her longer than you! ☹ I used to steal pot from her purse & her go fast pills from medicine cabenet.

I hold no anger, hatred, or bad feelings toward you. I understand she put a restraining order on you? (I have not talked to her since 1994.)

She took my money and yours. And used it for her Rabbit fur coats x2—1 mink coat—full length, $2000 water bed. Diamond rings on <u>all</u> her fingers & dope. She was/is very hot headed & <u>evil</u>. Yes I said it <u>EVIL</u>.

Could you please send more pictures.

I used to do wood working in Canada! We made chairs, sofa's, tables out of oak wood & made mini chair & tables for Ronald McDonald's Children's Hospital—As donation for very ILL children. Worked for COR-CAN Industrys in Canada. Dows & Glue are a bitch! So we developed a pre-glue dow plunger! Big drop of glue—"Dow plunger" forces it up out of hole so wood won't split on assembly & in vice. Had wood splitting problems & quality control issues from too much glue—no spreadage.

I think the meaning of life is to have fun whenever you can. Last night I went for a steack dinner & made funny faces at people and objects. But no Obama jokes! Hope this fella Obama can change—<u>not just U.S.</u> But the world ~~opion~~ (attitude) towards the U.S.'s short comings. It can't get any worse can it?—(Yes it can)…Hope it won't.

Hey! What happened with that address I gave you in grand Rapids? Michigan. That somebitch said "Hey your dad can send mail here."

Well, I fucked off to Iowa & lost track of you & myself. No jobs. No hope & I left never to return to Michigan, then about 1 or 2 months later went to get the Nova outta the back yard, in Taylor (police state).

I've got 5,000 cash on my card & in the bank. Thank you for sending money when I was in Michigan. Gosh that helped! Well Dad God bless!

—Jim

P.S. Went camping in Idaho in Shoshone Natl. Forest in Shoshone County Idaho for 3 weeks! Saw a bear (yearling) walk with in 20 yards of campsite. Also saw Moose. Rustic Campsite along Glacier melt stream & tributary of Shoshone River (in my $900 Buick)

CHAPTER TEN

Escape

Ineligible for other programs in the prison system because of antidepressants he was prescribed, Jimmy pursued his GED, passing the test in March 1990. His worst subject was writing, which he did not pass, but the 77 he got in social studies and the 86 he received in science, along with a 50 in literature and a 52 in mathematics, gave him a passing score of 53 overall. An average of 45 was the cutoff.

He also pursued a paralegal course by correspondence.

In October 1990, he wrote, "Im on my last lesson of my paralegal studies. It talks about writing a resume and what places to mail them to."

There is no record that Jimmy passed the course, but he did receive a certificate for referring other inmates to the program and later listed among his job skills "paralegal."

Getting into the automotive courses he hoped to pursue would have to wait until he was off Sinequan for a year.

The first occasion in which Jimmy wrote to Harry directly was around the same time he was denied training, August 1989, about two months after he stopped taking Sinequan. He seemed paranoid. The oppressor and molester had been put in the position of begging his victim to let him know their mother was okay. After relying almost completely on Charlene for the few comforts he had in prison, one of her letters had been returned to sender.

Jimmy mentions "harry" a scant twenty-five times in the nearly two hundred missives he wrote from prison. There are only a couple of letters actually written to his brother, and it is worth pointing out that Harry never wrote back. Rob doesn't even have any recollection of seeing Jimmy's letters at the time.

Nearly half of the twenty-five references to Harry are a simple greeting, thrown in at the close of a letter to Charlene, or a comment expressing his hope things are going well for his mother and brother. But with a letter to Charlene returned to him, Jimmy wrote directly to Harry. For once, Harry's name is capitalized.

> Harry, What happened to Mom? Did she die or something? I sent a letter to her and it was returned "Doesn't Live Here." It Doesn't look like her handwriting though on the letter. I've tried calling Alllll DAAAYY today and only the answering machine picks up. Harry Please let me know what's going on. Im scared to Death that something happened to her. It Just DidN't look like her handwriting. Your Brother, Jim.
> P.S. If shes mad at me or something tell her I'm sorry with all my heart.

Rob never knew of the letter at the time, and Charlene has no idea why the earlier one was returned to sender.

Jimmy may have been anxious to gain some skill or accomplishment. It did not escape Jimmy's notice that his little brother's life was taking off. Jimmy initially did not seem supportive upon hearing Harry's plan to enter the military. He wrote to his mom:

> Did you tell harry anything about the marines? They teach you how to shoot a machine gun. They teach you how to kill people. They tell you when to eat, shit & sleep. And they tell you when you can come home. Why, hell, I'm almost doing that now. If they gave us all machine guns in here we could cure the overcrowding problem!

Charlene, too, was against Harry joining the military. She believed he was too sensitive to withstand being yelled at by drill instructors. But with Harry living at Julie's, there was no way she could talk him out of it.

Jimmy wrote to Harry about his enlistment a second time, sounding supportive.

"I hear your going to be the Few, the Proud, The MARINES! Well, that's good an I hope it works out for ya."

In April 1990, Jimmy asked Charlene, "Has harry gone to the Marines yet? I know when he does, that I hope Im out by then."

Shortly after Harry and Julie's holiday visit in December 1990, Jimmy wrote what Rob believes is the closest thing to an apology he ever received from his abuser.

"I know I don't write you But sometimes I don't know what to say for myself," Jimmy said. "I'm not the same Jim you use to know. A New Jim has taken over and Is going to make something out of his life!"

Jimmy closes his letter to Harry with a reminder he's still hoping for a pen pal.

"Have you Found a sig single chick who wants to write me?" he asked Harry. "I don't care if she the uglyist girl in school! Your brother, Jim."

In a letter to Charlene in the same mailing, Jimmy elaborated.

> ...sometimes its hard to put my thoughts into words. I feel like a different person now, Its hard to describe, but I have new hope for my future. Even ~~thoo~~ though I'm nowhere in life right now because of my drug and alcohol problem, I'll have a fresh start when I get out, and things will only get better. I'm going to write Harry a letter and put it in this one.

The reference to Harry, immediately following the desire for a "fresh start," seems to indicate a fresh start is what he hoped for with his brother.

In another letter, written a couple of months after the Christmas 1990 visit, Jimmy wrote:

> HI Harry...Just a note to say hello...All day I hear nigger music plus every single day I have to look at them and hear their big mouths. I hate niggers. I'll be so glad to come back and live with you white folk. You see, there's hardly any white folk here...Eight days without a smoke. Smoking is a "dirty expensive habit." I'm still going through withdrals, sometimes I have fits of rage and anger, anxity and nervousness, but I don't have as many bad hea-dechs or feel tired all the time.

It almost seems to me as if, in Jimmy's mind, what happened in the past never happened. Is he looking for sympathy? Or is the mention of "fits of rage" an attempt to point out some outside stimulus may have caused the abuse?

Strangely, three of the letters reference Harry and the dog, Runt, in close proximity.

In a letter from 1989, Jimmy jumped right from, "How's the dog been?" to "Has harry got his brakes fixed?"

In a letter from February 1990, Jimmy wrote, "Is the dog doing well? Do you think you can send any money? Tell harry I said hi!"

Jimmy told Charlene how much he enjoyed the December 1990 visit with "harry." The letter closes with hugs and kisses for the family pets and mentions the dog, Runt, by name.

"I miss them," he wrote.

Jimmy wrote in another letter about listening to a tape recording Charlene sent in which she sounded sad.

"Did the dog die or something?" he asked.

It is almost uncanny. In fact, the dog did die of some unknown malady around that time. Harry found him bloated and dead in the back yard, but Charlene didn't tell Jimmy.

One time, Jimmy wrote at length about Runt and understanding what it felt like to be the dog—the same dog he raped before he went to prison.

> No Sex, boardom, lonlyness. When I get home I'm going to Take him For walk more often. I Remember when I use to take him out in the Field Behind Sears Surplus and he would sniff out all the Rabbit holes. You could Almost see him Smile as he would run around, then he would stand still & Perk his ears in one direction as If he heard something, and Take Off running.

If I didn't know how he abused Harry and the dog, I could almost imagine Jimmy had a great deal of affection for both of them.

Jimmy lamented in his letters the lack of contact with anyone but his mother.

"I haven't got anything in the mail yet from Paula or Shelly. It seems you're the one who writes most. It goes to show I have a mother who cares About me more than Any person on earth...I Love You!"

At first, Charlene was moved by her son's expressions of affection, but today she sees them as manipulations—trying to get the money and things he needed inside, through his only reliable outside connection.

At times, Jimmy's communication was completely inappropriate, like telling his mother he wanted to look like a Playgirl centerfold when he got out of prison and asking his mom to bring him *Hustler* magazines. Just as inappropriate were comments that crossed the line for a son writing to his mother.

"Have you lost more weight since the last time you wrote me? You sure would look sexy when you get skinny. You would have to carry a can of mace around to keep all the guys from attacking you! I liked that picture of you in that Pretty Coat! You look great!"

In a letter dated May 14, 1989, he wrote, "I joke with the guy in the bunk below, I tell him I ought to Marry you because youre the only one who cares enough to visit & write & send me money and clothes."

Of all the letters Jimmy wrote, one sent in the summer of 1989 is beyond the pale. This letter, like the one to Harry in which he expressed the paranoid concern that Charlene was dead, was written several weeks after Jimmy went off of Sinequan. He enclosed with the letter a clipping about a woman who went on a diet.

"Please read it. You could be Skiny and have all kinds of guys chasing you around! Maybe even me! I always had a thing for Blue eyed women. I miss you! Love Always, Jim, OXOXO."

Charlene does not immediately share this letter with me. She spent most of the night before Jimmy's memorial service rereading the letters, and this one was so disturbing to her, she removed it from the files she gave me to take home. Later, after considering awhile, she sent it to me.

His apology for inappropriate comments is also among the letters she saved.

"Im sorry you took my letters that way," he said. "I was just trying to build your self esteem. Love YA!"

At one point, Jimmy tried to draw Charlene into a "get-rich-quick" scheme involving Social Security benefits.

In the summer of 1989, Jimmy was bunking with a man he described as a drug "kingpin" who supposedly eluded capture by the FBI for a number of years before being arrested. Jimmy told Charlene he had learned from the kingpin of a sure-fire form of income upon his release. Jimmy was so excited about the information, he spent hours painstakingly copying down the exact instructions, which run to ten pages. Through information he said the kingpin found at the law library, Jimmy was convinced he could make a claim for Social Security once he was released from prison.

> Go immediately to the nearest Social Security Office. Ask to speak to a counselor so that you can apply for Social Security Insurance Emergency Supplement Benefits of up to $1,500. Explain that you are emotionally (mentally) unprepared to hold a job. Show them your parole or Mandatory discharge papers to prove that you are just out of prison. Note: You should have a check within 72 hours...$310 monthly disability for every month that you were incarcerated.

Since Jimmy hadn't worked long enough to qualify for the program on his own, he told her he could qualify with a parent's birth date and Social Security number. He wrote the instructions down for Charlene so she would provide the necessary information. At the end of ten pages, Jimmy wrote, "FUCK IM TIRED OF WRITING!!"

In a later letter to Charlene, he asked again for her birth date and Social Security number. There is no record of Jimmy's reaction but tucked in with a letter to Charlene later is a copy of a short bulletin, apparently from prison officials, advising that someone, "as a joke," was spreading misinformation about the availability of benefits for inmates. All of Jimmy's hard work to get on easy street was for naught.

My interviews with Julie consisted of a lot of e-mails, back and forth over a period of several months, and one telephone conversation. Rob and Charlene consider Julie an ally, and they both respect her take on everything that happened. When it comes to dates and details, Julie's recollection, they feel, is above reproach. It is great to have an outside party to confirm so many of the stories Rob and Charlene tell me. Julie has nothing to gain from sharing her opinions. Just the fact an ex-wife of Rob's is still on friendly terms with both Rob and Charlene tells me a lot about what kind of people they all are.

Julie's only request is that I shield her identity and details about her life today. She knows the information she can provide is fairly critical to the story I am telling, but she doesn't want the past invading her present life.

Julie remembers a lot of red flags during preparations for her wedding, but nothing was going to stop her from marrying Rob. The red flags were unconnected to Rob's estrangement from his whole family but served as little alarms Julie was determined not to acknowledge.

The down payment on the bridesmaids' dresses was lost when the store went bankrupt. Julie had a table on layaway and lost that money too, when another store closed.

"The whole 'getting married' thing was that high school girl 'la-la land.' I wish I would have been smart enough not to do that. Just to keep it simple. So many things went wrong," she says. "There were signs that somebody was saying, 'Hey now, is this really what you want to do?'"

Though she worried she might be making the wrong decision, she wasn't about to back out. Close friends were telling her not to go through with it, even though they liked Rob.

Charlene, Julie says, was "off the hook" at that time. Rob did not want her at the wedding.

"She was just so rude and crazy at that point...The whole family not speaking to each other, not being a family, was so unusual to me."

In short, Julie had doubts, but what young bride doesn't?

"I was afraid I would upset everyone if I didn't get married to Rob. He was always there, and I was worried that breaking it off with him would upset the balance in life."

"I have a broken family," Rob tells me in one of our interviews. It was never more broken than at the time of his marriage.

"They probably wouldn't even send a card if they did know," he says. "I don't think I invited anyone from my family because they would have told my mom. I couldn't picture her behaving—going through one entire night without making one snide comment."

Julie and her family had become Rob's support system.

"It was what I wanted—to be with Julie—and Julie was my whole life at the time."

Rob's biggest worry was that his mother would object in the middle of the wedding.

"Not having my family there didn't really bother me. It didn't faze me. I'm sure some of Julie's family must have been thinking about it—*Are there any Krimms here?*...I had made friends and my new life; that's what I wanted."

Today, Rob regrets the disconnect with his mother, no matter her part in causing it.

"I'm sorry that happened," he says.

Though Jimmy mostly expressed love and thanks for Charlene's help and attention, he also had the nerve, in his letters, to lash out at her. In a letter postmarked July 5, 1989, he wrote:

> Why don't you treat me as a person, as a son? YOU KNOW I would Never hurt you! Maybe you think when I come up outa here, That Ill be screaming For Vengance, Well Im Not, That's the worst thing that a ex-con can do. Instead I will Be Fighting to Be Free Forever! And yes, It can be done. I have to plan on getting out of that neiborhood, its Bad News.

In 1991, Charlene told Jimmy his gravy train was coming to an end, though it's not clear he received the letter—it is in an envelope that was returned with a bad address.

The dispute between the two centered around a $20 money order Charlene had purchased for Jimmy, but he said he never received it. He must have complained of not receiving it in harsh enough words that Charlene let him have it. It also appears he complained of money he had in the bank that he thought Charlene had taken from him or was somehow withholding from him.

> Dear Jim, I'm writing to tell you that you just Fucked Up. Enclosed is a copy of a $20 money order January 11 like I promised and you weren't very nice to me either on our last visit. But you won't have to worry about hearing nasty things I say anymore. Your money is in the bank in your name so give it your best shot. If you think I'm going to go out of my way for you anymore…you can think again. I saw a lot of hatred and animosity still in your face and in your words last week. After all the support—money—food—clothes I've given. I can't believe you sold all those nice things. But now you can sell the whole fucking mess because you'll not get any more money or time out of me. And for what—cigarettes. Sounds like you're into the drugs again—selling everything. But your gold mine here at home has ended.—I remain, Your mother.

Jimmy wrote a short time later, "Sometimes the letters I write show the mood swings I go through in this place. You probably wonder 'why' This place isn't racialy balanced that's why."

Another example of discord between Jimmy and Charlene comes in a letter dated August 13, 1993, after he had just found out he had 120 days, rather than the 61 he thought he had left to serve.

> I'm sorry you feel that I will Drink & do drugs when I get home. I just wonder how the Hell you Know these things before I do?! Ya KNoW—There was a mother who Always told her son 'you'll NeveR Amount to anything' and ya KNoW the son Never did.— See Ya, Jimbo. P.S. Ya think I'll start back smoking Ciggerettes too? And drinking coffee, And listening to Heavy Metal and working at Taco Bell pushin beans.

After nearly three years in the prison system, Jimmy was put in a minimum-security environment Charlene describes as a halfway house. He escaped and moved in with Paula. Paula tells me what happened when I call her a few weeks after meeting her at Jimmy's memorial service.

"I knew when he came to the door," Paula says, that he was in trouble. "He was always looking over his shoulder."

She took him in and tried to resume a relationship with him. But Jimmy's demons got in the way.

"He used to write to me that he would dream where I would cheat on him," Paula says. His lack of trust and fear that she would cheat came out in controlling behaviors—dictating what kind of music she could listen to and which friends she could see.

"I told him, 'You can't tell me who I can have for company and who I like,'" Paula says. She really wanted the relationship to work, but it didn't.

"You always have that person you think you can fall back on," she says, and given her long acquaintance with Jimmy, he was that guy for her. She saw good things in him.

"He always talked really good about his brother," Paula says. He would brag about how good Rob was with money; how he worked his way up and bought the car he wanted. Paula says Jimmy also spoke highly of Charlene.

"His mom was everything to him. She was the best cook, just the best of everything."

A picture from this period shows Jimmy and Paula smiling, with her son between them. Though Jimmy seemed to want to be a father figure,

Paula says, he didn't take much interest in her son, nor did he help out with the child or with any chores around the house. He got mad at her when she wouldn't get up early to drive him to work, never mind that she had an infant to care for and it was pretty inconvenient to have to bundle up the child to take him outside on those cold mornings and then come back to get herself ready for work.

"I wanted to be with him, but he spent a lot of time being nasty," Paula says. She actually began to hope he would get caught and put back in jail. She hoped it would teach him a lesson to "stop getting into trouble and grow up."

Though he was controlling, he was never physically abusive except for one time, Paula remembers, when he wanted to have sex and she did not. They were in bed, and she told him she wasn't up to it.

"He kept going," Paula says, even after she somewhat sarcastically suggested he let her know when he was "done."

"Most men, it would kill the mood," she says.

"He just kept going," and that was the moment when Paula decided she'd had enough. "That was the last he ever had."

Following a fight on Paula's birthday, Jimmy slashed her tires, and she told him he couldn't come back to the house.

Three months after escaping from the halfway house, Jimmy was arrested without incident at the place where he was working. A month after being returned to prison, Jimmy wrote to his mom.

"I finally figured out why things didn't work out between me & Paula. It's because I wouldn't baby-sit, (on a voluntary basis) her son. I also wouldn't hold him, change his dipers or feed him. Maybe that's why her 'I don't care about you' attitude started."

It appears Jimmy believed Paula turned him in.

"I've been keeping my cool and not calling or writing paula," Jimmy told Charlene. "In about a month I'll get recent copies of my Lansing file and see whats really in there (Just for my own piece of mind.)."

A second letter also seems to associate Paula with his recapture.

"I Drove for 4 months without getting pulled over, or having a crash. God works in mysterious ways…Sometimes it is annoying when the person you love has no or little respect for your feelings, like Paula."

It seems a strange lament to me, coming from someone who viciously abused his younger brother for five years, raped the family pet, and stole from his own mother.

CHAPTER ELEVEN

Every Man for Himself

Jimmy tried throughout his prison time to contact his dad, finally having some success in 1992. Every written reference to his dad is in quotation marks, as if Jimmy had bestowed the title "dad" somewhat grudgingly to his father.

Following his return to prison after his three months on escape, Jimmy wrote to Charlene. "Sent 'dad' a Christmas card and a short note saying what happened & how things are going. Told him if he could send money it would help out."

In February 1992, he wrote, "Wrote to 'DAD' told him to send a phone number—cause I like to call someday. Also asked him to send money if he could."

In March 1992, Jimmy wrote:

> Finally got a letter from 'DAD'…He finally gave me his phone number too. Sunday March 1st at Noon I called him. First Time in more than 10 god-m yrs. Since I heard him…We made small talk for a short time…Before I could get into the nitty-gritty of things—He said well 'James' it was good hearin from ya…Keep Your nose clean. So I took my Que and said OK I will. Told him I loved him—then he said the same to me (I love you too) And we hung-up. So much for long conversations with my Long Lost father, Huh? What a guy. You'd think that 10 yrs. Gone by without a word said he would have a lot on his mind or maybe explain some things before I Ask them.

Later the same month, Jimmy wrote, "'Dad' sent a birthday card, it said, 'Good to Talk to You' 'Love Dad' So today I wrote a thank you letter with a picture in it (same as yours) And a Newspaper Article about all the GM plants being closed."

Another time, he wrote, "Haven't got letters from 'DAD' or 'ROB'—especially 'ROB.'"

The quotation marks around Harry's recently assumed identity seems to me to convey that Jimmy held "Rob" in the same regard as his dad. A statement Jimmy made in the letter, that it was "every man for himself in this family" is one that raises Rob's hackles today.

"That's really ringing my bell," Rob tells me, given the fact Jimmy abused him so horribly.

Jimmy was upset with Rob, it seems, not just because Rob didn't write, but because he had to learn from his dad that Rob and Julie were getting married. In a letter to Charlene in November 1993, Jimmy relates that he had written to his grandma Crosby.

"She also said Harry didn't invite her to the wedding but invited Grandma Krimm who couldn't go anyway. I told Ms. Crosby 'don't feel bad he didn't even invite his own mother.'"

Rob tells me he felt at the time there were good reasons for not inviting Charlene to the wedding, but under no circumstances would he ever have considered inviting Jimmy.

Rob describes his marriage to Julie, at first, as "bliss."

"We weren't even old enough to buy alcohol, yet here we are, married. It was everything I ever imagined."

Rob was determined to forge ahead with his life, with no impact from the abuse in his past.

"If you're naked and you're with somebody, there should be feelings and response and reaction. When that time finally came, I was happy to find out he hadn't destroyed that."

Julie, too, looks back fondly on their early marriage.

"We had fun figuring out where to find things in the new places he was stationed…The band traveled a lot. So we were pretty happy to see each other when he was home."

Among the perks of Rob's duty was getting to play with the band at a performance in Carnegie Hall, and meeting former president Jimmy Carter.

Julie was in nursing school and worked part-time.

"We lived in base housing. We made friends, because we were all newly married, young, and poor. We did some silly stuff for fun.

We would get into water fights with our neighbors…We would walk at night around the neighborhood…and we would drive to places so I could take pictures. Rob liked to eat at Denny's so we would usually try to find a Denny's on the route…we would rent movies and watch them all night. Then other people would have parties…The boys would turn it into WrestleMania. The wives would stand back and laugh."

Though they were low on cash, Rob and Julie found ways to show one another they cared. He brought back little gifts for her from band trips. She packed his lunch every day.

"He would get so excited about the surprises I made him, just like my daughter has through the years. He has always managed to be a kid," Julie says.

Whenever the subject of children of their own came up, there wasn't much of a discussion.

"I think she was the main stopper in the whole thing," Rob says. "She was always the planner, finances, vacations, groceries, what we can afford to eat out on."

Julie's way of deflecting the idea was to point out to Rob, on various occasions when they might be on a trip or doing something fun, that children would complicate things.

Rob recalls Julie saying, "Can you see us doing that with a kid? Translation, 'Rob, you're too much of a kid.'"

But there was something else holding Julie back.

"I just had this feeling there was something about Rob that I didn't know," she says, and always lurking was the specter of Jimmy popping into their lives again.

Jimmy harped continually throughout his prison time on the lack of racial balance in the various institutions he was placed in. At least half of Jimmy's letters contain the use of the word *nigger* at least once. The attitude was so ingrained, the references crop up again and again.

"Don't buy me new T-shoes to wear here," he wrote. "The niggers will steal them. Bring my cheap Blue ones."

He made it clear he didn't hide his racism from fellow inmates.

"These poor niggers who have to live with me in this cube are baffled because I don't say one fuckin word to them."

In another, he wrote, "I'm not looking foreward to going to Washtenaw. Niggers, lots of niggers, but its like that everywhere I've been, except here in hillsdale. Its like being on a vacation away from niggers!"

In March 1992, he wrote, "I sure am Tired of waken' up and lookin at niggers every morning. After 3 yrs. You'd think I'd be use to it! Niggers are ugly repulsive people. I'll be glad when I can wake up and not see them, hear them, or look at them."

His distrust and dislike of black people was bound to come to a boiling point. The worst incident recorded in detail occurred before his escape in March 1990.

> A guard caught me in the act of sharping a piece of steel (shank). 8 gaurds ran up in the unit to see what was going on…So the gaurds took me to the control center, while one had to look on the other side of the fence for the piece I was sharping (I threw it far over the fence). I sat in the control center handcuffed & Ankles shackled For Two hours while a ticket was wrote…Now I am here at Adrian Temp. Fac. (Medium) its nice here. Im trying to beat the ticket…Its called a dangersous contraband ticket) God saved some poor niggers life by me getting caught.

In another incident, Jimmy wrote of making a shank to throw under a black inmate's bed so the other inmate would get in trouble for having contraband and be transferred out.

Jimmy complained repeatedly of the noise in the prison, particularly from "niggers fighting" and "nigger music."

"Niggers always want to run shit around here. That's why I don't watch T.V. They don't watch the news (Oh no, that's too educational)."

At one point, Jimmy said he was feeling better because of his placement in a new facility.

"I've made new friends in here, all white ones. I don't hear that fuckin nigger music 12 hours a day."

By the end of his prison sentence, he said, "I want a life, this is nowhere. And its not even safe to do time in here. These damn niggers! I've lived with Africans for 5 years and I'm fully fed up with it."

Jimmy expressed frustration when he signed up for an AA class at one of the centers and had to listen to a black woman talking about her addictions.

> The thing she talked about the most was crack and Bluntly told how she sucked Dick for it. I didn't enjoy hearing all that shit.

There's men In here who've been locked up for years, so, you can imagine how the Animals acted. What gets me is her story doesn't relate to me. Men don't suck dick to get crack—men rob, steal, and sometimes kill.

Jimmy seems to have had some homophobic attitudes, also.

I remember Ray telling me if I got to prison I'm going to suck Niger Dick, well, he must have been in a very bad prison or maybe he was trying to scare me strait. The places I've been there were Fags who did that. Some of them even try to dress, walk, act and talk like women. Fucked up Aint it?

Like many inmates, Jimmy exchanged letters for a period of months with a prison missionary. In one letter, Jimmy told Charlene he was born again and asked if she was.

"I got another Bible study course in the mail today," he wrote. "It was about when Jesus comes & how he rose from the grave. Have you accepted Jesus Christ as your saivor? I did March 11, 1990," the day after his twenty-third birthday.

His early letters are sprinkled with information gleaned through contacts with prison missionaries. In one letter, he copied down scripture that had meaning to him.

In Revenlations 2:10 it said "Fear none of those things which thou shalt suffer: behold, the devil may cast some of you into prison, that ye may be tried; and ye shall have tribulation ten days: Be thou faithful unto death, and I will give thee a crown of life." So I am a Beliver without a doubt.

He told Charlene he read his Bible at night, along with books and true stories of people who had turned their lives around after getting saved.

"In the Books, I read stories that made my skin crawl. Then they told how they found the Lord. They prayed a lot & Really Believed That Santan had Influinced there lives."

I can't help wondering how bad a story would have to be to make Jimmy's skin crawl. The ideas that Satan could have influenced his own actions and that God forgives appear to be concepts he considered, much to my surprise.

"I went to church again Sunday night," he wrote. "I think it would be good for me to keep at it, I need all the help I can get, mentally & spritully."

But later in his prison term, he appeared not to have incorporated Christian behavior into his routine.

"I got rid of my snotty, Christian Roomate today. I wrote a grievance about being a non-smoker in a room with a smoker (for 3 months). Boy was he pissed."

According to prison records in Charlene's possession, Jimmy had numerous infractions throughout his incarceration, all of which served to extend his time behind bars.

In October 1992, a report to the parole board recorded sixteen misconduct convictions, two major misconduct tickets, and three security reclassifications. Jimmy was issued tickets multiple times for substance abuse and for failing to produce a urine sample. He claimed he was kidney shy and couldn't urinate in front of a female guard. Several times, he received tickets for being "out of place"—in the weight pit when he should have been at the library, for instance.

One time, he was ticketed for disobeying a direct order to get out of bed. Another time, he was denied parole for having written a threatening letter to the parole board. Jimmy kept a running list of grievances against a nurse at one institution, complaining his medical needs were neglected.

"If hell is a place you may go to when you die, then I surely must be dead," he wrote of his ailments at the time.

Jimmy dreamed about how he would get his life back on track once he was released from prison.

"I tell myself I could have a mustang G.T. with a good Job and no partying. Do you know how much I'd like to own a mustang? All I have to do is think positive and remember the sky's the limit!"

The reference to owning a Mustang makes me wonder how Jimmy would feel knowing his brother attained that dream. The parallels between Rob and Jimmy, much as Rob wanted to believe he was so different, are unmistakable. But where Rob managed to overcome obstacles to make dreams into reality, Jimmy seemed stuck in a hell mostly of his own making.

No matter how much Jimmy dreamed, he was his own worst enemy. Infractions took away his points and good time toward an early release, until he came up with a new strategy: serving the maximum sentence to avoid having to report to a parole officer when he got out.

In one of the few examples of looking beyond himself to think of the welfare of others, Jimmy wrote to his mom begging her to reconsider her decision to join the volunteer patrols that were springing up in response to the crack cocaine epidemic, which was reaching its zenith in Taylor at the time.

> I would feel uncomfortable living at home if you went ahead with this. Maybe you Feel my opinon doesn't matter. I'm not trying to tell you what to do, but giving advise about what I already Know. Its dangerous. People are getting Killed over this shit. Please think about it. You can't beat 'em, not even Police can rid the area of the shit. If you Really are concerned about harrys safty and yours, then maybe we should plan on moving away from the getto. I don't know how else to say it, but the drug problem in our neibourhood won't just 'go away,' it's there to stay!

Charlene joined the patrol anyway. And Jimmy was wrong, because the patrols had a big impact on the crack problem, according to local historian George Gouth. Though it took a number of years, the neighborhood is very different today. Pine Ridge is no longer a crib for criminals and drug addicts. But it wasn't just the crime that was the issue in Taylor.

Gouth confirms a phenomenon Rob recalls from his youth. Looking back at a random sampling of friends he made over the years in his neighborhood, Rob can recall maybe one in four who had a father still in the picture. As a former teacher, Gouth recalls whole classrooms of Taylor kids in which not one child had a father present in the home. It was a segregated economic group, rather than a racial one.

"We had entire schools that were considered low income," because their mothers were either on welfare or their incomes were so low their children qualified for reduced-price or free meals.

With an absent father, a working mother, no supervision, and a school system and social services taxed to the limit, not to mention a recession bringing cuts in every aspect of local government, the Krimm boys grew up in a home and a society with no safety net. When things went wrong, they stayed wrong. At the time Jimmy was writing to his mother from prison, the cliché "falling between the cracks" may as well have been "falling into crack." It was easy to do, even in prison.

"I went to take a shower last night and the shower room smelled like somebody was smoking crack. Its been over 2 yrs since I smelled that shit, but I know the smell. IT (Crack) smells like boiling orange peels."

AA and NA meetings had some impact on Jimmy, helping him to stay away from drugs at least some of the time and teaching him about addictions in general.

"I used to think willpower had something to do with a drug problem—It doesn't—A lack of willpower or a wekness in character does not cause an addiction. Nor is willpower the answer to overcoming an addiction."

But after a few years inside, Jimmy seemed clearly depressed with his lot in life.

"Things have been hard for me lately...Ive been borrowing smoke and gone into debt...Things are boring here. I do a lot of thinking, daydreaming, etc. I wish I could spend a day with you outside this fence and show you how much a changed person I am."

As his time in prison comes to an end, Jimmy wants to find a place of his own—in response to Charlene laying down the rules she feels would be appropriate if he was going to live with her. For one, she didn't want Jimmy bringing strange women into her house. That didn't sit well with Jimmy.

"I don't like the idea of going from one prison, out to the world to the other," he wrote.

He complained more than once that he had learned little to help himself once he was free.

"Lifting weights and scrubbing toilets is not rehabilitation. So sick and tire of living like this. It can only get better. 7 more months till discharge..."

Jimmy responded positively to the news Charlene had given away a sled that belonged to her sons.

"I hope the little boy has fun with the tobboggen as we did. Life seems so short and goes by so fast..."

A growing maturity seems evident in Jimmy's final letters. He appeared willing to help his mom with things that needed fixing around the house.

"...like Paint, fill in holes in the wall, fix closet doors, fix my car, organize things. I'm going to be the white tornado!" he declared to his mom.

A few months before his release, he gave detailed instructions to Charlene on home maintenance.

> Before you turn on the furnace you should change the filter. If you don't have a new filter don't worry we'll get one soon enough... just pull old one out. If you feel energetic you may remove the vent cover in the hallway under the thermostate and vacume the furnace fan "blower" to remove all cat hair and dust...Another things is when you use the stove to heat the house or a kerosene heater, Remember They produce Carbon Monoxide—An odorless, Colorless Gas that can kill you.

He went on to warn, "There's no venting system in the house, not even in the Bathroom, nor in the Kitchen. That's why that mold builds up in the corners. No leaking Roof, Just high Humidity All the time. That's why the windows fog up and sweat when you cook...The only way to get fresh air in the house is to open a window or door."

I am impressed. Jimmy had diagnosed what was wrong with Charlene's house to a tee, and about ten years later, in a major rehabilitation project in some of the HUD homes in the neighborhood, the interior of Charlene's house was entirely gutted as part of a mold-remediation project.

"As for the truck," Jimmy continued in his letter, "I'm state Certified in tune-ups and more than likely could have did yours for a fraction of what you paid."

This letter, frankly, astounds me. It reads as if it is from a different person—a rehabilitated person.

"I don't know why you keep asking where I'll be in 5 yrs," he went on to write his mother, "when you yourself do not Know where you will be in 5 yrs. All that I can tell you is that I will try to better myself as best I can. And Five yrs from now I will be better than where I am today."

Even as I read the statement, I know Jimmy will not be better off in five years. But I am not unsympathetic to his frustration that no one, not even his mother, seems to believe in him. But who could blame Charlene, who had seen him fail—or try to lie his way out of trouble—so many times? How could she help but doubt him?

The exact date Jimmy returned to Charlene's house is recorded because Charlene was attending a Co-Dependents Anonymous group at the time and she was keeping a journal.

Jimmy had been released from prison a few weeks earlier, showing up at Charlene's on January 12, 1994.

"I feel happy in a sad way or sad in a happy way now I'm dealing with my older son...I told him he needed to relax and chill out and set goals that he can realistically achieve," she wrote at the time.

A few days later, Charlene recorded that Jimmy had been busy cleaning and fixing things around the house.

"I feel good that he's home but I don't want him to throw away something that I want."

The clutter in her life at that time was out of control, she tells me.

Charlene wrote a few days into the visit of the lack of a barrier between mother and son now that he was an adult, but barely a week later, he left home. The next day, Charlene wrote, "At first I just missed him but now I'm afraid, partly because I don't know if he did something wrong and he went to jail and partly because I gave him a key to my house and I wonder if he would steal from me like he used to."

Not knowing when he might return, Charlene decided to write him a letter, putting it in his room so he could read it if he returned. There had obviously been a fight over Jimmy's attempt to help his mom de-clutter her house.

> Jim, You are a 26-year-old adult. I will not try to control your life—where you go—who you see—what you do...If you do something wrong, you are the only person who pays the penalty. I am trying to provide a safe place for you with no pressures. So that you can safely go out into the world when you feel comfortable and have a good life—job, car, house...You do not have to lie to me. I will accept the truth without criticism because I love you and I want to allow you to live your life without my control...
>
> I realize that all the things you've done this week required quite an effort and you really are trying to help me get back to normal. However, I need your respect in order to start detaching myself from the things I cannot control.
>
> First of all to let me know that you're safe. You don't have to tell me where you are—who you're with or what you're doing—just let me know that you're safe and for me not to worry.

Second, respect my wishes and my property whether it is junk in your opinion or not. It is still my junk and I want the decision to throw it out. I don't want you to tell me what I need and don't need. I agree with you that things have to go but only when I can release them, not behind my back. That hurts me and makes me angry. I'm not sure I'm back to feeling that I care yet about dealing with these things. I'm sorry if it makes you angry but it took me a long time to get this way and I'm not going to recover overnight. That's why I'm asking for your help. I need to discover my boundaries, both for me and for you. I love you and I miss you, With unconditional love, Mom.

Around that time, Charlene wrote to Rob too, in her journal. It had been nearly three years since her youngest son moved out of her house and left for the military. It had been a year since they had even spoken on the phone.

She told him about the changes she was trying to make, including her resignation as a band booster and her decision to enter therapy.

My therapist said I'm Co-dependant, meaning the value of my worthiness is decided by how other people view me…I feel sad that I can't be a part of your life. I would really like to have contact with you…I'm angry with myself that I pushed you and tried to control you so much that you stopped really loving me.

As in all twelve-step programs, part of the process for Charlene was to own up to her past mistakes and ask for forgiveness. Unable to do that in person, Charlene poured her heart out in her journal. In a later letter, she elaborated on the ways she felt she hurt her younger son.

Believe me when I say I'm not the same mom that told you to get out of my house. That mom was controlling, narrow minded, demanding, jealous. Because you were the last part of my life and I was so determined to live my life through you that I couldn't let go gracefully.

I love you very much and will accept you for the person you've become. The Rob Krimm that I knew as Harry does not exist anymore. In order to have even communication with each other we would have to start like two people just meeting each other and learning the boundaries…

Memory has clouded the exact sequence of events for Charlene, but she remembers Jimmy returned home briefly, following a surgery she had in the spring of 1994. It was either at that time or earlier, when he came home in January, that Charlene tried to help him conceal the fact he stole another car.

She is sick to her stomach remembering the event, just as she was when it happened. Hoping to give Jimmy one more chance, she made him return a stolen car to the spot he stole it from, following behind him to bring him home after.

The action, making Charlene an accessory to a crime, stemmed out of her love for him but also illustrated her overarching codependency.

"In my heart I felt that if I could help him through this, maybe he could get turned around," she says.

Her biggest fear, in revealing the story to me sixteen years after the fact, is what Rob will think. She holds this secret close, never revealing it until nearly a year into our acquaintance.

It is not Charlene's only "secret." Inexplicable to me, and despite my delving pretty extensively into the family relationships she had when she was growing up, including details about physical beatings she received, somehow, it is not until we are nearly ready to go to press with her sons' story that Charlene's own sexual abuse as a child comes to my attention.

Startled that such a detail could have remained hidden for so long, I question Rob about it and learn he knew of his mother's history and assumed I did, too. I was nonplussed, because at the outset, I *expected* to hear that Charlene had been abused. It's the classic pattern in so many families. And somehow, in the hours and hours of interviewing, never mind e-mails and phone conversations over nearly a year's time, I believed the extent of any abuse in Charlene's upbringing was corporal, not sexual.

Given Charlene's inability to form a lasting and healthy relationship with another man after her divorce, as well as her self-described confusion of sex as love, it absolutely fit that she was abused as a child, yet I had not one hint or statement to that effect until it was almost too late to include in the story.

I feel horrible when it finally comes out, like I had failed her so terribly—that somehow, I'd misunderstood or overlooked the obvious clues and never asked the right question to pull this information to the forefront.

A statement she made to me after revealing the car-theft accessory incident seemed to me also to shed some light on Charlene's mind-set about her own past sexual abuse.

"I always want Rob to be proud of me, and that would tarnish it. I wanted my boys to be happy. I did whatever I could to guarantee that," she says.

It is characteristic of Charlene, I know, not to make a big deal of her own pain, because in her mind, Rob's abuse was so much worse than her own. And her sons are the focus of my story, not her past. Yet Charlene's past influenced her sons' lives pretty dramatically.

The fact their mother had been abused literally put them at risk before they were even born, not that it was Charlene's fault. She didn't learn until they were grown that being an abuse survivor is almost like carrying a genetic disease that is passed down from generation to generation. As a victim, Charlene was predisposed to attract men who would abuse her or her sons, but mostly, her abuse built up such a wall the chances of her ever finding a healthy male role model for her boys was almost nil.

Jimmy, I learned in my research, was charged with the theft of yet another car *before* he even showed up at Charlene's in January 1994—just days after being released from prison! Of course, Charlene didn't know that at the time. That charge was apparently why he left Michigan for good, never to return. In the summer of 1994, he sent Charlene some photographs taken in Colorado, and that was the absolute last communication she ever received from him, aside from an envelope stuffed with $2 bills, which he sent with no explanation in 2006.

On the back of one of the 1994 photos, he said he was "wishing things could be different."

He seemed to be alluding to the fact he couldn't come back to Michigan because of the outstanding warrant. He let his mother know that his car, the Nova she stored all the while he was in prison, was running fine.

The Nova Super Sport was the same model Jimmy's dad had had when he was a tyke and got to go driving with him.

"I'm sure his dad was showing off," Charlene says.

Jimmy would come home from these drives making "Vroom, vroom" noises, the way little boys will.

"I'm sure he had the ride of his life." Charlene laughs.

Written on the back of the picture of himself, standing next to his own beat-up Nova, is a note telling Charlene he was working full-time, making $900 a month, paying rent of $226 a month, and that he "cherish[es] every day of freedom."

With the road to any future relationship with Jimmy seemingly blocked, Charlene's desire to renew the relationship with her younger son was growing. And it was motivating her to try to become a better person.

She wrote in her journal, "I lost my son Harry a few years ago and I understand this person Rob has similar characteristics and I'd like to get to know him..."

She wrote of her sadness that she was not included in special occasions where Julie was involved and of her pride in his accomplishments. All of the things Charlene remembers about her younger son are memories of Harry, not the man who now calls himself Rob.

"And when I first met Rob he was mean to me and called me names... I've felt that Harry is hidden away and Rob popped out. I don't know Rob and he doesn't know me. He's only using the information that Harry has to cut me down. Big tough Marine."

The very next page in the journal is another letter, addressed to the complete individual, Harry Robert.

> Wherever you are whatever you do, I still wish you a happy life and I'm still here where you left me...I really want to be a part of your life. I'm sorry if I intruded where you didn't want me. It's hard for a parent to let go of that child that they loved and guided and "possessed." I felt that way, that you were "mine." I still feel that you are mine but like the dove I had to let you go free and I'm waiting for you to come back. I hope you do this before I die. I wouldn't want you to be reading this and regretting the fact that you never got to know me on the adult level.
>
> I have tried to be helpful in your life...but I know now that there are boundaries that I have to stay within.

She expressed hurt that her younger son would keep himself away from her for so long, especially over the holidays.

"What could be that important to keep you from remembering the fun times, too?"

Unable to do things for her own sons, in December 1994, Charlene provided gifts to other children with whom she came into contact. She wrote, "Now that the holiday is over I still feel empty even though I made a lot of people happy, especially kids. Except for my own kids—no call, no card."

On March 1, 1995, just a few days before both of her sons' birthdays, Charlene wrote:

> Not a day goes by that I don't think about my boys. I miss you both, Jim and Harry. I pray that your lives are comfortable and happy. I don't know why I'm going on. I don't have a reason to live. I'm only making the motions. Why would God want me to be in such pain all the time? Why am I living? Please God take me out of this Hell.

With Rob estranged and Jimmy gone, Charlene went through a dark period. A day after Jimmy's memorial service, we are sitting in her living room, and she talks about that dark period at length.

"I wondered why was I living, why am I here? They have their own lives, apparently they don't need me. Because they don't contact me…I'm just existing. I have a job, I go to the job, I come back…you know, the family in Pennsylvania at that time…They were just people to go to, to be criticized and then come back home again."

At first, Charlene comforted herself with food, trying to fill up the emptiness.

"I'm just shoving the food in my mouth. I told Estella, 'My hand feeds me,' you know? And I don't even know that I'm eating. Well, it came to a point where there was an advertisement on TV, and I don't know what it was for, but the advertisement showed a gun, and it fired. And right after it fired, the screen went blank; it was absolutely silent. And I took that silence as peace. And I wanted peace," she says, crying at the thought of how awful that day was. "I didn't want to go through this anymore. It wasn't peaceful for me."

Tears stream down her face at the memory of that anguish. As a mother myself, I can only imagine what it would be like to feel my children are lost, never to be seen again, never to be hugged again, with nothing to look forward to for all of my pain and effort in raising them and no grandchildren to play with in my old age.

Charlene's thoughts, at that dark time, turned to the little .38 special she kept for her own protection. Estella and her husband came over and took her bullets away from her. With Charlene's disconnect between brain and hand, they were worried her hand might fire the gun before her brain registered what she was doing. By taking the bullets, they reasoned, Charlene would have time to think should she ever be tempted to hurt herself.

"I haven't had bullets for my gun for years; I still don't have them. I don't think I would do anything, but I don't want to take that chance, because it was so real. It was real, the peace."

Even before this episode, Charlene began to face her demons, in her journal. She reads the passages now and recognizes a guilty parent, but also, someone who is just trying to get it together.

"I was just so lonely because I didn't have a direction—and God knows I was not going to go to church! Because church, they tell you you're going to go to hell. I don't believe in hell. Our hell is right here. You know what I'm saying?" Charlene asks, with a laugh that rises from her gut. "I'm not going to hell, because I'm already there!"

It is a statement made with much conviction, but also by a person who feels she has mostly left hell behind. The journal helped lift her out of it, even if her motivation for writing it, initially, was very different.

"If I died, I wanted my boys to know that I loved them," she says, tearing up again. "Regardless of where they were. Just because they were somewhere else, and they had another life, if they ever wondered...I didn't want them to wonder if I loved them or not...I wanted them to know that I loved them both, and whatever I did, I did it with love."

Charlene came to realize many ways she did the wrong things, even though her motives were loving.

"I can't have a healthy relationship because I want to do too much for them," she says, not just with her boys, but with other men, too. For that reason, as much as any other, Charlene never let another man into her life for any length of time.

"The only person that would want to hang around was someone who was just as sick as I was—take advantage."

Slowly but surely, Charlene made progress, and life began to make sense again. Medication, along with therapy, helped her overcome the dark feelings that once threatened to consume her. She saw at least the possibility of renewing a relationship with Rob, if not with Jimmy.

In August 1995, the stalemate was broken, and Rob contacted her. Charlene wrote in her journal, "Well, Rob called me and I'm very relieved. At least I know he loves me and that he never hated me."

Over time, and at Julie's insistence, Rob began to reach out to his mother more and more.

"He called and gave me a chance to talk. We didn't talk very long, but I think he could see I was a little different."

Slowly, they rebuilt a connection.

"I was grateful for any amount of time that he would give me...And I'm not that same person. I'm just not anything like that person. And he's grown up now, too," Charlene says. Perhaps most amazing of all, the girl Charlene once called a "hussy" became her ally.

"Julie saved both of us, I think," or at least she set the stage for mother and son to reconcile.

Rob recognized his mother's effort to try to change.

"It was hard to talk to her and get a word in edgewise. She's just so emotional. I didn't know what to say with all those emotions," but he did keep in contact, and he continued, with Julie's support, over the next two years, to let his mother back into his life.

None of them knew Rob would soon need as much support as both Julie and Charlene could give him.

Just when it was beginning to seem that Jimmy was long gone, he victimized his brother one more time, only this time, they weren't even in the same time zone.

CHAPTER TWELVE

Bank Bandit

Charlene believes Jimmy found an old Social Security card for Rob while she lay in a hospital bed. He had free run of her house for several days in the spring of 1994, following her surgery for sleep apnea and before he left Michigan for good.

Jimmy had already made clear his disdain for his brother's adoption of the name "Rob"—referring to his younger brother in letters from prison the same as he had his "dad."

I wondered whether Jimmy was truly annoyed with his brother for not inviting Charlene to his wedding or if he was just trying to curry favor with his mother. It seemed plausible to me that Jimmy could have seen Rob's actions as an "in" since Rob and Charlene were estranged when he got out of prison. He couldn't use it to his advantage because if he stayed in Michigan, he would be arrested again for another car theft. But he could "punish" his brother and have the benefit of a clean record by stealing his brother's identity.

In the spring of 1994, Jimmy became "Harry Robert Krimm"—four years younger, with a fresh Social Security number. Just as Rob had grown accustomed to having people call him by a new name, so did Jimmy. It was uncanny. Here again, their lives paralleled one another. Rob was leaving behind the identity of Harry. Jimmy was assuming it.

When I met them, Charlene and Rob knew very little of the places Jimmy went or the crimes he was convicted of after he left Michigan. Aside from the notification of his death and the odd detail—that he also spent some time in prison in Canada—the last sixteen years of Jimmy's life presented a void to his family.

Probing into Jimmy's past reminded me of an exercise I had in a high school science class. Each of us was instructed to put something into a black box made of cardboard and then seal it. Next, we had to exchange boxes with a classmate. Our exercise was to deduce what was inside each other's black box through any means available. We could shake it, smell it, test it in any way we chose, but we could not open it and look inside.

Initially, looking at the black box that was Jimmy's life was no less intimidating—and frustrating—than that old high school science lesson. I remember I was stymied by the assignment as a high school junior. How on earth was I supposed to figure out what was inside of this box?

Jimmy, it turns out, was a much easier mystery to solve than the experiment with the black box. I couldn't ask Jimmy any questions. But for someone who only sporadically held a job and rarely had a set address, I was amazed at the information it was possible to learn about him. What made Jimmy's life traceable, in fact, was a string of crime. Everyone wants to leave a mark on this world. Based on what I could find, Jimmy's marks were all negative.

After leaving Michigan, he went to Iowa and promptly got charged with possession of stolen property. That's when he crossed the Mississippi into the western United States. It would be nine years before he crossed that river again. He was still driving the Nova one night in Salem, Utah—about twenty miles from where he lived—when his beloved car finally let him down on a dead-end road, near a cemetery.

Officer Scott Dibble of the Salem Police Department remembers running the plates on the car while working the graveyard shift on April 15, 1995.

"I haven't thought about this case for fifteen years," Dibble tells me when I call him. He has spent his whole career with the Salem Police Department and is now a sergeant. With the aid of notes from his written report reinforcing some of the finer details, he tells me what happened.

Jimmy's 1974 Nova caught Dibble's attention because it was parked half on and half off the roadway. The car came back as registered to Harry R. Krimm of nearby Orem. He wondered why the driver would have left the car parked so haphazardly. Figuring the car had broken down, Dibble left it for the night. Around 3:30 AM, a man who had just gotten out of bed for a drink of water looked across the street and saw the garage door on his elderly neighbor's house opening and his car backing out. The man called the neighbor to see what was up.

The man had left his keys in the ignition and his garage door unlocked. All Jimmy had to do was enter the garage, back the car out, and drive away. Upon hearing of the car theft, Dibble remembered the Nova parked up by the cemetery. *What are the odds,* he wondered, *that the person who abandoned the car could have stolen the one missing from the same neighborhood?*

An officer was sent to a large apartment complex where the Nova's owner lived.

"Sure enough," Dibble says, "they find my stolen car."

Dibble loaded up the car owner, and they drove to Orem. They retrieved the car and inside found a bottle of Mountain Dew and also a number of sundry items like shampoo and shaving cream. None of the items belonged to the car's owner. Dibble processed the car for physical evidence but found nothing tying his suspect to the car. He released the car to its owner.

They found "Harry" Krimm asleep at his apartment, along with three other guys—two roommates and a fourth guy who claimed he was just crashing there for the night. "Harry" admitted to being in Salem because he was "visiting his boss." He said his car broke down, and he hitchhiked home. Dibble doesn't need his notes to remember his suspect's demeanor.

After being awakened by police in the middle of the night, "He wasn't nervous at all," Dibble says. "He should have been an attorney the way he lied…For every question we asked him, he had a quick answer."

I get a kick out of Dibble's statement. Maybe Jimmy did pass that paralegal course, after all.

Though Dibble had no doubt Krimm was guilty of car theft, he couldn't arrest him.

"To convince a judge of that is tough without evidence. I felt I didn't have enough."

But he did have the Nova impounded.

In the morning, another residential burglary came to light, in the same neighborhood where the car was stolen.

"The people report odd things missing," like a shaver, shampoo, sunscreen, a bank card, and a .22 shot pistol with five hundred rounds of ammunition, some tapes, and cologne, according to Dibble's report. He talked to residents in the area who said they saw a guy walking around carrying a green pop bottle.

"It looked like his car broke down," one witness said.

The witness saw the man under the car looking like he was trying to fix it, "but finally he got fed up trying to get it running, kicked it, saluted, and walked away."

Dibble figured he could tie Krimm to the car theft because of the pop bottle, "but that's easier said than done."

He obtained a search warrant on the apartment but managed only to get the roommates on some minor marijuana violations.

The roommates claimed not to know where "Harry" was. They said he had a girlfriend somewhere in the apartment complex, but they didn't know her name or which apartment she lived in. Police searched Krimm's apartment, finding what appeared to be items from the burglary but not the credit card or the gun.

Dibble went to ProSteel in Provo, where his suspect worked. It was a steel fabrication plant, now closed.

"The boss said he didn't show up for work," so police continued their search. "We hit the apartment three or four times the next day trying to catch him there," but he didn't show. Dibble tracked down the man "Harry" claimed as his boss in the neighborhood where the car was stolen. This guy worked in a tire store. He said he recognized the man in his neighborhood that day, but when he drove by with his kids in the car, he didn't want to stop.

"Harry flipped me off as I drove past," the guy told Dibble. On the way back, without his kids, the man stopped to see if "Harry" needed some help, but his old employee waved him off. When police got to ProSteel the following day, they learned "Harry" had pulled up at work the day before in a black Toyota Corolla with no license plates, collected his paycheck, and quit, saying he had "legal problems."

Dibble could do nothing except have the county attorney draft a warrant charging Harry R. Krimm with two burglaries and a car theft.

Six days later, and eight hundred miles straight north of Orem, Utah, there was a bank robbery at Lethbridge, Alberta, Canada.

I already know Jimmy served time in Canada. Seven years was the figure that kept popping up. My local sheriff tells me, "You have to do something pretty bad to get that steep a sentence in Canada," but he doesn't have Jimmy's Canadian record to show what crimes he had been convicted of.

Knowing there were crimes in Canada but also believing the FBI is going to provide that information to me, I don't go looking for it right away. Then, about six months after Jimmy's death, the FBI makes a total reversal from earlier statements. They are not only unable to provide Jimmy's Canadian record, they refuse to share what they know about banks robbed in the United States. Aside from the Williston robbery and one in Wahpeton, North Dakota, they aren't going to tell me anything without a Freedom of Information/Privacy Act request.

Telling reporters to file a FOIPA request is akin to telling them they can wait till hell freezes over. It could be years, I knew, before that avenue produced any information. I file the request anyway, but unless I can do my own sleuthing, I have a book about a serial bank robber whose U.S. spree includes exactly two banks. So I start making calls. One bonus comes from a source who tells me he can't confirm Jimmy robbed any banks, but he can give me a list of towns I should look at. He suggests I call authorities in those jurisdictions. The FBI planned to share their findings with local agencies, and it would be up to police in each jurisdiction to decide whether or not to close their own files. There are fourteen towns on the list, all with unsolved bank robberies.

Next, I get a break from a prison official in Canada, who tells me Jimmy had been convicted of seventeen robberies, but because of the way bank robbery is charged in Canada, the only way I can determine the type of robberies is to get the court records. Getting any actual prison records from Canada would turn out to be impossible. Canada's privacy laws dictate no release of prison records until twenty years after the death of an inmate! It is a huge disappointment. Jimmy's Michigan records, saved so long by Charlene, had been very illuminating, providing his psych evaluations and a list of infractions inside. The only morsel I am going to get out of the Canadian prison authorities, albeit, a pretty juicy one, is that in Jimmy's seven years in jail there, he had not one visitor.

I get Jimmy's Canadian court record, with a list of towns where crimes occurred, and confirmation he had, indeed, been convicted of seventeen bank robberies and one attempt, but I still am not home free. There are no details about any of the crimes. The speed with which Jimmy began serving his sentence after his arrest suggests a plea agreement, rather than a trial, which means no court transcripts.

I turn next to newspapers and libraries, looking for the same sort of write-ups my own newspaper carried about the Williston robbery. After weeks of calling and e-mailing people, the picture of Jimmy's bank robbery spree in Canada comes into focus.

According to a press report at the time, the Lethbridge robber entered the bank and indicated he had a handgun but didn't show it. He was last seen walking away from the bank. The robber was described as twenty-five to thirty years old, with sandy-blond collar-length hair and no facial hair. He wore jeans, a green bomber-style jacket, and a white and green ball cap. The height and weight of the robber don't match Jimmy Krimm, but the police sketch of the robber's face is a good likeness.

On May 4, there was a robbery in nearby Medicine Hat, two hours to the east. A lone male matching Jimmy's general description passed a note to a teller demanding money and claiming to have a gun. A news article described the robber as "chubby" and about six foot three inches tall. Jimmy probably did not like that description, I think. But it's more accurate than the description in the Lethbridge robbery. A bank manager was quoted as saying tellers were trained to hand over money when a robber requested it, because the money was worth "nothing to the bank" compared to someone's life.

The statement served as an open invitation. The same bank was hit again the next day by a man who could not have been Jimmy Krimm. Authorities ran police sketches of both suspects, neither of whom looks much like Jimmy. Speculation centers on whether the second man was a copycat or someone connected to the first. A few days later, a new sketch of the first robber was circulated, and it looks remarkably like the man in the last photos Jimmy sent to his mom after leaving Michigan. News articles talk about police "pouring" into Medicine Hat to search for the two suspects.

But the robber was already far away. On May 19, he turned up 565 miles to the west in Kamloops, British Columbia. A few weeks after that, a bandit hit a bank in Vernon, in the Okanagan Valley, about an hour east of Kamloops.

My research tells me the Okanagan Valley is a picturesque landscape centered around Okanagan Lake, where lore has it a creature similar to the Loch Ness monster resides. The area is known for its orchards, vineyards, skiing, and mountains, including the tallest of the Canadian Rockies. A waterfall twice the height of Niagara Falls is located in the region, and each year, visitors flock there to hike, ski, fish, camp, and enjoy the scenery.

In the Vernon robbery, there are details that don't seem to match the twenty-nine-year-old Jimmy. Witnesses described the robber as being in his early forties or fifties. But the rest of the physical description is spot on: a six-footer weighing 200 to 220 pounds. The press reported the robber wore a white dress shirt with blue pinstripes. The collar of the shirt was open, revealing "a large amount of chest hair."

That sounded like Jimmy. There was no other way to describe his chest other than "hairy," based on photos I'd seen.

Once again, at Vernon, the robber claimed to have a gun but none was seen. He handed a teller a holdup note and collected over $2,000 from her before disappearing on foot. It was the third robbery of the branch in fifteen months, but it is unclear whether the robberies are related.

On July 4, 1995—Independence Day in the United States but just another workday in Canada—the robber hit again, this time in Salmon Arm, less than an hour's drive north of Vernon. Robbing a bank on the Fourth of July struck me as the perfect "Jimmy" touch. Maybe he bought fireworks with his loot!

If authorities were starting to suspect the same man, I cannot find press reports to reflect it. Though the region is decidedly rural in nature, the population is relatively large, with a big influx of transient people year-round. Bank robberies are not all that uncommon. It is the perfect place for a stranger to get lost in a crowd. And Jimmy seemed to have a knack for blending in.

Rob tells me Jimmy's chameleon-like ability dated back to high school, when he deliberately dressed to fade into the background. He even believed certain colors made it less likely people would notice him or were less apt to make him stand out in memory. Even in high school, Jimmy's motivation for "blending in" was about not being noticed for doing something wrong.

Following Salmon Arm, Jimmy must have figured the area was getting hot, so he traveled farther west for the next robbery, about four hours, to the town of Sardis, just north of Seattle, along the U.S.-Canadian border, on August 8, 1995.

Next, he hit Revelstoke, five hours to the east, on September 21, 1995. This robbery is closer to the scene of earlier Okanagan Valley crimes.

At this point, press reports reflect, law enforcement was growing wise to the possibility of a serial robber. They were close-mouthed about the Revelstoke robbery, and the local press reported police were concerned about tipping off the suspect. The general description of the robber and the method of the robbery were similar to those of five other robberies in the region in five months' time. A police sketch looks eerily similar to the one in the Lethbridge robbery, though the Revelstoke robber wore glasses.

In October, the robber struck at Kelowna, on the southern end of the Okanagan region, before leaving British Columbia and driving all the way to Calgary, Alberta, eight hours to the east. This trip did not go well. On October 26, he entered one bank and got scared off, leaving with no money. In a second attempt the same day, at a different bank, he reportedly made off with only a "small" amount of money. I'd read reports of other robbers hitting more than one bank on the same day, so the fact Jimmy did wasn't all that surprising.

However much the second holdup yielded in Calgary, it must have been enough to tide him over until mid-December, when he traveled back the way he had already been once, to Kamloops, where he robbed another bank. Two months later, he headed east again, to Kimberley. The MO was the same as always—a man approached a single teller and passed a note demanding money. This time, the tall suspect sported a beard and moustache. Though the Royal Canadian Mounted Police (RCMP) used tracking dogs in their search, he got away on foot with $1,200.

According to the *Kimberley Daily Bulletin,*

> At the time of the crime he was wearing light-coloured blue jeans, a beige hand-knit sweater with matching toque. He also had a black leather fanny pack around his waist, which he used to deposit the stolen money…Despite the presence of an off-duty officer in the line behind the robber, nobody but the teller knew what was taking place. The man handed the teller the note without saying a word.

The robber struck next at Trail, about 165 miles west of Kimberley, on February 27, 1996. It would appear this was a good haul. The robber was content to wait until April 22, 1996, before traveling back through Kimberley to strike a bank in nearby Fernie. He got away with $1,200, but the police artist's sketch was the best yet. The man, wearing a cowboy hat and aviator-style glasses, sported a close-cropped beard. The police sketch was a remarkable likeness of Jimmy Krimm.

The detail of the cowboy hat cracks me up. Jimmy, who grew up enjoying artists like Ozzy Osbourne, fell in love with country music while in a Michigan prison. One of his letters to Charlene, written from prison, talked about wanting to dress like a cowboy, in tight jeans and a cowboy hat!

According to the *Fernie Free Press*, police "swarmed" into the area following the "daring" daytime robbery.

The RCMP in the region now had twelve robberies in a period of just under a year—all with a similar MO and a similar suspect. A constable from the area was later quoted as saying he knew after this robbery, it would only be a matter of time before they got their man. The bandit seemed in no hurry to leave the area. He brazenly went back to Trail for a robbery on May 13, 1996, in which he was labeled the "cowboy" robber.

Following the second robbery at Trail, he must have sensed his luck was wearing thin. Why else would he travel more than twelve hours to the west, all the way to Port Albernie?

Tourist literature describes Port Albernie as a waterland paradise and the "gateway to Vancouver Island." It is located just across the Puget Sound from Bellingham, Washington. Just as in the Okanagan Valley, an unfamiliar face blends into the crowd.

It was June 10, 1996, and the RCMP at Port Albernie were "releasing few details" about the robbery, but the MO matched the rash of holdups plaguing towns to the east. The physical description of the bandit was a match, except this robber was reported as having red hair.

After Port Albernie, the bandit obviously felt he couldn't go back the way he came. Instead of heading to more familiar haunts, he turned north, possibly taking in any number of scenic vistas and camping out along the way. He was headed into the northern interior of British Columbia, finally turning up again fourteen hours north of Port Albernie.

The robber hit a bank at Prince George, the region's largest city, which is home to some seventy thousand residents. It was July 20, 1996, and the haul was not particularly good, so Jimmy decided to leave the area, heading east.

In July 1995, Rob took leave, and he and Julie planned to renew their Michigan driver's licenses when they went back home. But Rob was denied his renewal. He was told he would have to surrender his Utah license first.

Julie tells me Rob's response.

"It's got to be my brother," he said, but Rob didn't follow through immediately to find out what he needed to do to clear up the matter. Finally, Julie pursued it.

Julie made repeated phone calls to Utah over a period of eight months. She learned there was a warrant out for Rob's arrest because no one in Utah had any reason to suspect Jimmy's true identity. Rob was even getting notices from the Internal Revenue Service for unpaid taxes from a job he never worked in Utah. Julie provided evidence to the prosecutor in Orem so they could charge Jimmy with forgery for impersonating Harry.

Sergeant Dibble remembers lots of paperwork being sent back and forth. The military gave Rob an airtight alibi.

"They certainly can account for every second of his time," Dibble tells me.

Finally, in September 1996, the prosecutor let Sergeant Dibble know the identity question had been cleared up.

"This Harry, in the Marines, is not the guy," Dibble agrees. But for Dibble, there remained the issue of the real criminal, Jimmy Krimm. What about pursuing him?

"That was my question," Dibble says. "Are we going to put out a warrant for this James Edward Krimm? And it was decided it would almost be a moot thing at that point."

The prosecutor in Salem was comfortable with the fact the real Harry was not their guy but not comfortable they could prove in court it was really Jimmy who stole the old man's car and broke into his garage and into the home where the sundry items were missing. There were no fingerprints, only circumstantial evidence tying Jimmy to the stolen car. And besides, no one knew where Jimmy was. Or did they? That overarching question is answered for me in public records fourteen years after the fact, and it is a detail very important to Rob and Julie. Newspaper reports I found showed the FBI knew exactly where Jimmy Krimm was as early as August 1996.

At the time, Dibble says, in Utah, "The prosecutor felt it was a dead case."

But the damage to Rob's sense of security was already done. And it would be compounded by events that, even now, Rob and Julie have a tough time understanding.

Julie looks back on that period as a turning point for Rob.

"When he found out Jimmy stole his ID, he started getting really quiet," Julie says.

"Little Krimmy went through some problems," Rob says a little sheepishly, recalling the domino effect that seemed to take hold of his life at that time, from trouble at work to meltdowns at home and, at times, complete withdrawal into the world Julie dubbed "Krimmland."

"It was like he was walking around in a haze," Julie says. She knew there was a serious problem when one of Rob's co-workers reported seeing him blow through a red light.

"Rob said he was scared 'cause he did not mean to go through a red light and didn't remember doing that."

"I guess my depression sort of went into full swing," Rob tells me. "I was tired all the time. I'd come home, fall asleep. She could pound on my chest, and I wouldn't wake up."

Julie remembers, "He'd have two alarms set, and I'd be calling [from work or school], just to get him off to work. And he would still be late...I was literally pasting him together Monday through Friday, and then on the weekends, he would fall apart."

He also had trouble staying awake on the job.

"His staff sergeant was able to take his rifle right out of his hands, and Rob didn't wake up for an hour after that."

Even when Rob was fully awake, he could be totally absent.

"Rob can maintain eye contact with you, and he's in another world," Julie says.

"My brain was not there," agrees Rob.

Jarred back into the role of victim after the identity theft, Rob could no longer mask the identity he had hoped to leave behind forever—that of Harry, the boy Jimmy abused.

"I was reliving the whole hurt from my childhood, and it was like, fuck, you know? He's fucking with my life as an adult now," Rob says.

Rob's past was affecting his relationship with Julie even before that, though he didn't realize it until later.

"After we got to that comfort level [in the marriage], I think I just kind of expected things to be a certain way," Rob says, but his clinging annoyed Julie as much as his withdrawals. Adding stress was the atmosphere of the post. Rob and Julie describe Camp Lejeune, North Carolina, where they were stationed, as a "hard-core" division headquarters.

"There was a gunny who was bullying Rob and giving him a really hard time. I could see he was channeling anger from somewhere else towards that gunny. He looked at that man as if he really were Jimmy... and he just literally shut down every time he spoke to him," Julie says.

"My abuse has given me a real problem with authority figures," Rob tells me. "I'd be reduced to tears because I was so emotionally screwed up."

Rob was also having trouble learning the ever more complicated drum routines necessary to advance in rank with the Marine Corps Band. Julie explains, "You have to make a certain cutting score playing your instrument," and Rob's scores weren't cutting it. He was placed on remedial practice, but it didn't help. More practice time only produced average results and took more time away from Julie.

"This pattern of constantly screwing up is due to stuffing down so many repressed memories," Rob believes. "It made me forgetful, and I had to learn to be responsible with limited brain power."

At the time of the abuse, that ability to shut out the rest of the world helped Rob survive, "but as an adult this coping device is unsuitable."

In addition to how the identity theft thrust him into the role of victim once more, Rob worried about his mom and how Jimmy could hurt both of them.

"I was always worried...that at some point, I was going to have to deal with him personally, whether he showed up on my doorstep—highly unlikely—or...on my ma's doorstep."

Having renewed contact with Charlene, Rob and Julie came up with the idea of giving Charlene a code word.

They told Charlene, "If anything ever happens, i.e., Jimmy shows up, it's like, just give us a call and use the word 'fish' in a sentence."

Just the possibility he might ever receive a call like that from his mother weighed on Rob. But he and Julie knew exactly what they'd do if it did. They would call the FBI.

What the Krimms couldn't know at the time is that the FBI already knew Jimmy's location. A bank robber the Mounties dubbed "John Doe" was believed to be an American, suspected of more than twenty robberies over the previous eighteen months. The FBI was called in to help identify the suspect.

It was August 20, 1996, in Grand Prairie, Alberta, Canada, that Jimmy's first bank robbing spree came to an end.

According to the *Grand Prairie Herald-Tribune*, Jimmy walked into a bank intent on pulling his usual note-pass robbery. He didn't count on the teller fainting.

"This lady needs help!" he hollered to the people around him, but no sooner than other people rushed to the woman's aid, Jimmy was helping himself to her cash drawer.

Witnesses gave a good description of the getaway car and also noted his British Columbia license plate. Checkpoints were set up all over the city, which had a population of about fifty thousand. Police in Valleyview, about an hour east of Grande Prairie, were also on the alert.

Valleyview Mounties soon spotted the suspect's car.

"He stopped," Constable Dennis Groenhof told the *Herald-Tribune's* reporter. "I was going to cut him off from the front…And that's when he took off."

A chase ensued, covering about five miles. It sounds to me just like Jimmy's confrontation with a Montana trooper after the Williston robbery, but for one thorny detail: a spike strip deployed west of Valleyview disabled Jimmy's car.

Jimmy jumped out of the car and tried to run away.

"He fell a couple of times," Groenhof told the newspaper, and four or five Mounties were right on his tail when he did.

Based on the information in the clipping, Jimmy was carrying an "imitation" handgun. He was lucky not to have been shot on the spot! He threw the gun down as Mounties approached, and he was taken into custody.

Over the next several days, Jimmy refused to give his name but, according to multiple press reports, the FBI was called in. It was the FBI, they said, that provided the positive identification of James Edward Krimm, age twenty-nine, who was born in McKeesport, Pennsylvania. The FBI supplied information that Krimm was wanted for car theft in Michigan and for possession of stolen property in Iowa, but nothing from Utah was mentioned because charges had never been filed against Jimmy in the Salem cases. The forgery complaint Julie and Rob filed in Orem did not exist yet.

A report in the newspaper at Kimberley said the robber was suspected in more than twenty holdups, but it was doubtful they would have enough evidence to charge him with all twenty.

On October 26, 1996, Jimmy was sentenced on twenty charges—including seventeen bank robberies and one attempt. With Canada's mandatory release laws, he had to serve three-quarters of his ten-year sentence—seven years—and then he had to be set free.

Less than three years after his discharge from the Michigan prison system, Jimmy entered the federal prison system in Canada on December 2, 1996. Later that month, the prosecutor in Utah concluded the paperwork exonerating Harry and supplied Rob and Julie with documents proving Harry's record was clear.

"The district attorney even enclosed a note telling Rob he needed to take me out to dinner for me being so persistent," Julie says.

On Julie's birthday, in mid-January 1997, she was home in the afternoon, nursing a knee injury. She took a pain pill and fell asleep.

"I heard the doorbell ring, and I was so tired." It was hard to wake up, she told me. "I went to the front door, and I didn't see anyone. I heard someone whispering heavily that I was at the door. I was scared. No car was in the drive or in front of the house. I yelled, 'Who is out there?'

"And a man yelled at me 'The FBI! Open the door!'"

Still not seeing anyone, Julie didn't know whether to think someone was playing a joke or what.

"Then I looked out the window next to the door, and a man started edging his way around the fireplace with gun in hand and holding a badge."

Scared out of her wits, Julie let the officers know she would comply. Ten agents barged in, guns drawn.

"There was a lot of them," Julie says, not that she stopped to count them at the time.

"I just remember the gun on me, my hands up, and them yelling at me asking me if we had any weapons and trying to tell them that it was a mistake, they had the wrong guy. They were asking where Harry was."

Julie had the document from Utah, proving Harry's innocence.

"That is when they stopped treating me like a criminal. I told them where it was—that I didn't understand why they were there—that the Utah DA had cleared Rob. They showed me a copy of the driver's license. It was Jimmy, with all of Rob's info. I remember I was sobbing, and I thought I was going to have a heart attack. I called the duty desk at the band hall, and the duty started giving me a hard time about getting Rob. I started screaming into the phone."

Photos of Rob in the home, in uniform, including wedding pictures, further proved to the agents there had to be some kind of mix-up. This was not the right guy. Once they were satisfied Rob was not there, "the

FBI filed out of my house as if nothing ever happened and went to the base."

Rob remembers being called to the drum major's office.

"You don't just go into his office to chitchat," Rob says, and given his increasing difficulties at work, "I knew something was up."

He recalls seeing several "squared away" civilians in the hall, obviously acting in an official capacity.

"Next thing I know, I'm sitting in a corner," with the drum major at his desk, an FBI agent questioning him, and four or five staff NCOs listening in. At first, it seemed like the agent was just asking basic questions about Jimmy. Once Rob volunteered the information that he'd last seen his brother in prison in Michigan, it was if he'd committed a crime. The questioning, at that point, took a harder line, with the FBI agent insinuating Rob was somehow guilty by association.

That was the moment Rob came a little unglued.

"I realized, like, I'm a fucking suspect! You're now accusing me of aiding and abetting this total fucking asshole?"

The superiors he worked for every day were saying nothing in his defense.

"I'm yelling, 'You guys are gonna sit around and let them talk to me this way?' I'm thinking, wow, all my leadership has really got my back on this one."

The agent thrust a blowup of a Utah driver's license into view, with Rob's name and Social Security number and his brother's picture. Being confronted so harshly, let alone the suggestion he could have aided or assisted his brother's life of crime was like waking up in a horror movie.

"If they knew me—if they knew anything about me," Rob says, "they would know I could never help him."

To be a victim and then be further victimized with false accusations of helping the person who harmed him so greatly felt to Rob like being violated all over again. At that point, one of his superiors suggested Rob calm down.

"Calm down?" he answered. "You guys aren't even backing me up!"

The agent finally dropped the insinuations, showing Rob some of the information the file contained.

"I guess they just wanted to see my reaction or something," Rob says, but "obviously, there wasn't any concern about how they fucked up my life."

Or Julie's.

"That really did not help our marriage," Rob says. "Not a damn bit."

Rob went home that day to a hysterical wife he was ill equipped to comfort.

"I was pretty much unaware of the trauma that awaited me at home with her," Rob says. So long accustomed to Jimmy wreaking havoc in his life, his reaction to Julie's upset was low key. The episode was over. He wanted to be done with it, while Julie needed to dissect it.

"I just wanted people to leave me the fuck alone," Rob says, so he could move on, just as he'd moved on after high school, putting the identity of Harry away.

The FBI seemed to know everything about "Harry Krimm"—except the fact he was at work when they stormed his house.

"The gist of it was they went and had access to my military files in the Marines—found out my rifle score is the highest of the high," Rob says. "I've scored expert every time...I guess it counts to my ability to block out things and focus on one thing...you aim center mass...Pretty basic shit," Rob says.

It would be laughable, Rob says, except the FBI obviously believed he was dangerous, either leading a secret life in Utah, or somehow aiding his criminal brother.

"They just really bullied their way through this and didn't prepare," Rob says, or they would have known, first of all, that he was at work when they came to his house and second, that he could not have been in Utah—not to mention the military had already provided Rob an airtight alibi and the Utah authorities had already fingered Jimmy as the real criminal. Besides, someone in the FBI already knew Jimmy was sitting in a Canadian jail, because the FBI had provided the positive ID for the John Doe bank robber in Canada.

The FBI had all of the real Harry Krimm's past addresses, from Taylor through boot camp and music school to his first posting in Albany, Georgia, and finally, at Camp Lejeune.

Rob and Julie figured Jimmy must have done something really bad to warrant an FBI raid. But a couple of burglaries and a car theft?

"What are they not telling us? What's the real story?" Rob asks. He wishes he knew. "Why were they even involved?"

Unless it had something to do with a bank robbery investigation—it was a possibility that loomed large given the fact so many of Jimmy's Canadian bank robberies were so close to the U.S. border. It's easy to imagine the FBI could have been looking at Jimmy for robberies in the United States, too, after his convictions in the Canadian spree.

Months later in my own investigation, when my FOIPA request finally begins producing a trickle of information, a document seems to confirm my suspicions. It reveals Jimmy was investigated over the years under a number of aliases, but it doesn't give the names, making it impossible to trace those investigations.

In a report dated April 8, 2010, around the time the FBI reneged on a promise to share information with me, the reporting agent writes, "Current and prior investigations of Krimm have shown that he also frequently engaged in identity theft. He was convicted under at least two separate aliases in Canada, *with a strong possibility that he may have been identified by U.S. law enforcement authorities under different names.*"

Reading the document, I can't help but wonder if the FBI has ever been able to put the whole puzzle together, or if they even tried.

At the time Rob was dealing with his own identity being stolen, and with no knowledge of Jimmy robbing banks, "I never delved that deeply into it. I was just working through a depression. My way of dealing with it was to just push it aside," Rob says. He just tried to soldier on.

The only other explanation Rob and Julie can come up with for the FBI raid is the same one Sergeant Dibble offers. That it was part of a military clearance investigation. Rob recalls filling out paperwork around that time, in advance of pursuing a different career field in the Marines. But it still didn't add up that the FBI would have gone to such great lengths to nail Harry Robert Krimm when Utah authorities had already cleared him and the real criminal was already sitting behind bars, which the FBI knew all along.

The memory of looking at his brother's picture that day in the drum major's office, Rob says, "It's kind of haunting...past memories...You tell yourself, 'That's then. It's not now; it's not who I am. I've risen above it.' You just gotta reach deep down inside and say, 'I'm a bigger person for having made it.'"

But Rob hadn't really made it—not yet. He still had a long road to travel toward putting his abuse behind him, and his marriage would not survive the trip.

CHAPTER THIRTEEN

Meltdown

With Rob already feeling abused from the identity theft, the FBI "raid" served only to ratchet up his distress.

"Rob just started falling apart," Julie tells me.

She would ask her husband, "What's wrong with you? Did someone molest you or something?"

She doesn't know what made her ask such a question, and Rob's reaction was to stare at her blankly and walk away.

Around this time, a boss suggested Rob attend a retreat with other soldiers having difficulties. There, for the first time ever, at the age of twenty-six, Rob admitted aloud some of the things his brother had done to him when he was growing up. He was amazed at the level of acceptance he received, and yet, he still couldn't tell his wife about the abuse he'd suffered.

"He started melting down," Julie says. He was becoming more and more withdrawn at home. "He was hiding things."

Still not aware of the issues her husband was really dealing with, Julie insisted he needed professional help. At the time, and in the Marine Corps especially, Julie says, emotional disturbance had to be dealt with covertly. They could go to marriage counseling, but if the Marine Corps knew the extent of Rob's emotional upset, he could lose his job.

Julie and Rob ostensibly began couple's counseling. Julie was able to find a counselor who would prescribe medication to her to hide the fact Rob needed antidepressants. But she still had no idea what really ailed him.

Exhausted from dealing with Rob's calamities, including the unraveling of the identity theft and the FBI raid, not to mention working twelve-hour shifts as a nurse, Julie came home one day to find her husband in a state that scared her. He was outside, washing their Jeep, when she entered the house.

"The ironing board looks like you dropped a weight in the center of it. In the kitchen, there was dirt and muddy footprints all over."

Taped to a kitchen cupboard were two pepper plants Rob had pulled from their backyard garden.

"One pepper plant was wilted and dying, and one had ten or so peppers on it and was full of life. He had pulled them out by the roots and duct-taped them to the cupboard," Julie says. He'd posted a note next to the plants.

"This is my life," Rob wrote, with an arrow pointing at the wilted pepper, "and this is Julie's life," with an arrow pointing at the thriving one.

Julie contemplated running from the house, concerned for her own safety. It looked, suddenly, as if Rob had come completely unhinged.

"So he comes in the house, and I'm like, 'What is this all about?'"

Rob couldn't answer.

She asked him, "Are you gonna hurt yourself?"

"I don't know," Rob answered.

"Are you going to hurt me?" she asked.

"No, I don't want to hurt you...That's just how I feel," he told her.

When I ask Rob about the episode, I can hear in his voice both his regret in having to own the incident, as well as his upset that Julie had to witness it.

"That haunts me to this day. I don't want to burden somebody with that ever again."

He remembers he and Julie had fought earlier that day.

"Everything's come to a peak. I'm getting therapy, and our relationship is screwed up...all this shit is going on." Rob felt unable to express his feelings.

"That garden was something we did together. She had yelled at me that day, and it was tough; out of all people to yell at me, to have her down on me, it was really tough."

So, Rob directed his frustration toward a project they had worked on together.

"We made this garden in our backyard, filled it with this manure stuff, even grew, like, wildflowers and stuff...six-foot-tall tomatoes. The pepper plants was just the sort of expression I was trying to portray—some vocabulary that I didn't have back then. When she yelled at me, it was for real. When the love of my life and high school sweetheart had the same outlook [that he was a screw-up], it was really just a punch in the face. I wanted to be heard, and that was my only way of expressing myself...It was me grasping at something, wanting her to kind of accept me."

Pulling the pepper plants out by the roots was Rob's cry for help. He couldn't find the words, didn't want to express to Julie the sexual abuse that haunted him. I can sympathize. Many times in my own life, when some upset occurred, I wished I could just hold up a sign that said, "Please excuse me. I am a sexual abuse survivor."

I knew what it felt like, whenever my own life seemed to spin out of control, to drag along the added baggage of "survivor." Every challenge, every upset always seemed to come back to that underlying victimization. If only the abuse hadn't happened, I told myself, I wouldn't be in the current situation or I would be able to handle it better.

Unable to admit the real problem, Rob used the pepper plants to try to convey to Julie the sorry state of his psyche without having to reveal its true cause. Julie answered Rob's cry by taking it upon herself to up his dosage of medication, hoping it would help stabilize his moods.

When she visited the therapist not long after the pepper plant incident, the therapist asked Julie if Rob had told her anything recently.

"No," Julie answered. "Was he supposed to?"

As they were walking the dog that night, Julie demanded Rob tell her. He wouldn't answer, and she decided she'd had enough.

She told him, "If you can't communicate with me, I want a divorce. I'm done."

Julie was tired of the drama, tired of feeling as if her life was out of control, never knowing what Rob would do next or what calamity might assault them from the outside.

"She literally threw her ring on the ground," Rob tells me, imitating the "ping-ping-ping" sound of it landing on the street. Julie kept walking as Rob scrambled to retrieve it.

"I knew she was serious, and I wasn't about to throw it away that easy."

Afraid to admit the secrets he'd long hidden from his wife but figuring their relationship was over anyway, Rob finally blurted out the truth, right there on the street.

Faced with Julie's ultimatum, he screamed, "My brother fucking raped me when I was little!"

The words stunned Julie. But it was also as if, suddenly, everything made sense. Now she understood why the identity theft hit Rob so hard. Now she could see why the gunny who reminded Rob of his brother was such a thorn. Now she realized just how traumatic it must have been for him to be accused by the FBI of aiding his brother—his abuser.

"Rob's Pandora's box was opened up, and Jimmy taking his identity was like raping him all over again," Julie says, but now that it was out in the open, she insisted on getting the whole story. She and Rob walked back to the house together, and she urged him to tell her everything.

"I really didn't want to put the words out there," Rob says, because of the shame he felt. It was for his own self preservation, not Jimmy's, that Rob kept his secrets so long.

If not for the shame, "I would have told on him right after he was arrested."

Even if he'd been tempted, as a defense to the FBI agent's insinuations, to admit why his brother would be the last person he would ever help, the whole scenario in the drum major's office, with not one of his superiors coming to his defense, reinforced the notion that to reveal more about Jimmy would only add to his own victimization.

"That was just total proof to me," Rob says. "That lack of support really just blew my mind."

He made Julie swear no one could know.

"It was such a mind fuck in my head, of what would people think of me?" Rob says. Even though he'd been warmly received when he'd made the admission to fellow soldiers at the retreat, he still feared being judged, especially by his wife.

It was the same for me, through the years. While that label "sexual abuse survivor" may have helped me at times when people didn't understand what my problem was, I also abhorred the connotation that came with that label: "damaged goods."

Unlike Rob, I spent my early adulthood telling everyone I was in relationship with about how I had been victimized. The reaction—much as

I'd hoped it would help my friends understand me—just as often created distance. Rob, anticipating those sorts of reactions, chose not to reveal information to those closest to him, but we both arrived at the same conclusion: it was better to keep the mask on. People didn't really want to know—didn't know how to handle—what the mask hid.

And for a man, societal ignorance made it even tougher. "Men aren't supposed to be victims." "Only fags take it in the ass." "Abused boys always become child molesters." These stereotypical beliefs kept Rob's mouth firmly shut for ten years after the abuse ended, so fearful was he of being judged in these ways.

It took Julie's threat of walking out on him to finally convince Rob he had more to lose by keeping the mask on than taking it off.

The full story came out, as Julie probed for the answers Rob was so reluctant to reveal.

Rob recalls, "After I started talking about it, she said, 'You might as well just tell me everything now.'"

In rapid fire, Rob spewed the details, telling Julie he had been penetrated, repeatedly, over a period of five years. He told her about Jimmy raping the dogs.

"And she's like, 'Is that it? Is that it?' It was just like one after another. And I told her, I think that's about as much as I can handle for now, and she's like, 'All right, if you remember anything else, just tell me about it.' And it was just a relief to have told somebody about it and have this warm response of wanting to get me help for my problems."

With Rob's permission, Julie called Charlene, telling her if she had any medication, she better take some and sit down.

Julie relayed the story Rob spilled to her.

"I was so upset," Charlene remembers. She couldn't even talk at first she was sobbing so violently. "I said, 'Oh my God, Oh my God. My sweet little baby boy!' *Someone hurt him that bad? Where was I? What was I doing? How did I not see this?*"

Julie told Charlene how Rob had kept the secret when they were kids because of the threat of more violence from Jimmy.

"Jimmy threatened him to not say or not tell, and Jimmy acted like things were just fine when they were home," says Charlene. "And why didn't I see any bruises or why didn't I see any—you know? I don't know what I would have done. I might have killed Jimmy. I might have actually killed him."

Julie sympathized with everything Rob had endured, but it also added to her stress. She was angry, not only because Rob hid his abuse for so long, but because of how their marriage was harmed by it. On the one hand, Rob says, "She had this newfound respect for me because I'd dealt with it for so long." But at the same time, "I realized I was an emotional drain on Julie."

Taking Rob's mask off was like relieving the steam on a pressure cooker, but the contents still boiled inside. Rob was in serious danger of losing his job. He'd received a nonjudicial punishment for failing to make a band performance and was docked a month's pay but didn't tell Julie. Meanwhile, they were paying $200 a month out-of-pocket for medications they didn't want the Marine Corps to know Rob was taking.

Rob feared if Julie found out about his punishment, it would be the last straw. While Julie's reaction to the abuse was sympathetic, it wasn't enough to override Rob's conditioning, which taught him to keep secrets.

"At that point in our relationship, we fought about everything," Rob says.

When Julie did find out, "I was not happy to know that he would not have a paycheck coming in for a month. Where was that money gonna come from? It was a mess."

Rob made an appointment for them to talk to the chaplain on base. Julie just wanted to figure out how to pay off their bills and split up.

"I was tired of him crying about everything that happened," she says. She was frustrated that he wouldn't help himself by staying on the medications the therapist prescribed for depression and attention deficit disorder. Those twin ailments, either caused by or exacerbated by his victimization as a child, Julie saw as the reason for Rob's present-day issues—his lack of attention, his ability to withdraw into another world and sleep through alarm clocks, not to mention, his failure to meet the daily demands of a job and a wife.

Julie was frustrated Rob wouldn't take the medicine that would "fix" these problems.

"I felt bad about what happened to him, but I also felt he wasn't trying to get out of it. That was his drug, his sob story about his abuse," Julie says.

When the chaplain asked Rob who he thought was hurting more, him or Julie, Rob answered, "I am."

The chaplain told the couple, in his experience, the person who has the plan to get out of a marriage is probably the one who is hurting the most. Julie had a plan.

The chaplain said if there was any chance they were going to save the marriage, they would need to date each other, get to know one another again.

"We were supposed to play 'pick up,'" Julie explains.

She and a girlfriend went to a bar. Rob was supposed to come to the bar—and in essence, pursue his wife.

"Rob was supposed to be there at ten. He wasn't there."

At 11:30, Julie started drinking. By 12:30, she was trashed.

"My husband stood me up," Julie tells me.

"Things were already on shaky ground," Rob says. He was uncomfortable with the setup and arrived very late.

"When I got there...it was kind of like she was on the other side of the room playing coy, or whatever. She made her presence known but wasn't approaching me. She wanted me to sort of initiate the approach...I don't know what to say, so I asked her, 'Can I get a hug?'"

"Unh-uh," came Julie's answer.

Julie remembers the episode a little differently. She remembers Rob asking her to dance. She told him to "Fuck off."

Whatever the actual words exchanged, "That night was a train crash," Rob says.

It was time for Rob to reenlist, but his immediate supervisor, the gunny he was having trouble with, didn't want him. With all of the disciplinary actions Rob had faced, he looked forward to becoming a civilian, but Julie was adamant.

"You need the Marines," Julie told him, for the insurance benefits, as much as the structure. Though the odds were against him, Julie told me, "Rob has angels on his side."

A military career planner helped him figure out his next step. The planner went behind the gunny's back and got Rob reenlisted, and he was able to attain the next rank. His test scores showed he was eligible to become a linguist, and he was signed up for Arabic language school in California.

"He went to California, and I stayed here," Julie says.

Rob left for Monterey in July 1997, with a laptop computer purchased so he could keep in touch with his wife while he was gone. But he rarely wrote to Julie, or he would send her silly forwarded messages other people sent him.

"I'm his wife, and that's what he sends me—forwards?"

She went, one time, for over two weeks without hearing from him.

Midway through his course, Julie suggested legal separation.

"He came back from Monterey for a visit," and Julie learned he hadn't been taking his medication.

"He's not calling, and I'm paying money for medicine he's not taking? I'm working twelve-hour shifts to pay for this medicine. This is a slap in the face," she says, and she told him so.

She declined to sleep with him, telling him their separation would be voided if they had sex and it would take that much longer to get divorced.

"Whether that was true or not," Rob laughed, recalling Julie's pronouncement, "I wasn't getting any."

His efforts to woo his wife made no impact.

Julie came home from an overnight shift to find a trail of Hershey's kisses leading to the bedroom.

"I wanted to pick up the Hershey kisses and throw every single one of them at him," Julie tells me. "For months he ignored me, and then he comes home, throws some kisses around, and I am supposed to be action ready? Yeah, I remember wanting to yell and scream at him at the top of my lungs."

Instead, she locked herself in the bathroom and took a shower.

"That was a really tough week," Julie says, but she enlisted the help of friends to help her get through it.

"Three good girlfriends came over a lot and hung around a lot. We went shopping, one of them went with us. We went to the movies, one of them went with us. I needed that."

For Julie, the icing on the cake was a statement Rob made about a particular girl in Monterey. He told Julie if not for the fact dating a fellow student would be considered fraternization, "it would be *on.*"

"I was done by the end of that week," she says. "I told him the plan and how we were going to divide things up. I know he was hurt. I could see it in his eyes. I just couldn't do that anymore and be so insulted like that. I was tired of trying."

They agreed to stay together long enough to get some bills paid off.

Rob says, "She gave it everything; she did. Even though I gave it everything too, it wasn't enough. She was really the foundation. She was like my foundation. I miss it. If I were to say I didn't miss that, then I'd be lying."

Today, Rob blames himself for the breakup of the marriage, but he swears he didn't cheat. If he was guilty of anything it was of taking his wife for granted.

"At the time, I didn't realize how great of a life I had. A lot of guys would tell me they would give their left nut to have what I have. But I think they were literally saying they would *give their left nut* to have what I had. They envied what I had...I was lucky. For a period of time, Julie was a gift—a gift for me for all the bad things that happened. She's a good person. And I did some asinine things."

"All the friends were my friends," Julie tells me. "All our couple friends were my friends. The person I was turning into, I was hating."

After seven years of marriage, they divorced in February 1998.

After school was over, Rob flew to North Carolina, and Julie gave him the keys to their pickup. She would keep the house. They didn't talk for nearly a year after that, but when they did, they talked for hours. The pair remain good friends. Julie's assessment of Rob is that he "has a good heart," despite whatever pain he once caused her.

Charlene and Julie are so close today, Charlene considers Julie's children her grandchildren—the only grandchildren she has.

When Charlene learned of Jimmy's death, ten years after Rob and Julie divorced, she called Julie first.

"It didn't surprise me that Jimmy was a bank robber," Julie says. "That he killed himself was really more of a relief. Not so much for Rob, but I feared that he would come back and do something to Charlene."

When Rob returned to California, his score on his final Arabic test was failing. He had passed the class, flying Charlene out for his graduation in the fall of 1998, but he could not be placed in a job as an Arabic linguist.

"I studied for sixty-three weeks and took a test at the end and failed. But I still passed the class."

Rob was disappointed that, once again, his effort translated into only marginal results. With less than two years to go to finish out ten years in the Marine Corps, he received orders to serve the rest of his time at Camp Pendleton in Southern California, as a bulk fuel specialist. This was a job that required no schooling and could not have held less appeal.

But, Rob says, "The weirdest thing happened."

Not long after arriving at his new post, he came face-to-face with the battalion sergeant major.

"How much you bench?" the sergeant major asked him.

"Two-forty," came Rob's reply. Like his brother in prison, Rob was into weight lifting.

"How would you like to be our intel officer?" came the next question.

"Seriously?"

"You don't seem like a bulk fuel specialist," the sergeant major told him, and after he heard Rob's whole story about passing Arabic school but failing the test, not to mention the fact he had computer skills, the deal was sealed.

Julie's assessment, that Rob has angels on his side, seemed, once again, to fit.

As Rob explains, "You're a Marine first," so the fact he was in good fighting shape, apparently, made an impression. Working out had allowed Rob to increase his chest size and whittle his waist. In short, he looked the part.

"I guess I just had that squeaky-clean appearance."

Following investigation, he received top secret clearance and became the man in charge of updating the security clearances of the battalion's 150 to 200 E-6's and above.

"I was the collector of the raw material," Rob says. He encrypted and e-mailed the data for investigation elsewhere.

One of the most enjoyable aspects of this duty was getting to participate in simulated war games against top-ranking brass. Basically, it was a computer war.

And heads rolled.

"Majors and lieutenant colonels lost their jobs in the middle of this. I sat there and witnessed this."

Information Rob had been able to collect off a classified military Internet system before the exercise gave his team the advantage.

"I came back with these folders filled with satellite photos of the actual bridges and stuff," which allowed his team to put up a better fight. "Besides having a blast for two weeks, we helped them learn a lot."

If Rob could have stayed in that job, he might have considered staying in the Marines, but the update on the battalion's security clearances came to a close, and his record still reflected the bulk fuel specialist job title.

"I had my chance [at Arabic school], and I blew it. If I was gonna stay in the Marines, I would have to be a bulk fuel specialist the rest of my career."

He opted instead to leave the Marines in November 2000. But it wouldn't be long before the military beckoned again.

Rob wasn't out of the Marine Corps for six months before he enlisted in the Air Force. He spent those six months training with two different trucking companies before concluding he was not cut out to be a truck driver.

Julie was right, Rob decided. He needed the structure of the military, and he was already halfway to a lifelong pension. What was ten more years?

Rob chose the Air Force based on observations he'd made while traveling with the Marine Corps Band. Any Air Force base in any locale he ever saw bested the best of the Marine Corps bases he'd visited. If he was going to spend another ten years in the service, he figured, he may as well go top shelf.

But he would also be held to a higher standard.

"Marines have your big bull-hunk dumb asshole," Rob tells me, "while the Air Force has the college graduate asshole. Instead of making you do push-ups, he'll make you write a five-hundred word essay on why it was screwed up, whatever mistake you did."

It was a trade-off Rob was willing to make, even though he would have preferred the push-ups.

"I needed to see if I could retire, and so, it's given me structure, and I'm thankful for being able to deal with it, but the military is not for me. It wasn't for me, and I knew it wasn't for me, and I kept on it anyways. Now that I had gone halfway, it's like I'm not going to throw a halfway mark away—you're halfway there! Just think how fast the first half went, all you got to do is *that*, one more time. And I'm like, I can do that. Just sort of stick it out, get my retirement, and then I'll move on to something more along my personality."

The Air Force would take Rob in at the rank of staff sergeant. He was offered a course in avionics, and early in the summer of 2001, Rob was on his way to Texas for training.

On September 11, 2001, Rob was still in training. If he'd remained in the Marine Corps as a bulk fuel specialist, no doubt he would soon have been headed to Afghanistan or Iraq. There, his training in Arabic might have been useful, but the odds of anyone intervening to keep him outside of a dangerous combat zone were not good—angels or no angels.

Rob was content to work in support of the air war, Stateside, making repairs to the infrared camera pods that help pilots identify and confirm bomb targets. He was posted to Las Vegas, where he bought the house he planned to retire in one day. He flew Charlene out on his dime. He was proud to show off the unique and artful paint job he'd employed on the blank canvas that was the interior of his new home. Life was pretty good, even without medication.

Following his divorce from Julie, Rob had discontinued taking the depression and ADD meds prescribed to him. The biggest ache in his heart these days was getting over his first post-divorce relationship with a young woman who was in the navy. He'd met Mary* during Arabic school.

The relationship developed slowly. Nineteen years old when they met, Mary was inexperienced, but the romance blossomed. He even visited Mary a couple of times in Hawaii, where she was eventually stationed. The distance proved too great a strain on the relationship, and they broke up.

Having tried at love and failed twice before, Rob turned to the Internet for social connection. It was too much trouble, he decided, to try to form relationships within the military. The odds alone were not in his favor.

"Most women in the area already have their 'bitch shield' up and don't even notice the gem before their eyes. Just another shaved head. That's a big factor in why I haven't found Mrs. Right. I have found 'Ms. Right Now' a few times."

---

*   Not her real name.

While in Vegas, Rob met an older woman in an Internet chat room. Carol* was six years his senior. Chats gave way to phone calls. Then they agreed to meet in person.

Just as in the movie, *"Same Time Next Year,"* Carol and Rob met once a year. She would fly out to Vegas for a week's vacation. By the time he found out Carol was married, with a teenaged son from a previous affair, Rob was too far into the relationship to walk away.

"We'd play 'boyfriend-girlfriend,'" Rob says. They'd spend each week, more or less in bed. The relationship, and occasional visits, continued over the next seven years.

Carol, Rob decided, was like an unpolished diamond. He loved her ease in dealing with people. She was a great cook, and besides, "it made me feel special to have this woman flying out to see me. I liked the attention."

Rob figured he'd tried going by the book romantically, and it hadn't worked. "Weird" was his new standard of normal.

The only year Rob didn't see Carol was when he was stationed in Korea.

"Everyone has to put their time in overseas," Rob explains, at least in the Air Force. If he wanted a tour in Europe, a year in Korea was the most likely way to get there. He was promised a tour in England immediately following his duty in Korea. And at least in Korea, he wouldn't have to worry about Jimmy showing up.

---

*   Not her real name.

"Going for World's Longest Fart—12 seconds. Holding your letter as good luck charm."

January 31, 2009

Hello

Finally more pictures to send! A picture is worth a thousand words.

Nice job on your wood working & Thank you for the pictures. You look better with a shave. No more Bigfoot! ☺

I quit drinking 5 days ago—Let's see how long this lasts...

For a long drive to see you it would help to stay sober. And drunk people are not always the best company to have over—even if they are Functional Alcoholics.

In 2004 I spent $12,000 at the bar in one year. And $6,000 more on "Jack" that same year! (Smiley face with gritted teeth)

Bought a used car for $1,800. 96 Galant with 113,000 miles. I got the little puppy up to 130 mph! Then took my foot off the gas cause front tires were dry rotted. The speedometer goes to 140 mph. And it still smells new inside. Starts in -20F temps. But trans has issues...Like being overfilled when I bought it.

I did 4 trans flushes—first one looked like motor oil with metal shavings in it. 2,000 miles on it so far & its doing okay. 2.4 liter 4 cyl. Engine. Made tires smoke bad—then bought new ones.

Hey, your email address is giving me problems. Like it says—invalid—or some crap. So I will try again. I couldn't get your email maps So thank you for mailing them cause I'd never dam find that place on my own.

Would've come this week but "ice storm of the century" happened. Hope your okay & trees didn't break and fall everywhere. Tree almost killed me in Canada. F-2 tornado in Rockies? You bet. 30 miles north of Idaho/Canada boarder at Yahk Provincial Park. There are 2 different spelling on each side of the Boarder. (For Yahk)

Today, someone at Wal-Mart scuffed up my front bumper on my green car—paint damage mostly—And yesterday I got a chip in the windshield by a semi truck. But it still smells new! Glad it's not new off the dealership lot or I'd flip.

Insurance Company is cancelling my insurance on my cars. Their reason—no drivers license. I don't crash—nor in the 3 ½ years of Preogressive Insurance have I filed a claim. We'll talk about "The Rest of the story" (Paul Harvey) when I visit you! And that rolled for $500 in west Detroit story.

Keeping track of ice storm #2 in your area—when all that power goes out it means (No Gas, Curfue, Full motels, Desperate people, National Guard) so…on to page 4—

We'll see what happens & play it buy ear.

Pigeon city up by Dollyworld has a lot of hotels <u>cheap</u>. 25.00 a night???

Keep in Touch,
Love Ya—Jim

P.S. the Canadian Geese with Turbans was fartin, pukin & Cryin out loud <u>FUNNY.</u>

CHAPTER FOURTEEN

Fast Forward

As Rob was leaving the country in the summer of 2003, Jimmy was reentering it. Jimmy had served seven years of a ten-year sentence for bank robbery at Kent Institution, a maximum-security prison in British Columbia, Canada.

Kent houses up to three hundred inmates. More than half of all offenders, like Jimmy, serve sentences longer than forty months. A fourth of all prisoners at Kent are lifers.

The experience should have been a great deal more productive for Jimmy than his time in the Michigan system. According to Corrections Canada material, Kent is big on education, socialization, and employment programming, but his stay there also put him in touch with many more hardened criminals.

He was released from Canadian custody on August 1, 2003, and extradited to Iowa on a fugitive warrant dating back to January 4, 1994. He was wanted in Johnson County for theft in the second degree/possession of stolen property. He sat in jail for nearly three months, but his case was dismissed when a necessary witness could not be located.

Jimmy would live the next eighteen months "off the grid." Though I pretty easily followed his trail from Michigan to Iowa to Utah and Canada, there were only a few hints of where he was during this period. With no other means of support, the only question in my mind is which banks did he rob and where?

For Rob, Korea was at least a safe haven from Jimmy. Rob developed a taste for spicy Korean kimchi and other delicacies, did a lot of jogging, and learned what a "juicy girl" is. Servicemen visiting clubs were encouraged to buy the club girls overpriced juice drinks or roses to keep their attention and conversation. Rob befriended one juicy girl in particular—a Russian—but the relationship had no future.

Being in a foreign country, being recognized as a U.S. servicemen, Rob felt called to a higher standard, and he tried to do it justice in small ways, if not big.

"It's just tough, wearing that uniform...constantly being this symbol of the United States, like an ambassador. Whatever you say and wherever you go, they say, 'Oh that's what an American is like.'"

One day, he boarded a local bus, paying about 80 cents for a memory he considers priceless.

"I'm clueless as to where I am," Rob says. But if all else failed, he figured he'd take a taxi back to the base.

When a little old lady boarded, Rob felt duty bound to show her some courtesy.

"Here I am, this big, tall white guy with round eyes," in a bus filled with Koreans. "I stood up and gave my seat to her. I thought the people around me were going to shit a brick. I was all proud of myself because that's probably the only time they'll have that close of an encounter with an American. Those are the moments that are just—Ah! That's what you do it for—make a good example of America and show them people are people."

Defying his upbringing in a community that offered few positive role models for a kid, Rob was acting as a goodwill ambassador. The contrast for me, between the way Rob and Jimmy made their way through the world, was interesting—parallel, but opposite. Jimmy went to a foreign country to steal, while Rob went mindful of leaving a good impression.

Rob was seeing things and experiencing things it was hard to imagine Jimmy ever seeing or doing. At least in Korea, Jimmy wasn't likely to come knocking on Rob's door.

Absent a steady girlfriend and with the threat of Jimmy as far removed as possible, Rob concentrated on his career. Though he could never leave behind entirely his tendency to show up late for work, he was determined to advance in rank.

Once he arrived at his next duty station at Lakenheath in Suffolk, England, Rob volunteered to serve in the honor guard, attending military funerals and flag-folding ceremonies. He started going to college for computer science and had advanced in his job assignment.

"I was promoted to production supervisor as a staff sergeant, and that's not always done," Rob explains, unless the troop is soon going to pin on the stripes of a tech sergeant. Rob was giving his all and expecting it to pay off. He'd passed his test for tech sergeant, a feat in itself. A uniform with a tech sergeant's stripes had already found a home in his closet. It was only a matter of time, Rob believed, before he would be wearing it.

"After sixteen fucking years in the military, I finally get to put on an E-6. By that time, most people are master sergeants debating on whether they want to go toward senior.

"Everything was just good, good, good," he tells me, including his performance reviews. For once in his life, Rob believed, his extra effort was going to pay off.

He was evaluated on a scale of one to five, five being the best. "If I was ever gonna earn a five, it would have been then."

When he learned he would receive a four instead, it was a slap in the face. A four, according to military literature, reflects "above average" performance, but not the stellar effort Rob felt he was putting out. With so much competition for promotions and every point on an evaluation counting toward promotion, not receiving a five was like saying Rob didn't do enough to earn the "clearly above" average mark.

"You can't turn around and give me a four," Rob thought. "I did the work to get the A, A-plus ratings, and it was just a personal blow to me that I was marked down."

Ronnie McGee, who knew Rob in England, as well as at his last duty station in North Carolina, tells me Rob was stabbed in the back by a guy he thought was his friend. This two-faced friend, Ronnie and Rob believe, had a hand in Rob's markdown on the performance review.

Long off the medications he'd been prescribed for depression and ADD, the blow was devastating to Rob. Life seemed so unfair. He'd struggled and struggled in the Marines, trying to make a go of it and reaching a career dead end instead. He'd started fresh in the Air Force, determined to do the things necessary to advance in rank, and now he wasn't being recognized for it.

When setbacks like this happened, it seemed to Rob like the universe had it out for him. How well I knew that trap! Like Rob, I'd look at my accomplishments or inability to achieve at the level I thought I should and wonder how being an abuse survivor hampered me. If I achieved a certain measure of success, always, I had to wonder how much better I could have done if I'd had a good male influence in my life, instead of an abusive one.

Being abused messes with a person's confidence. It acts like a weight when other things go wrong, giving us that extra little shove into feelings of utter worthlessness. At times like that, survivors can become their own worst enemy—sabotaging themselves.

Plenty of airmen would probably be thrilled with a four rating, seeing it as praise, not an insult. But for Rob, it may as well have been a neon sign flashing the words "not perfect."

Dragging the abuse baggage around felt like an injustice, like God saying, "Here, I am going to give you a challenge that will color your whole life, and at the same time, it's going to create a desire in you to prove to the world you're a person worthy of praise. The kicker is, when you do get praise, you'll be unable to absorb it."

Piled atop his abuse issues, getting a four on his performance review was enough to make Rob feel as though he had failed utterly.

After learning he did not achieve the top mark, Rob went home and smashed nearly every piece of glass and all of the dishes he owned, in his driveway, then he called his shop, lip quivering, tears of rage rolling down his cheeks.

"It's a blur. I don't remember it all...I'm in tears...I said, 'I got a four on my EPR, and I just broke everything in my house, and I'm going crazy.'"

Help was on the way. Rob was sent to The Priory in Richmond, England, for ten days of intense mental health treatment. He could not have landed in a better spot, he said, even if he'd been in the United States.

The Priory, I learn, is a leader in acute mental health care in Europe. Many high-profile celebrities have spent time there. Considering the ways the visit changed Rob's life, The Priory certainly lived up to its reputation.

"It was like this big gigantic house that was one of those mansion-sized things, converted to a hospital," he says. In the center of the complex, ringed by the walls of the house, was a grassy square with trees.

When he first got there, he told them, "I need ADD drugs."

Though Rob had been diagnosed with ADD before he and Julie divorced, it wasn't on his military health records since the medication had been prescribed in Julie's name.

"Literally, I'm there half a day, and the doctor comes in and explains there's this drug, Straterra, and it's experimental, and it's being used to treat adults with ADD."

"Okay, I'll do it," Rob told the doctor, who continued to impress upon him the experimental nature of the drug and the fact long-term effects were unknown.

"Okay, I'll do it," Rob affirmed, willing to try something—anything—to smooth over the rough patches in his brain. Virtually overnight, on Straterra, Rob's emotional state improved.

"I know when something works on me," he says.

With the Straterra, it felt like someone had flipped a switch.

"The next morning on my way to get coffee, I said, 'Hello,' and 'Good morning,' to three people," instead of stumbling after coffee and grunting to the people around him.

He remembers thinking, *This is some good shit!*

Today, more than five years into taking the medication, he continues to regard Straterra as a miracle drug, even if there were somewhat troubling physical side effects at first. Rob was motivated to put up with a few minor blips for the clarity Straterra brought to his thoughts. On Straterra, he could sit and read a book—for pleasure—instead of struggling through required reading or falling asleep after a few pages.

"And I'm actually interested in the book. And you know, I can read about twenty pages before my brain gets overwhelmed with information, but that's pretty good for me. And I'm talking in full sentences and talking until I have cotton mouth, and I'm like, *Wow, is this really me talking?* I wasn't able to do that the majority of my life."

Along with Straterra and the antidepressant Zoloft, Rob was administered an alternative form of intense psychotherapy, known as eye movement desensitization and reprocessing (EMDR). Rob tells me the therapy, borrowing from hypnosis and other techniques, was explained to him as something outside the norm, but based on Old World concepts, to rewire or reframe negative events in memory.

"If it's worked in the past, I don't care if it's accepted in polite society—that counts me out." He laughs.

According to literature from the EMDR Institute, the therapy "tends to the past experiences that have set the groundwork for pathology, the current situations that trigger dysfunctional emotions, beliefs and sensations, and the positive experience needed to enhance future adaptive behaviors and mental health."[*]

---

[*]   http://www.emdr.com/index.htm

Dual stimulation—bilateral eye movements along with tones or taps—is employed as the reprocessing phase begins.

"The client attends momentarily to past memories, present triggers, or anticipated future experiences while simultaneously focusing on a set of external stimulus."

One of Rob's sessions focused on his breakup with Mary.

"I never really got closure with her," Rob explains, and years later, the hurt remained. Through the EMDR session, Rob entered, in his imagination, a pure white room where he could feel the positive sensation of Mary's head on his shoulder as they danced at a navy ball. "Then she just sorted of faded into the distance, and I went through this door…I felt so much closure."

Mainstream or not, the method worked wonders.

I am interested to learn in my own research that EMDR has frequently been employed in treating patients with post-traumatic stress disorder, which Rob believes he suffers from, even if the military doesn't acknowledge it. Recent studies indicate soldiers with trauma in their childhoods are predisposed to develop post-traumatic stress disorder following combat. Rob never fought in a conventional war, but the triggering dynamic is the same. In his case, the identity theft and FBI raid, rather than combat, served as the catalyst reigniting the trauma of his childhood. EMDR proved a particularly effective tool in dealing with those memories, just as EMDR has proven effective in helping combat veterans.

Several sessions focused on events involving Jimmy, "but I don't want to dwell on it," Rob tells me.

His answer startles me. Rob's assertion, from the beginning, that he is an "open book" has proven true. But suddenly, here is a private chapter. In months of interviews covering every aspect of his life, there is only one question he declines to answer: what was an EMDR session on Jimmy like? I had expected him to recount the details of such a session with the same ease as he described the session with Mary.

The fact Rob won't go there, he later explains, is more a case of can't. Following EMDR therapy, he says, it is almost as if many of the most traumatic of his abuse experiences have simply been removed from his brain to a sort of data dump where they are no longer accessible. There are limits to what he can recall about the things Jimmy did to him—not because he doesn't want to relate them, but because they are stored somewhere from which he can't retrieve them.

The most he can share about his EMDR sessions related to the abuse is that he "vanquished" Jimmy.

I don't push. He doesn't need to go there, and neither do I. For me, it is a little like seeing that picture of Jimmy, the first time I laid eyes on it. His face somehow zaps me back in time, tapping into some look I remember on my abuser's face. Like a train wreck, it is hard to tear my eyes away, but I do. No good is going to come from remembering a particular event or a specific degradation. It is important to deal with the feelings abuse left us—not wallow in each ugly episode.

Rob tells me he will be forever grateful for the help he received at The Priory and for his introduction to Straterra, a drug he expects to take for the rest of his life.

Though the treatment was covered by the military, it cost Rob dearly. He would never wear the uniform he hung in his closet in anticipation of a promotion to tech sergeant.

"It's frustrating for me, because I'm not a numbers sort of guy," he says, but it stung, not attaining the next rank.

Unlike when he was in the Marines, Rob was open with the Air Force about his therapy and for the first time, about the fact he had ADD. In the Marines, he had worried about losing his security clearance, but the Air Force was much more accepting—at least to a point.

"In some ways, I've gotten a lot of leniency," Rob tells me, "but they eventually get tired of being lenient."

Straterra had flipped a switch in Rob that needed flipping, but there was an adjustment period involved. And for a time, he says, the meds were making him, literally, too smart for his own good.

"There's personal work that goes on with taking these types of pills," he says, it isn't just an instant fix.

On Straterra, his response to a mild reprimand, such as one he received for dipping smokeless tobacco in the shop instead of in a designated area, became a little too flamboyant. Printing his response on blue paper with pink ink, Rob figures, is what cost him his tech sergeant stripes.

"I was giving the image of being rather immature, and they didn't like that."

Rob figured the military could suck it up this time.

"You don't like what I do? Fuck you! I don't like getting a haircut every two weeks."

It was not an attitude likely to win Rob his long-anticipated promotion, but it was necessary emotional work.

"It was just my way of trying to find out who I am as an individual and not many people appreciate individuality in the military."

Rob no longer wanted to be covered by the "grey blanket" of the Air Force. Straterra returned color to his world, and he wanted to use it. In a way, he was fighting back against Jimmy. Rob had entered the military seeking a positive paternal influence, but too often, what he found was a brand of authority no less arbitrary than his brother's.

If he wasn't going to wear a tech sergeant's stripes, Rob decided, he wasn't going to act like one.

"I should have been a tech, and I'm not, so I'm not gonna do the work of a tech and not get paid for it."

Bringing Charlene to England was a highlight of both Rob's time on duty there and in the continuing development of their mother-son relationship, which had been so fractured when he'd left home as a teenager.

"I realized how much she really had done for us and what it must have taken for her to raise us, and I just had a lot of respect for that...I wanted to give something back for her efforts," Rob says.

It was the summer of 2006. While one son was flying her out to England, the other was continuing his career of crime. Unknown to either Charlene or Rob at the time, Jimmy was just getting out of jail—again.

Jimmy had been arrested May 28, 2005, in Polk County, Iowa, for possession of marijuana and having a firearm as a felon. His bond was set at $11,700. According to the court record I found, Jimmy waived a bond review, preferring instead to sit in jail until his case came to court. A few weeks later, he waived his right to a preliminary hearing and refused counsel, apparently figuring his paralegal background would suffice in representing himself. He pled guilty to the charges and received a sentence of two years. He was released on July 17, 2006, while Rob and Charlene were touring England.

Charlene had always wanted to see England, and because of a re-signing bonus, Rob could afford the plane ticket.

"She had never really traveled overseas to Europe," and if she was ever going to do it, this was the time.

Rob decided his mother would fly first class.

The round trip—first-class one way, coach the other—would cost $2,100, which was about the amount Jimmy was collecting when he was robbing banks in Canada.

Rob had not forgotten his mother's attitude when it came to spending extra money.

"If I could do a little extra for her, I would do the extra; if I had it, we would do extra, and that's the way she's always done things. We haven't always had extra in our lives."

It felt good to give his mother so extravagant a gift.

"Something as intangible as an 'experience,' flying first class."

But the ticket Rob purchased turned out to be much more than first class.

"She got the Maharaja first-class seats, and she was all excited about that."

Charlene picks up the narrative, explaining how there was a mix-up when she went to check in for her flight. There was a problem with her seat and the gate agent had to do some checking.

"She looked, and she's like, 'Oh, here you go. I have the best seat in the house for you,' and I'm like, well, I thought I had the best seat in the house."

When Charlene boarded the plane, she entered the first-class cabin expecting to be seated there, but instead, she was directed to a seat just behind the cockpit.

"My seat is like this wonderful recliner seat, this big old leg room, and I'm thinking, *Oh, I really want to get my camera.* And here all those people over there they already had their laptops out...and I know they would think, *What a country bumpkin this woman is. Who paid for her to come up here? Why are they letting her up here in our space?* This is what's going on in my head." Charlene laughs.

Rob wanted his mother to feel pampered, and he definitely got his money's worth.

"As soon as we were seated, she came with the hot towel. Oh my god! And I just wanted to oh, wash my face with it—Ah la la la la la." Charlene laughs, going through the motions. "And then, before we even took off, she brought champagne...Sure, you know, I'd love some! I was just happy, like a little kid up there, and I'm like, wait until I tell *Rob!* Because you know, it wouldn't have happened if I'd had coach. But him doing that allowed me to have this wonderful, marvelous experience."

The vacation was not without a few bumps.

"We arrived; of course, the first thing was Lego Land," Charlene remembers. "'Ma,' he says, 'They have a Lego Land,' and I'm thinking, *Okay, that's good. You know?* 'Want to go to Lego Land?' Well, that enthusiasm was so much, I didn't want to say no...Because he wanted to go there, let's go...and I just kind of followed him, and they're cute and all that but he was just mesmerized. He's like, 'Look at this, Ma! Come here, look!'"

Charlene was pleased to share something with her son that excited him that much.

"We saw Big Ben, and we drove through, and we saw the London Eye," she says. They were on the way to Stonehenge, which for Charlene, held special significance.

In the years since hitting rock bottom with her own depression, Charlene had discovered a church with beliefs she could put her faith in. Novus Spiritus, founded by psychic and author, Sylvia Browne, provided a spiritual home where Charlene felt loved, guided, comforted, and accepted.

The tenets of Novus Spiritus include the belief that the purpose of life is to scale the mountain of self, to love oneself, and to purge all negativity. The concept of knowing—or gnosis—is the root from which the church's belief system stems.

Gnostics believe each life is a path winding toward perfection. The path is chosen by each individual before birth, to work on and perfect the soul. The tenets encourage simplicity and the avoidance of judgment, even of oneself. Fear will only impede spiritual growth. Gnostics discourage belief in demons, seeing such belief as a block to communion with God. The body is to be treated as a living temple. Karma is merely a balancing of experience, not retribution for past wrongs. God allows each person as many lives as necessary to achieve perfection. Death should be accepted with grace and recognized as the act of returning to the other side—the soul's true home.

Gnostics believe in a Mother God, who co-created the Earth with an all-loving Father God. They believe Christ was crucified, but did not die on the cross and lived to father children in France with Mary Magdalene, his wife.

With her alternative religious views, visiting Stonehenge, for Charlene, was akin to making a trek to Mecca. Just getting there was an experience.

"I said this is just an adventure, whatever happens…the only way I can get through certain events, I go into the situation with no expectations," Charlene explains. "I just go for the ride, and that's how I handled England."

At Stonehenge, Charlene felt a special energy, "like 'aliveness' that whenever you breathe in, it just kind of gave you that good sense of well-being."

At the same time she was sharing that special feeling with the son who flew her to England on his dime, Jimmy was celebrating his release from jail on July 17, 2006. He'd served fourteen months on the Iowa charges. The very next day, he robbed a bank in Jackson, Minnesota.

According to an online news report,

> Officials in Jackson, Minnesota, are looking for a suspect in a morning bank robbery. At 10:20 Tuesday morning, the suspect walked up to a teller at United Prairie Bank and handed the teller a note with demands. The teller gave him the money and the suspect ran away…Police are looking for a white male wearing a long sleeved blue and white pin-striped shirt. He stands about six feet tall and weighs around 200 pounds. At the time of the robbery, the suspect was wearing dark sunglasses, a baseball cap, and blue jeans.

Surveillance photos from the robbery leave little doubt.

"Looks just like him," Rob tells me when I send him the Internet link to a bank surveillance photo.

A shirt just like the one worn by the robber in the Jackson robbery is among the possessions returned to Charlene by the FBI three years after the Jackson robbery, after Jimmy's death. The shirt also sounds exactly like one he wore in one of his Canadian robberies ten years earlier.

After Stonehenge, Charlene and Rob toured the Thames River. It was July 19, 2006—one day after Jimmy's first documented bank robbery in the United States. That day required some patience for Charlene and Rob, who were oblivious to Jimmy's activities.

There was an altercation with a Frenchman, in which he and Charlene exchanged words after the man cut in front of her in a line. As Rob walked up, "I was saying to the guy, 'You're an asshole,' and then the guy said, 'You're an asshole' back to me! Ohhhh!"

It was one thing for Rob to give a bus seat to a Korean in order to show Americans are good people; it was quite another when a Frenchman messed with his mother.

"Rob reached over to the guy, grabbed him by the shirt in the front, and pulled him around, and he said, 'Apologize to my ma, right now, or I'll smash you right in the face.'"

The man apologized, and Rob let him go.

Later, "We ran into a couple who pointed out that the French hate Americans, so the guy was just an example of what France would be like if we were to go to Paris, so then we were glad we didn't go. With my big mouth and Rob's temper, we would both get in trouble over there. I won't tolerate rude people, and Rob won't tolerate someone being rude to me."

There was a record heat wave that summer, exacerbating Rob's ill mood. Earlier in the day, he'd hit his head on a low tunnel while sightseeing and drew blood.

Later, they got lost riding trains to different points of interest.

"We were very confused, and we both had a different opinion as to where we were," until a woman got off the train with them and pointed them in the right direction.

Despite these minor disturbances, Charlene looks back on the vacation as the trip of a lifetime.

As Charlene boarded the plane at the end of her two-week visit, Rob began packing, preparing to return to the States for his last duty station, at Seymour Johnson Air Force Base, in Goldsboro, North Carolina.

Still adjusting to life on Straterra, it was as if Rob's brain were undergoing a renaissance. Artistic skills he had had as a youngster began reasserting themselves. His career in the military and his desire for self-expression were more at odds than ever. And he still couldn't completely escape some of the complications of life with ADD.

"Sometimes, I say things just to get a rise out of people, like at work… It's just made me have this twisted sense of humor, and nobody really understands so I've had to change my approach."

Talking to people, earlier in life, meant exposing himself and possibly holding himself up to ridicule.

With Straterra, Rob feels more at ease dealing with people, if not showing everyone the complete spectrum of who he is. Above all, Rob was learning to accept himself—and his limitations.

"I just never really grew up…and it sort of like made me the out-cast—they're like, 'You're goofy; you're weird,' and after a while, I just started saying, 'Thanks.'"

For every positive the medication brings, there is a trade-off. But Rob hasn't missed the lows.

"It's an exchange I'm willing to deal with in order to have a coherent mind. I wish I could get the highs back…but I'm not willing to go off it that long in order to achieve mediocrity…The meds help me to think, speak, comprehend at higher levels. I still like to daydream, but it no longer consumes me."

While still in England, Rob began studying Richard Bandler's theory of neurolinguistic programming (NLP).

"If there ever was something I was into, that would be 75 percent of what I consider religion. Because it's the way you form language. That's what hypnosis is all about."

In the past, "being the constant troublemaker I am, whenever I would talk to people in that setting—'Let's sit down and have a talk'—I would just say the wrong stuff."

Studying NLP, Rob learned to tone down the "nots and don'ts" in his vocabulary.

"When I started changing the way I talked to people, I noticed I was getting better responses from them…Whenever they get ready to yell at me or scold me or counsel me, I just kind of agree with them. I say, 'I see where you're coming from.' They're like, 'Shit. I guess I got nothing else to tell you then.'"

It almost became a game, pushing the limits, and then playing contrite. The change in tactics worked, to a point.

"I pushed it pretty far," Rob says. He received about three dozen reprimands, big and small, during the course of his military career. So many, he says, it should have been enough to kick four airmen out of the Air Force.

"Am I pushing it because of my sickness, or am I just a neglectful person?" Rob asks himself.

At the same time, on Straterra, "I'm growing mentally at this exponential rate."

Looking back, Rob feels it was all just a necessary phase in his recovery—one that came at a pretty high cost to his career. After nearly twenty years of trying to fit into the military and often coming up short, he didn't exactly make peace with his lot, but he did decide to quit beating himself up so much about his lack of advancement.

"So what if I got a five or a four? What if they gave me a three or a two? I didn't care anymore."

When he got to North Carolina, he declined a supervisory role because he didn't have the attendant rank. Earlier in his career, he might have recovered from a decision like that, but it effectively took any chance of advancement off the table permanently.

The military, for all that it provided—stability, direction, a steady paycheck—never fit Rob and never could. But it did provide the opportunity to make peace—as much as will ever be possible—with his past.

"Nobody understands what it's like wanting to do the best job, whatever it may be, then having the results come up average at best. But, in the Marines, they had a saying, 'The key to being a good Marine is to do ordinary things, extraordinary.'"

Another saying meaningful to Rob came from President Ronald Reagan, who once remarked, "Some people spend an entire lifetime wondering if they made a difference in the world. But the Marines don't have that problem."

And a third, "Once a Marine, always a Marine."

"Just don't say 'ex-Marine,'" Rob jokes.

Even though he will leave the military after 20 years with an honorable discharge from the Air Force, Rob still takes as part of his identity the discipline instilled in him in Marine Corps boot camp.

"I think I've served my country well," Rob says. "No matter the results I produced, I've always given my loyalty."

Rob resigned himself to the notion of finishing his twenty years. He just wanted to get to the end of his enlistment and move on to something more suited to the man he had become. He could live with the failure to gain more rank, but he never would have imagined his testing of limits would actually result in a demotion.

The year leading up to his demotion brought calamity after calamity. Carol, his Internet girlfriend, moved out after they tried for a year to make a go of a daily relationship. He was evicted from two different rental homes—once because of the chaos Carol's son created and once over a dispute with a landlord that had nothing to do with paying rent. He wrecked his dream car, a 2004 Ford Mustang, requiring surgery for himself, as well as car repairs. To top it all off, he was issued two nonjudicial punishments in six months for failing to deal promptly with paperwork and appointments related to being over Air Force weight guidelines.

The year 2009 proved one of the most challenging of Rob's life. It was a year when nothing seemed to go his way, and everything that could go wrong, did—all culminating with a summons to his commander's office on the afternoon of September 14, 2009.

Bank robber, like Marine, is another occupation for which "ex" does not apply. Once a bank robber, always a bank robber. In the fall of 2006, as his brother's military career was winding down, Jimmy's career as a bank robber was picking up. During the same period in which Rob was trying to get his emotional life firmly and finally in order, Jimmy was reverting to the only way of life he knew—taking what he needed, no matter the cost to his victims.

September 14, 2009, would bring Jimmy to his own day of reckoning—one he probably expected all along.

CHAPTER FIFTEEN

Leaving Michigan

November 6, 2009

At the end of my three days in Michigan with Rob and Charlene, I do not want to go home. I have immersed myself in their stories, finding in them so many familiar emotions it is almost as if I already knew their story and just needed reminding.

I can identify with Charlene's experiences, both with her romantic losses and her losses with her sons. I can empathize with the utter exhaustion she felt, working three jobs just to keep a roof overhead. I think of my own children and wonder how I would have fared with the same challenges. Too often, I used that line, "Just wait until your father comes home," but for Charlene, that threat was never an option. As much kinship as I feel with her, sympathizing with her pain as the mother of a child who inflicted such trauma on others, the kinship I feel with Rob goes much deeper.

At every step of the way, as he shared his story with me, I recognized myself—the same fears, the same defenses, the same demons. Our abuse experiences were very different, but somehow, they shaped us in almost the exact same way. Before me, for the first time in my life, is a man who understands what it means to be a sexual abuse survivor, because he is one! Instead of allowing his victimization to turn him into a drunkard or a druggie or a predator, he'd done the hard work necessary to try to be the most whole human he could be. And, in my admiration for him, I am finally able to give myself credit for trying to do the same.

All my life, I've carried that abuse baggage thinking I would never find someone else who really understood what I went through. I knew there were millions of survivors like me, but I'd never met one whose coping mechanisms mirrored mine.

In telling Rob's story, I see the chance to give him what no one has ever given me—a medal of honor, a badge of courage, recognition for fighting the valiant battle of self. I had set out unsure if Rob was the kind of person anyone else would describe as a hero. I had an idea he could be, but in those three days in Michigan, he proved it with every admission of failure and every instance of getting back up to try again.

Perhaps most startling, these people, who opened up their lives to me as completely as any interviewer could dream, were shining light on the ways I was still hiding from the truth in my own life.

In Charlene's recounting of the ways she felt she'd let her children down, I see how my lack of attention to my own kids put them at risk. In the disintegration of her marriage to the boys' father, I see how I was editing who I really was to keep my husband's affection.

Any notions I'd had that I was somehow "farther along" than Rob in facing the issues abuse left me were shot down just as cleanly as Rob could test "expert" as a marksman in the Marines. He'd spent a lot more time focused intently on coming to terms with his abuse than I had and in many ways, had been much more successful. He knew who he was; he knew that he sometimes just needed to give himself a break; and though he often grew frustrated with his own limitations, he'd actually survived in a military setting in which his every misstep was scrutinized. In the process, he'd gained so much insight into the human condition, he constantly amazed me. Every word he uttered carried so much weight and wisdom, it was like reading a book of knowledge born of every heartache he ever endured.

His journey toward health and wholeness made him beautiful in my eyes, the way an angel is beautiful—with a spirit so earnest and trustworthy, it was almost childlike.

Above all, what makes me want to stay in Michigan is the sensation of being utterly myself and finding complete acceptance. How many years had it been since I'd felt that? Had I ever? Once tasted, that feeling is as addictive as any drug. In a matter of just a few days, I'd been shown almost a complete review of every emotion I'd ever felt as an abuse survivor, recognized some of the big ways I was still letting that history affect my life, and come to the realization I had a great deal of work to do if I was ever going to align the "real" Cecile with the life her stand-in had been living.

That last evening in Michigan, Charlene and Rob go on and on, thanking me for wanting to tell their story, for bringing Jimmy's ashes home, for listening to them. I am embarrassed. They have given me so much more!

"I wish I could take you home to North Carolina with me," Rob says.

I agree it would be fun to go to North Carolina and see where Rob works and meet some of the people he works with.

"I might just have to come for a visit," I say, as part of my book research.

It is actually quite early in the evening, but I make motions to leave. Because I don't really want to say good-bye, I ask Rob if he wants to go do something—go bowling, for a walk at the mall, anything. I haven't really thought it out. What activity is appropriate for a thirty-eight-year-old single man and a forty-six-year-old married woman? I just want more time with my hero; it's as simple as that. I enjoy his company.

"It's been a pretty exhausting couple of days," he says.

True, that.

Finally, I just have to go.

I hug Charlene good-bye, much as I'd hugged her on my arrival three days earlier, with tears and smiles, all at the same time. I promise to guard Jimmy's letters with my life and get them back to her when our project is done. I tell her what an amazing son she has in Rob, and he hears me say it.

Then, I turn to Rob.

This hug is very different than our first awkward embrace at the airport. So many thoughts and emotions crowd my heart and brain I can hardly sort them out.

The first wave is gratitude. I am so grateful Rob decided to share his story with me, trusting me to portray him in whatever light I see appropriate given his struggles in his career and relationships.

Next is empathy. I am hugging the little boy inside of Rob, the same as I would hug the little girl in me, if only I could comfort either of the children we used to be. I have never understood another human being's hurts the way I understand his. I know how devastating the loss of innocence and the nightmare of being violated over such a long period of time.

There is also admiration. Rob has spent his adult life feeling like an outcast, around people who don't give him the credit he deserves for acting anywhere close to "normal." There are so many reasons for Rob not to have turned out to be a good son, a good man, and he has turned out to be both. Despite all of the hurts inflicted upon him, he cares about people, and he isn't afraid to show it. The way he respects and honors his mother alone is exemplary, but he has also helped others less fortunate than he is, I have learned in the course of our conversations, sharing what little surplus he has with people in greater need than himself.

This hug is lasting a long time. I sense, though I don't actually see, Charlene go into the kitchen and busy herself with pots and pans. I worry we are making her uncomfortable, but Rob isn't letting go either.

I should say something—should be separating from him, but I can't speak, can't push myself away.

"Are you going to be all right?" he asks, finally breaking the silence.

His concern makes me hug all the harder. I simply do not want to let go—of him, or of the identity his story has helped me, finally, to unfurl.

Still embracing, I realize I am on dangerous ground. What is it I really want from this man? His story, or something more? I haven't forgotten I am married, and I know the overriding emotion surfacing in me is one that will require me to change my life so completely, I can hardly believe the certainty washing over me.

With that, the spell is broken, and I pull away. Thank goodness I know better than to make a fool of myself. Number one, Rob is eight years younger than I am. Number two, he can't possibly feel as strong a pull toward me as I do toward him, because he doesn't know all of the ways our stories match up. Number three, I am not about to mess up the biggest story ever handed to me. The direction my thoughts and feelings have taken over these three days startle me, but I am not about to trash my marriage and the biggest story of my career because of some crush I have developed. I am not going to add pathetic "cougar" to my new identity.

"It's probably just as well that I go," I say, while reaching for the doorknob. I need to get away before I say something I will regret.

"Ditto," Rob says, as I hurl myself across the threshold and out of his mother's house.

What the hell just happened? I ask myself as I drive back to my hotel room. *Have I just thrown myself at the hero of the story I want to write? 'Ditto'? What does that mean?* However Rob meant it, the way I take it is that, yes, given my obviously raw emotional state, my age, and the fact I am married, it is best if I leave. The fact he did not take me up on my invitation to spend more time together only proved I overstepped. I feel so foolish. He is obviously the healthier of the two of us because he is wise enough to protect my marriage even if I have just made a suggestion, which, while entirely innocent, could also prove explosive.

How could I have been so unprofessional? How could I have let myself get so drawn in? How could I have so completely lost my objectivity? I have a book to write—about how abuse shaped two brothers into two totally different kinds of men. That is the story, not some romance.

Perhaps most frustrating of all, I worry Rob has misunderstood my suggestion that we spend more time together. Of course, I find him attractive. He is just the kind of tall beefcake I have always appreciated, with the kindest eyes I have ever seen. But this isn't about a physical attraction. I want to spend more time with him because of the intellectual and emotional communion. I had no idea, having operated my whole life without the kind of connection I found in him, just how hungry I was for it.

The suggestion might have been inappropriate, but I didn't even really think it out. I'd simply been acting on the desire to extend the chance to be this new person he brought out in me, this real person I liked very much. Our whole connection, up until that hug, was completely professional.

After entering my motel room, I throw myself facedown on the bed and sob.

Aside from the possibility I might have compromised my ability to tell Rob's story effectively, it dawns on me that I now have to go home and act as if nothing in me has shifted or been changed by this trip. This thought makes me sob all the harder.

How can I go back to the dead existence I lived before Jimmy Krimm shot himself four miles from my house? I was sitting there that night he robbed the bank, the same as I had for months and months, escaping into some other person's story through a movie or a book—anything to remove me from my actual life story, the one where an imposter acted like she was fine.

Just as it would have been inappropriate for me to reveal only one side of Charlene's divorce, it wouldn't be fair for me to recap here, the issues in my own marriage. But the truth is, I am at least half of the reason it wasn't working. It's pretty tough to have a relationship with a woman who is hiding who she really is. Until that night in Michigan, I didn't even know I was missing!

To realize, at the age of forty-six, all of the ways abuse is still causing me to mask who I am, is quite a blow. I have had counseling over the years, tried to be aware of the traps, and I never hid my abuse background from my kids or my husband. But just admitting it wasn't the cure. This was going to require changing behavior, changing attitudes, changing the way I responded in my relationships. Once given sight, I couldn't go back to being blind—agreeing when I actually disagree, saying "yes" when I really mean "no." I couldn't go back to putting up with behaviors I find unacceptable or offensive.

I realize I have not stood up for myself in the simplest of situations to say, "I don't want to do it that way," or "I don't like it when you treat me like that." These words ceased being a regular part of my vocabulary as a child. Only with the greatest of effort and upset could I call them forth as an adult. It sickens me to realize I rarely called them forth because it was *easier*, more comfortable, not to. And that meant I was still acting like a victim, victimizing myself with my own lack of courage in revealing what I really felt about issues big and small. My very survival as a child depended on acting like what was not okay was fine with me. So I became a master at holding in hurts. That is not my husband's fault. It is mine.

I leave Michigan knowing I need to work at my marriage, but I hold out little hope it will do any good. I'd chosen this marriage twenty years earlier, as a person who didn't know who she was, hoping to find my true self in the identities of wife and mother.

Now, if I changed, it would cause conflict. If I pointed out things that bothered me, it would create friction. If I started making demands, it would cause upset. If I started acting on the outside the way I really felt on the inside, it would make my family feel like a stranger had taken my place.

My options are: reveal myself and let the chips fall, or lose myself forever. Playing the martyr, the way I have inside my mind for so long, will only lead to my own destruction. It is an easy choice, really. I choose me. Finally.

A storm is about to descend on my family, and I am the only one who knows it is coming.

Seventy-one days after coming home from Michigan, I tell my husband I want a divorce. Two weeks after that, I move out, leaving behind every bit of security I have amassed in forty-six years of living—everything except for my job at the newspaper, a few personal possessions, a ten-year-old van, and a pile of notes about a bank robber and his family. And yet, I feel rich.

Thirty-odd days after declaring my independence, I fly to North Carolina to see Rob in March 2010. Together, we are going to meet his dad. Rob has not seen his father in fifteen years. Even when Jimmy died six months earlier, Rob and Jim did not speak. It isn't until I ask Rob to find out if his dad will talk to me that he breaks the silence and calls his father.

This is going to be an intense meeting for a lot of reasons, but I never could have guessed the surprises awaiting us at Jim's place.

James Edward Krimm Charlene Krimm Harry Robert Krimm

The first photo I ever see of Jimmy Krimm is published widely in North Dakota following the Williston robbery. Charlene sends me a photo of herself to run with a story in The Journal. The first photo I see of Rob is a relief, with none of the menace I see in his brother's eyes.

(Clockwise) Charlene, Jimmy (standing) and Harry, around the age the abuse began; Rob, senior band photo; Jimmy, prison ID card; Rob, after Marine Corps boot camp.

At left, Rob and Julie married after he finished music school in the Marine Corps. Rob described the marriage, at first, as "bliss." He and Julie divorced seven years later, but remain on friendly terms today. While on escape, above, Jimmy and Paula, with her son. Rob has no recollection of the prison visit below, at Christmas 1990.

Hi Harry,
It was good seeuen ya!
I'm not the same Jim you
use to know, A new Jim
has taken over and Is
going to make something out
of his life!
I know I don't write
you But sometimes I don't
know what to say for myself.
Theres more drugs & Alcohol
in this camp ("Prison") than
any other one I've Been
to.
But that does'nt matter
Because I'm "Free" From
Drug & Alcohol Addiction.
Have you Found a sig
single chic who wants to
write me? I don't care
if she the uglyist girl in
school!
well, I guess that About
all For now, talk to ya
later.
your
brother,
Jim

Following the Christmas 1990 visit, Jimmy wrote the letter (excerpted left) to his brother, Harry, claiming "a new Jim has taken over" and that "sometimes I don't know what to say for myself." Rob calls it the closest thing to an apology he will ever receive.

Cherish every day of Freedom, wishing Things could be different.

Sent from Colorado in 1994, Jimmy is pictured with the Nova he spray-painted black. Written on the back was a message to his mother, below. Unbeknownst to Rob or Charlene was that Jimmy had stolen Rob's Social Security number before leaving Michigan.

BANK BANDIT: Fernie RCMP have released a police artist's sketch of a suspect believed to have robbed the Toronto Dominion bank at gunpoint last Monday morning. The thief is described as between 35 and 45 years old, six foot to six foot, three inches tall, between 200 and 230 pounds with well-groomed hair. When last seen, he was sporting a short-trimmed brown beard and wearing glasses, a jean jacket, blue jeans and a straw cowboy hat. Anyone with information regarding the crime or the suspect is asked to contact Fernie RCMP at 423-4404.

RCMP SKETCH
Artist's sketch of suspected robber.

Canadian newspapers print a series of artist's sketches following a rash of bank robberies in 1995 and 1996. Below, Charlene flies to California when Rob graduates from Arabic School.

Rob graduates from Avionics school in the Air Force (left); Jimmy robbed the bank in LeMars, Iowa, in August 2006, netting $47,500; around that time, Charlene visits Rob in England, while he was stationed at Lakenheath, in Suffolk. He serves in the Air Force honor guard for 18 months, including attending a Memorial Day event in Mattingley, with members of the British Armed Forces.

PART THREE

CHAPTER SIXTEEN

Bread Crumbs

Jim Krimm lives atop a hillside in the Smokey Mountains of North Carolina, in a prefab home made to look like a log cabin. Since the death of his second wife two years earlier, Jim has been more or less alone in the world.

"I deserve to be alone," he tells me, because of his failure to provide guidance to his sons as they grew up.

Rob and I have driven six hours to meet Jim in the parking lot of a grocery store not far from his house. The directions to get to his place are so complicated, he tells us, it is simpler just to lead us in.

We have some idea what Jim looks like because Charlene only that week received from the FBI pictures of Jim that were in Jimmy's car the night he died. The photos prove Jim and Jimmy had had some contact in recent years—a revelation in itself—but we have no idea the extent of it.

"I think that's him," I say, as an older man pulls into the lot in a new white Ford pickup. We get out of Rob's Mustang as Jim approaches.

"You've put on some pounds," Jim taunts Rob.

Considering Jim last saw his son as a twenty-four- or twenty-five-year-old, the remark is understandable. They hug, that way guys will, opposite shoulders making contact. I shake Jim's hand before he gives Rob driving instructions on where he might encounter some icy patches going up the mountain. He also advises Rob to floor his car the last little ways, before slamming on the brakes at the top of the hill. This is going to be interesting! I am already feeling a little motion sickness from hurtling across winding roads in Rob's little car.

Given the project it is just to get up to Jim's house, we are planning to spend the night. Jim insists. No matter how awkward this meeting becomes, we are committed to spending at least the next twenty-four hours with a man who, for all intents and purposes, is a stranger to both of us.

Jim is as eager to hear the details we can share about Jimmy's crimes as we are to hear what Jim might know.

Jimmy Krimm reentered his father's life shortly before Christmas 2008—about nine months before he died.

"Is this the other Jim Krimm?" Jimmy had asked his dad, having found a phone listing for Jim on the Internet. The notion of Jimmy searching for family members on the Internet sends a chill down my spine. If Jimmy found his dad, he had to know Charlene was still in Michigan and likely knew Rob's location, too!

As startling as those revelations are, nothing could have prepared me for what Jim was about to reveal: the existence of eight letters and 105 photographs documenting Jimmy's whereabouts over the last year of his life. Jim brings the letters out, one or two at a time. Seeing how blown away Rob and I are by what we are seeing and reading, Jim brings out more and more.

Whatever crimes he committed, whatever horrible abuse he inflicted on Rob, Jim Krimm wants one thing known about his older son.

"He was a person."

If sharing the letters will help Rob gain closure, show Rob his brother was not 100 percent monster, Jim is willing to share the words and pictures.

There is a clear contrast between the car thief who wrote a couple hundred letters to his mother from a Michigan prison cell as a young man and the forty-two-year-old serial bank bandit who wrote to his dad in the last year of his life. Gone are the racial epithets. The humor is heightened, as is a curiosity about the world around him and the possibility of a higher power. Still evident is a daily struggle with substance abuse. He wrote in detail about the things he'd seen in his travels. His letters document a failed attempt to visit his father over Christmas 2008, provide clues to his state of mind in his final months, and reveal the loneliness of a man who has had to isolate himself because of his criminal activities.

A letter written on March 27, 2009, hints at a busy spring. It is a couple of weeks after a bank robbery in Dilworth, Minnesota.

"Finally got a minute to write! I've been so dam busy. I'm just glad I can sit here and talk to ya. You're the only one who listens!!"[*]

Most of the letters come with a fistful of photographs, all but a few of which contain clues about Jimmy's travels.

They are like bread crumbs illuminating the path of Hansel and Gretel in the old Brothers Grimm fairy tale. They show where Jimmy was and even what he was driving, down to a couple of his license plates. As Rob and I see these photos and read his letters, we can't help wondering why Jimmy would provide so many clues that could result in his identification as the serial bank robber plaguing the Dakotas and surrounding states? It's almost as if he wants someone to have a record of his final days.

For every positive character trait illuminated, for any good deed related, I cannot read his words without remaining just a little skeptical. As Charlene points out, "Jimmy was conning his dad just like he conned me in his letters in prison…He said whatever he thought Jim would respond to."

"Do people change?" Rob asks. "Yeah, they do. I'm living proof of that. Mom's living proof of that. Dad, he's made a lot of changes, too."

Jimmy's words show me he changed, but not enough. He is still taking what he wants, no matter the consequences for those around him.

Rob believes his brother reached out to the only family member who might be receptive.

"The only one who would listen would be Dad. There's a trust level there…He knew Dad wouldn't judge him."

Jim's aim in nurturing a relationship with Jimmy stemmed from a latent sense of duty.

"I did those boys wrong. I recognize that," Jim says.

He hoped to be a positive influence on his oldest son, finally. He assumed Jimmy was working as a welder, making good money, and need only cut down on his drinking in order to get his act together.

The earliest letter, and also the shortest, carries no date and a PO Box in Valley City, North Dakota, for a return address. It is scrawled on the front and back of a piece of paper from a small scratch pad like something you might find in a motel for guest convenience. It is the start of the trail, filling in some of the blanks after Jimmy left his mother's home in Michigan in 1994.

---

[*] Quotes from letters preserve the spelling as written.

"I fled to Iowa and tried to start new," he wrote. "I then went to Canada nine months later. Cause of warrant in Michigan for yet another car theft."

Jimmy doesn't mention the Utah charges, which were the more immediate threat to his freedom at that time.

Fifteen photos accompany the note.

One shows an Air Force jet displayed in a park in Valley City, with the notation that his old apartment building is a quarter mile away and visible in the background.

Several photos show muscle cars Jimmy discovered on his travels and also, the first of a series of pictures of cars he owned himself, including a Grand Am GT.

"The color was giving me problems," he wrote, in reference to the bronze paint job, but he doesn't elaborate as to what those "problems" were.

Ten of the photos document earlier travels: Central Iowa in 2007; British Columbia, Canada, in 2007 ("Tree fell on my car, while I was in it. I walked away shaken with a bump on my head. Rear of car was like a smashed beer can."); Isabella State Forest in Minnesota (each summer for the previous four years); Theodore Roosevelt National Park ("You can drive up to buffalo in this park."); Arizona 2007 ("The Road to Nowhere leads to me. Last winter's vacation."); Lake Okanagan British Columbia ("Fifth deepest freshwater lake in world. I camped here 13 years ago for two months").

Jimmy says nothing about his travels in Saskatchewan, Canada, in 2007, in which Weyburn police now say Jimmy robbed a bank of $1,100, or of the time he took off on park rangers in July 2007, losing them along the Saskatchewan-Alberta border, or anything about how he supported himself in the Lake Okanagan area in 1995. There are no known records of him having contact with police in the other locales he mentions, but given that every place Jimmy went, trouble seemed to follow, it is not a stretch to assume crimes were committed in those places too, though they were never attributed to him.

A letter dated January 10, 2009, documents the failed attempt to visit his father over Christmas. He mentioned he searched "Google Earth" but couldn't find the road his dad lived on. Finally, he stopped at a church in the town where his dad's mail is delivered to ask for directions. He complained that someone was following him around, he thought, because of the buffalo on his North Dakota license plate, "so I left and went on to Lynchberg, T.N. to Jack Daniels Distillery Tour."

Jimmy then recounted an earlier visit to Lynchberg in 2004, when he caught on camera, at Jack Daniels Hollow, the image of what he believed to be a "poltergeist."

"Showed a few people and they agreed. A few said Wow! What's that?"

The 2004 visit to Tennessee is one of Jimmy's few references to that time period. October 2003 to May 2005 represents the longest period in his adulthood without some documentation of criminal behavior on his part, begging the obvious question: was there no criminal behavior, or is there just no record of it?

Jimmy wrote his dad about his addictions and shared that he was glad his dad was alive and well.

> I though the Camels and Budwieser would have got ya by now. You must have quit? I quit smoking in 1991. Took me 5 tries— cold turkey. The only drug I do is whiskey, and yes that's a drug. I quit drinking for 2 months then started up for a month. Then quit for a month then something would piss me off, and, to get even I'd go drink.

"I've kicked coke—last I did it was 1996. I smoked it," he wrote, indicating it was because he was not a "needle fan."

The admission does more than let his dad know he is no longer a drug addict. It gives a clue about his lifestyle until the moment he was captured and imprisoned in Canada at the conclusion of his earlier bank-robbing spree.

Pot did not always agree with him, he told his dad.

"When I was in Canada 2 summers ago I smoked pot with some campers. I got so sick I puked! 3 times! So that's not a habit for me. I'm on asprin reginmen—four years ago had a blood clot in leg while in Canada visiting. Leg swelled up like ball-bat & almost died 'again.'"

Jimmy claims he was diagnosed with deep vein thrombosis. He also relates having a bum knee from a "logging injury" in Canada, which solves the mystery of why, when Charlene found video of one of Jimmy's robberies online, she thought his legs looked "funny."

The reference to a "logging injury" struck me as questionable, unless he did that kind of work in prison.

Jimmy told his dad he went to a $2,000 welding class, the implication being that he was then working as a welder. He lamented the loss of the Nova he owned when he left Michigan—but didn't mention abandoning it when he left Utah. He gave an e-mail address where his dad could contact him.

On the back of the last page of the letter are two pieces of information that are surprising to Rob. One is that Jimmy had a hobby—one Rob had also pursued in the past.

Jimmy wrote, "For shits & giggles I play with 70 mph radio controlled cars and 4 wheel drive trucks in the snow. I also fly radio controlled (electric) (Lithuim Polymer Batt) planes. Lost three planes, they just flew away."

On a photograph, the information "Drinkin' and flyin' don't mix," further illuminates the trouble. As Rob learned for himself when he flew radio-controlled airplanes, a plane with a dying battery can lose the signal from its controller and fly off, never to be seen again. That his brother learned the same lesson, repeatedly, is a source of hilarity for Rob, but also part of a growing recognition that as different as they were, there were many similarities they shared.

The January 10 letter also made reference to a "spiritual moment" experienced on the Blue Ridge Parkway, while he was traveling in the Smokey Mountains.

Prior to visiting his dad and before reading any of Jimmy's letters, Rob studied a map of the area near Jim's house and formed the desire, inexplicably, to travel the same parkway that apparently touched Jimmy deeply.

Knowing his brother, though, Rob isn't sure how to take Jimmy's comment about a "spiritual moment," which could as easily have referred to getting drunk as glimpsing God.

That particular letter closed with a "Song of Day." It is Trace Adkins' "Muddy Water." The song ties in with a photo, sent later, from Jack Daniels Hollow, where Jimmy says he did a "self baptism."

The video for "Muddy Water" tells the story of a young man who hitches a ride in an eighteen-wheeler, back to his hometown. He enters a church, where a man (Adkins), in the role of a father or an older brother, welcomes him. They walk to a stream where the young man is surrounded by the congregation. A minister waits for him in the river. There, the young man undergoes a full-immersion baptism amid cheers from the crowd.

Jimmy stayed true to his love of country music, discovered while in prison in Michigan. Jimmy wrote that he liked Montgomery Gentry and owned three of the artist's CDs. He also referenced a perfect setting for "the next Alan Jackson video" on the back of a photo of an antique pickup left to rot somewhere near Williston, North Dakota.

A companion photo, of the same pickup, carries the eerie pronouncement, "Williston, N.D. Where time stands still. Period." He seemed to consider the locale in some way backward—apparently because no one had restored a truck like that.

"I bet I could make this truck run—er, maybe," he wrote.

The photo places Jimmy in the Williston area at some point in the summer of 2008—a full year before the Williston robbery. Other photos in the package show an antique auto parked in Jimmy's old neighborhood in Dilworth, Minnesota—a town where two bank robberies are unsolved. But that wasn't his only law-breaking activity there.

"I was arrested in my backyard while cutting the grass, for a DUI warrant (No show Jimmy). ☐ One DUI in my whole life! Working on a second?"

Jimmy was taken into custody with no one the wiser that he was involved in any more serious criminal activity.

He had included in the mailing pictures of wildlife. There's the photo of a magpie, a reference to a bear walking thirty feet from him in a photo of a North Idaho campground, and the photo of a chipmunk he claims to have fed for two years while camping in northeast Minnesota. Given Jimmy's past abuse of animals, Rob is floored by his brother's self-reported assistance to any wild thing.

"I'd like to see that chipmunk." Rob laughs ruefully.

Charlene is a little more charitable.

"I remember Jimmy being kind to all the animals that we had…but that's what addiction will do to you—whatever it takes to get the next fix—with Jimmy it was sex, and he violated two of the things that he loved. I believe he loved Rob and Runt…But in addiction, you don't care who you hurt."

Jimmy's humor is on display in a letter and picture captions dated January 17, 2009. The return address reads, "270 lbs. Little Jim ☐ Need Slim Fast? Kinda…"

Thirty-three photos are enclosed, many with humorous notations on the back. Of nine self-portraits, all but three were snapped in front of a mirror, or by holding the camera at arm's length. The number of self-portraits reveals to me both a yearning to be known, as well as a lack of contact with other people. The photos would have given police a good look at a serial bank robber—and a pair of sunglasses so frequently photographed in bank surveillance videos over the previous three years.

"Makin faces at the camera," Jimmy wrote on the back of one photo. "I didn't realize how I could scare women and children with this picture (shits & giggles)."

The photo is of Jimmy curling his lips in to show his teeth, with his eyes wide. He is sitting behind the wheel of his car. He wears a blue knit cap and a grey-colored distressed denim jacket. Both items of apparel are later returned to Charlene by the FBI, among Jimmy's personal effects. She sent the items to Rob, who brings them to Jim, who promptly disposes of them at the Goodwill.

Another self-portrait sent to his dad in the same series, also snapped from behind the wheel of his car, says, "A few drinks of Jack Daniels at 7 a.m. and this is the result. True happiness. Without sunglasses! Was thinking of you!"

Jimmy related that another self-portrait was taken at the end of the tour at the Jack Daniels distillery. He is wearing the mirrored sunglasses.

The sunglasses are significant, not only because they appear to be the same ones Jimmy used as his only disguise in several bank holdups, but because the cheap, nonprescription lenses are held in the frame by some JB Weld—a compound Rob is very familiar with. Rob has used JB Weld to fix his own prescription sunglasses. The wraparound style and color of the two pairs of shades is virtually identical, as are the mirrored lenses.

"It's like parallel lives," Rob remarks to his dad.

To which, Jim replies, "Well, you *were* brothers."

Before the conclusion of their first visit in fifteen years, Rob will hang Jimmy's sunglasses on a drapery rod in his dad's house, next to a framed photo of Jimmy. He decides to leave their fate to Jim. Rob is okay with the fact his dad gave away his brother's clothes.

"That's, perhaps, the single most decisive act I've ever seen," Rob says.

Sophomorically hilarious are two photos, both obviously taken on the same day, at a motel. The first was taken in the hallway by a set of stairs and is identical to one the North Dakota Bureau of Criminal Investigation released within a few months of Jimmy's death because it wasn't believed to be material to their investigation. It was a good call. The copy from the police was missing the caption Jimmy sent to his dad: "Going for the worlds longest fart—12 seconds. Holding your letter as a good luck charm."

The photo shows someone's finger got in the way when the shutter snapped, as Jimmy stands near the staircase about twelve feet from the camera, in a pose reminiscent of a cartoon character ready to run in place. A companion photo, snapped to catch Jimmy's reflection in the mirror of a hotel room, shows him winking: "Still holding your letter—going for 2nd attempt of world's longest fart."

Apparently snapped in the same session in front of the mirror, a third photo carries the caption, "I have conquered death. No[t] even bloodclots & trees can kill me."

The caption on one of two photos taken at an Air Force museum in Fargo sounds a similar note, with a quote from a Montgomery Gentry song about how he cheated death and felt lucky to be still be alive.

The setting is outside the museum, in front of a missile. These are the only two other photos which appear to have been taken by someone else. Jimmy is dressed in winter boots, jeans, sunglasses, and the knit cap, with a zip-up grey hooded sweatshirt under his denim jacket, hands in the front pockets of his jeans. His physical presence in the photo is imposing. With 270 pounds on his six-foot-two to six-foot-three-inch frame, he is a hulking figure, but by no means does he appear morbidly obese or physically impaired by his weight. In short, he is not a bad-looking guy, as the tellers in Williston later relate to me, though he obviously lost in the neighborhood of forty pounds before the Williston robbery eight months later. It is just another coincidence—Rob had to lose forty pounds during the same period, in order to meet Air Force weight limits.

Not every self-portrait Jimmy snapped made it into an envelope to be sent to his dad. A shot of Jimmy, bare-chested, in a he-man pose, and reflected in another motel room mirror, was returned to Charlene with Jimmy's possessions. This photo shows the once heavily muscled prison weightlifter grown paunchy, with a flabby chest—man boobs—as one detective on the trail of a serial bank robber labeled it.

Also in the January 17 mailing is another photo from the Jack Daniels tour, of a NASCAR race car sponsored by the distillery. "I drove it there myself," the caption reads. "Lemonade anyone? Number of Jack bottles thrown out after police incidents—2."

Jimmy apparently drove through Kansas on his way home from the failed Christmas trip and reveals still more contacts with police. On one photo, he wrote, "Somewhere after state trooper tore after me and followed me 6 miles. For no reason! Even on back road. Threw 1/2 full bottle of Jack out the window just to be safe L No show Jimmy J."

Also taken on the trip home was a snap of a jacked-up truck in Kansas.

"Remember your 4 x 4 Bronco in 1979? We went off-roading for shits and giggles…I saw a dead cat fall out of the rims of this truck at the McDonalds Drive through."

If the reference to dead cats seems crass or uncaring, a photo of an injured deer taken near Devils Lake, North Dakota, shows compassion, if true.

"Someone hit this deer, not me. (Broken Jaw) Red and sideways in Pic. (Broken leg) walked up to it after it hobbled 10 feet and fell. Patted on head and called game ward to put it down."

Rob finds the story amazing.

"I didn't see him as such a peaceful person."

But the notion of Jimmy feeling compassion for the animal doesn't totally jive. I have to wonder why he didn't use his own pistol to put the animal out of its misery. It is that discord, between past abuse of animals and a possibly self-serving description of himself as something of a hero, that makes it almost impossible for Rob to believe Jimmy went out of his way for any living thing.

For a man constantly on the move and seemingly leery of too much contact with people, Jimmy's letters reveal detail after detail placing himself in a certain place at a certain time, or even in a certain vehicle with specific license plates.

"This is what I drove down to see you in. '95' Grand Am GT. She washed up good. Very shiney. No rust. And it flies! Set cruise control at 114!"

This Grand Am is a deep red color.

A caption on a close-up photo makes reference to the "buffalo" on his license plate. Also curious are two photos of snow piled up at a storage garage in Valley City. One of Jimmy's cars, in fact, was recovered at a storage unit in Valley City after his death.

In the January 17 letter, Jimmy responded to questions his dad had obviously posed to him. He said he was single and believed he had a "kid or two," whom he was trying to locate on the Internet by looking up old girlfriends.

It is this possibility, that Jimmy may have left her grandchildren, that fuels Charlene's interest in telling his story. But there is no way to know where to look.

In this letter, Jimmy gave his dad his cell phone number and begged Jim to call him. The number is the same as one on a TracFone Charlene would receive from the FBI after Jimmy's death. Charlene was able to purchase a charger for it and called some of the numbers in the history. She spoke to a guy at a hobby shop in Utah who remembered Jimmy, but found no one who had had a personal relationship with her son.

Jimmy told his dad he was not on parole or probation.

"Have money & good guy. Also spare kidney. So call & just say hi—Please?"

He went on to speak of "struggles with women" and said he understood what his dad went through with Charlene.

It is frustrating to Charlene that Jimmy revives in his letters the notion she put a restraining order on Jim.

"I never put a restraining order on him. I wanted him to come see his kids," Charlene says. If any warrant existed, she says, it was filed by the Friend of the Court, which pursues nonpayment of child support.

Jimmy asked his dad to send more photos—photos later retrieved by police from Jimmy's car, which show the wooden train models Jim made as a hobby. The trains are a testament to the memory of the old iron Lionel train set Jim played with as a child—the same set Jimmy hocked as a teen for a few bucks to get high or drunk. The loss of the toy train haunts Rob to this day, not only because it was his dad's, but because of the memories of Christmases past. For Rob, it just isn't Christmas without the train set and the little puffs of smoke that came out of the engine as it made its way around the track, which was set up beneath a Christmas tree.

Jimmy shared with his dad his own belief about the meaning of life—a philosophy somewhat evolved from his statement in earlier letters that it was "every man for himself."

"I think the meaning of life is to have fun whenever you can. Last night I went for a steak dinner & made funny faces at people and objects. But no Obama jokes! Hope this fella Obama can change—not just U.S. but the world attitude towards the U.S.'s short comings."

In a single paragraph, Jimmy reveals an ability to laugh at himself and perhaps most amazingly of all from a self-professed "nigger beater," a tolerance for the nation's first black president. It's a glimmer of a start of a conscience in a man who admitted that fifteen years earlier, "I fucked off to Iowa & lost track of you—& myself.

"No jobs, no hope & I left never to return to Michigan. Then about one or two months later went back to get the Nova outta the back yard, in Taylor (police state). I've got 5,000 cash on my card & in the bank... Well Dad, God bless!"

He leaves out the fact it was Charlene who helped get his Nova running in 1994. Or that he had a warrant in Iowa when he left. The reference to $5,000 in the bank, presumably, is the money he still had on hand following a robbery in Jamestown, North Dakota, the previous December.

That Jimmy was robbing banks, both before, during, and after these letters were written indicates to me that his baptism, any change of attitude, or developing compassion for animals was not enough to keep him from continuing to take what he wanted from those more vulnerable than himself.

A letter addressed to "James 'Evil Knevil' Krimm," dated January 31, 2009, and mailed on February 2, paints a stark picture of Jimmy's alcoholism.

> I quit drinkin 5 days ago—lets see how long this last(s)...For a long drive to see you it would help to stay sober. And drunk people are not always the best company to have over—even if they are functional alcoholics.
> In 2004 I spent $12,000 at the bar in one year. And $6,000 more on 'Jack' that same year!

I could see how the admission of spending $18,000 on alcohol in a single year would tend to reinforce the notion that Jimmy was working in a job that paid well. Jim couldn't have known that Jimmy's only career was as a bank robber.

It appears to me, once again, that Jimmy seemed to be supplying clues about what he was doing at a particular point in time—a point in time when he had just gotten out of a Canadian jail and was extradited to Iowa on an old charge. It is a reference to a time period for which no record exists of where he was or what he was doing: October 2003 to May 2005.

I can't help putting myself in his shoes for a minute. I am a felon released from a Canadian prison after seven years. After being transported to Iowa and having an old case dismissed, I am dumped on the street. I have no assets. I have no friends, no family, and no money. But I have one skill that has served me pretty well in the past, and the pay is good. Even though I tell myself I'm just going to rob one bank, what's to stop me from robbing several?

If Jimmy resumed the single-teller-drawer, note-pass-style of robbery he pursued in Canada, he might have had to rob seventeen or eighteen banks to keep himself in booze for a year. But if he honed his MO and displayed a real gun with a takeover-style robbery method in which he cleaned out multiple teller drawers in each bank, he could up his take. At least, most of the time.

A thwarted robbery in Mansfield, South Dakota, is one hilarious possibility. A detective in South Dakota told me about a robbery on March 31, 2005, in which a guy pulled up on a motorcycle. When the demand for money was made, the old guy who ran the bank told the robber, "The guy before you took all our money out."

The would-be robber said not a word, turned, and rode away. Witnesses said the man was so large he made the motorcycle look small—he looked like an ape on a tricycle. The motorcycle was later found in a tree grove. All efforts to trace it were unsuccessful. It appeared to have been a bike completely assembled from junk parts. The case has never been solved, but it sure sounds like Jimmy. He learned how to ride a dirt bike as a kid, his mom by his side. And though he was never employed as a mechanic, he certainly had mechanical abilities.

There is no proof Jimmy robbed more than the eighteen banks for which he was convicted in Canada and the sixteen banks identified as likely matches by a Devils Lake, North Dakota, police detective, but if Bill Rehder had to guess, "There are more."

The retired FBI agent bases that presumption on thirty-three years of experience with cases just like Krimm's. He retired in 1999 as the head of the bank robbery unit in Los Angeles. Rehder made a career out of predicting what serial bank robbers would do. He is the coauthor of the 2003 book, *Where the Money Is*.

If there is a lapse of time between robberies, Rehder tells me, you can practically count on there being more crimes that simply have not been attributed in the spree.

Hearing Jimmy's tale, Rehder is sure Jimmy was as addicted to bank robbery as he was dependent on alcohol. But he doesn't just base that belief on Jimmy's history.

"To a man, every bank robber is a serial bandit. Nobody gets caught doing just one," Rehder says.

The average is six robberies before an arrest.

"You can't *not* do a second one. Once you pull one, that's it. You're hooked on it."

Jimmy had obvious addiction problems—not to mention that he had few other skills, no job history, and no Social Security number that wouldn't link him to a prior criminal record.

"He's a subsistence robber—he's robbing to support himself, just depending on how much money he needed," Rehder says. He had seen the type often enough.

"He's got a lifestyle. This guy doesn't need much to get by; he's just existing, moving from place to place…motel to motel…paying for auto storage."

Usually, Rehder says, it is an addiction to drugs that fuels a spree. Drug addicts need more money to get their next fix, whereas an alcoholic just needs a few bucks for his next bottle. Jimmy may have started out robbing banks as a means of doing drugs when he was in Canada, but with middle age approaching and the majority of his adult life spent behind bars, he had hardly a chance of making a legitimate life for himself and no idea, except his mother's example of slaving at three jobs to keep a roof overhead, of how to go about it. Robbing banks had become a necessity.

When he was arrested in May 2005 and spent a year in an Iowa prison, Jimmy was convicted of a crime that shows he had the means to perform the one job he knew: he was a felon with a firearm in his possession.

There is something else about Jimmy, which Rehder sees as indicative of what he calls the "classic serial bank bandit."

"He's a loner…no pals…He's living this lone-wolf lifestyle."

But at the same time, "These guys usually can't keep their mouth shut."

Jimmy knows he can't tell his dad he is robbing banks, but he gives his dad clue after clue, seemingly begging for someone to ask him how he could afford to spend $18,000 on booze in one year—one year after serving seven years for bank robbery.

At some point during the nine months or so that Jimmy was in contact with his dad, he called, seemingly fishing for just such a question.

Jimmy said, "Is there anything you want to ask me?"

Stunned, Jim asked, "What?"

"Is there anything you want to ask me?"

"No," Jim answered, and Jimmy hung up.

Jim has no idea what Jimmy might have been after.

Could he have been asking about the traffic warning he sent his dad one day in February? Jimmy got the warning for driving eleven miles per hour over the speed limit in Nebraska, pinpointing, once again, where in the country he was on a given day. Why would you send something like that unless you wanted someone to ask you why it was important?

The significance of the ticket is a mystery, but Rehder says, "I think if you look back, you're gonna find a robbery there somewhere on that day."

Or perhaps, nearby, a few weeks earlier? Mining the Internet for a connection to the ticket, I found a report on the Web site of the Nebraska TV station, WOWT. The robbery has never been solved.*

> Jan, 15, 2009: A bank was robbed in the town of Carleton, Nebraska Thursday. The Nebraska State Patrol has released pictures that will hopefully lead to an arrest.
>
> Carleton is in Thayer County, which is in southeastern Nebraska.
>
> Investigators say a man entered the Citizen State Bank about 3:15 pm Thursday. He demanded money and took off with the cash. He claimed to have a weapon but did not show one.
>
> He fled in a maroon Pontiac Grand Am, which can be seen in a bank surveillance photo.
>
> The bank robber is described as a white male, in his 40's, with brown hair. He stood about 5'11" and weighed about 220 pounds. Witnesses describe him as having a fat nose and fat fingers.

---

*   http://www.wowt.com/home/headlines/37686904.html

He was wearing baggy blue jeans, a flannel shirt, a blue t-shirt, and a dark brown heavy winter coat.

The photo accompanying the story is consistent with Jimmy's style of dress in photos he sent his dad. Letters to his dad tell me Jimmy was driving a reddish Grand Am at the time. He was on his way home from trying to see his dad at Christmas, traveling through Kansas and then Nebraska, where he got the speeding ticket.

By March, Jimmy was driving a new car, a 1996 Mitsubishi Galant with 113,000 miles on it. It cost him $1,800.

"I got the little puppy up to 130 mph!…The speedometer goes to 140 mph and it still smells new inside…starts in -20 degrees F temps, but the trans has issues…2,000 miles on it so far & its doing okay."

He wrote on the back of a photo of the car, "The color?" as if he was concerned about it for some reason. On another photo, he referred to the car as his "green monster."

He said his insurance company was unfairly canceling his policy because he didn't have a driver's license.

"I don't crash, nor in the 3½ years of Progressive Insurance have I filed a claim," Jimmy lamented.

Rob knows millions of people are insured with Progressive, but the fact both he and his brother are among them is just one more weird coincidence.

A letter dated March 27, 2009, and postmarked the same day contains a two-and-a-half page diatribe from Jimmy about trouble with an auto dealership he felt messed up a repair on one of his cars. The writing in this letter is clearly more haphazard and sloppy than that in the others, a fact Jim attributes to the probable intoxication level of his son when he was writing it, having sat around a dealership for four days waiting on repairs.

He also made reference to having visited Nebraska and north Georgia. Heavy snow from the winter of 2009 resulted in spring flooding along the Red River in North Dakota, forcing Jimmy from his usual haunts. Jimmy predicted the flood would be a Katrina-sized disaster. It did require mass evacuations and resulted in near ghost-town conditions for a couple of weeks.

A group of pictures sent with the letter show Jimmy's knowledge of the news in the region. There are several photos of a broadcasting tower and a series of photos of windmills that were springing up on the North Dakota prairie.

"North Valley City. No windmills here a year ago. Now about 100 of them as far as you can see," reads one caption.

Jimmy displayed knowledge of agricultural enterprise, too.

"Many fields of corn unharvested Due to fall floods of 08 12,000 acres of sugar beets left in the ground," he wrote.

On another, "Behind this picture of a car is a mountain of corn. Fuck Africa, we're making 'Jack'—er—a—no—Ethenol!"

His comments also illustrate Jimmy traveled the same roads more than once, over a period of time.

"Remember that purple Grand Am GT I sold for $1,500? Some Indian woman drove it 4 months and run out of oil on the Highway. It's sat here a year. Parts car," he wrote.

He mentioned camping at Lake Oahe, South Dakota, and also spotting some wild turkeys near the Nebraska border.

A newspaper clipping from the *Daily Republic* of Mitchell, South Dakota, about the Red River flooding, accompanies a letter dated April 20, 2009, and mailed the same day.

In the letter, Jimmy referenced a call to his dad the day before, in which they apparently talked about the extent of flooding in the Valley City area.

Jimmy shared he was up to 277 pounds and needed to chop wood all summer "like last year." It appears he was prone to seasonal weight gain—and loss. Photos from a Lisbon, North Dakota, bank in early summer 2008 are of a man much larger than one who robbed the bank in Williston a little more than a year later—at the end of the summer. He also gave a hint as to how he might have gained some of the weight: "K.F.C. = chicken—Krimms Fuckin' Cookin'."

There are more flood pictures, more old cars, and a picture of some wild horses with the notation, "Wild horses. Do not eat."

On a photo of a Nova, like he used to own, he wrote, "It hurt to take this picture."

And on a photo of his favorite model airplane, he explained a motel "maid" later broke it: "$180 in the garbage."

The last of Jimmy's letters arrived just a few weeks before his death, detailing an incident in which he claimed to have saved a kid pinned beneath his ATV when it flipped at a campground. Rob and I are floored. What would that kid think, we wonder, if he knew he was rescued by a serial bank robber and sexual abuser? But there is no way to trace what actually happened, or where.

Jim learned of Jimmy's suicide in a phone call from Williston detective Mark Hanson. He told Hanson he hadn't seen his son in thirty years, implying he knew nothing about Jimmy.

When I broach the subject of an interview with Jim on the night he showed us the letters, it does not go over well. The next morning, he apologizes for his reaction, which was a little hostile. He agrees to answer questions by e-mail. I send him a long list on my way home from North Carolina. He decides not to answer, preferring instead to let Jimmy's letters speak for themselves.

The FBI has never contacted anyone in the Krimm family to ask if they have information about Jimmy's activities in the final years of his life.

"Still holding your letter—going for 2nd attempt of worlds longest fart."

March 27, 2009

Hello

Finally got a minute to write! I've been so dam busy. I'm just glad I can sit here and talk to ya. You're the only one who LISTENS!!!

The dealership deal really fucked me up timewise—4 working days. I was in Iowa 1 day when car took a shit. Iowa people are very polite & friendly nice people. Except dealderships—

Nebraska & N. Georga are bad attitudes. (Middle fingers in the air?)

(My God Yankee plates in N. Georga. You are the enemy!! ☐

Back to Iowa event—Dealership put "modulator" under coil on car when battery issue got "squased." Modulator did not fix stalling. "Different mechanic" worked on it next 2 days, put fuel pump in tank & fuel filter on day 2. "That did not work."

Just filled up gas tank at a punjabi shit hole gas station and ask mechanic "wonder what the gas looks like, I filled up in the backwoods station."

He said, "Gas in my Jug looked Cloudy."

I said "Gas should be <u>clear</u> not cloudy." Gas left in a tank will go bad in 60 days, when it does it looks <u>milky.</u>

He says let me call my buddy and see what he thinks might be wrong.

Day 3 – 8 am Im at dealership seeing what's going on telling them gas is bad drain it & try good gas! (gritted teeth face).

I go back into shop and this punk is telling me "Its crank shaft sensor. And if its not that then it's the fuel injectors"!!!!

He broke the crank ses & now has to pull the oil pan! To which I was told I'll have to pay for his Fuck-up! I called the manager—told story—got bill cut in half. Went to service desk—said "Your done, push it out back and bill me out."

So these Auto Repair rip-offs steal for a living and don't go to Jail/ Why? They punch a time clock, which is attached to bussness lawyers, corporate lawyers, and insurance companys. And the public is on a need to know basis.

NEXT Page as Paul Harvey would say—he died last month. Good-day? Or he would say "Goooood day!"

Floods up here have made all wildlife come out onto the roads so they can be run over by fleeing flood victims like me. I'm out of Fargo now. My "geo" is in Valley City in a storage garage high up on a hill. Wait I gotta go take a shit.

Okay I'm Back, good thing we were'nt on the phone. Of Course we have all done that once in our life Right? Noooo…Not me…Nope…Maybe pissin once.

(Okay next page)

I've never seen so much water. Almost All Roads are closed up here. (100 miles of water) Words Cannot describe it except one—Biblical And it not because Bibles are floating everwhere! Hint-Hint. But the Mayor and City Counsel opened up the morning briefing with a prayer! One guy on T.V. Asked "is this Gods wrath?"

I wonder if Bibles FLoat? Can Garth Brooks make another unanswered Prayers song? This winter was worst in more than 10 yrs.

Live stock died, pets died & wild animals & yes people Died this year, cause of this shit. Yesterday I saw a newscaster wipe a tear from his eye. (While I was still up that way) (watching worst flood in 500 yrs to happen)

Bismarck has had bad 100 yr flood cause of ice jams. S. Dakota (land of ass holes) is flooding as well as west Minnesota.

So I'm in Mitchell, S.Dakota. Cause by the time you read this Fargo will be a Katrina disaster. You'll see…I'm doing good on money no worrys. Livin in a $150 a week motel.

Finally got to fly my airplane! Wait Im going to fly it again! Right now! Be back in 5 mins.

Okay, Frostbite dam near on hands but didn't crash! Did 2 loops Record is 5 loops. Picture of plane in next batch of pictures. Runs 7 mins wide open on cellphone battery. Goes as far as eyes can see! Broke plastic propeller on landing—cause its so big—no clearance hardly. Motor still idels on landing too. So Im not pushing the Right button?

Buyin' Digital Camera! Just figured this shit out. Cause Wal-mart stoped 1 hour photos!

Gotta go shit again—Nope Just kidin Ya!!!

Love Ya—Jimmy

CHAPTER SEVENTEEN

Obsession

By the time I meet her, Sue Schwab, a police detective in Devils Lake, North Dakota, has spent three years on the same trail I am now following.

Schwab's obsession began when a man in sunglasses strode into a branch bank a block from her office, committed a robbery, and walked away, seemingly into thin air.

"It was reported at about 3:05 in the afternoon," Schwab recalls, on March 29, 2007.

The Ramsey National Bank branch is so close to the combined law enforcement center—police, sheriff, and highway patrol—officers were on the scene in seconds, "but he was long gone."

Schwab shares the story on a Saturday afternoon, in her office. She is dressed casually. Her petite frame and blond hair, at first glance, probably make criminals think she is a pushover, but this lady, I can tell, is tough as nails. I have driven nearly five hours across the state to meet her. Three months earlier, Schwab put away her files on her mystery bank bandit, but when I called, she was willing to dig them out again.

Shortly after the robbery, Schwab interviewed some of the tellers, who told her the subject walked into the enclosed entry, walked up to the glass window, and made his demand.

"The girls were very upset," she says. "He pulled out a white envelope," with a demand for money, and also stated verbally, "Give me the money, big bills."

Witnesses recall the note, written in black pen with sloppy block letters, said, "THIS IS A ROBBERY, I HAVE A GUN," but the robber did not show a gun. Afterward, "He walked out very casually, like he was strolling out of a grocery store," carrying $4,000.

A teletype with the man's description was put out.

"But we had no vehicle so that really cuts things down right away. We had officers checking motels for descriptions. They stopped some people who were walking who matched the general description...It was frustrating. After probably an hour or two of immediate action, we were still looking, looking..."

It was the first bank robbery ever in the town of seven thousand people. The impetus to solve the case, Schwab says, had as much to do with wanting to provide closure to victims, as trying to clear the case.

"People want to feel safe in their community, so there's a lot of questions. The press would always ask, like, they would do a story like every couple of weeks at first, then every couple of months, they want to know. And they would say, 'Police Department frustrated' because it was unsolved."

For all anyone knew, the robber could still be in the community, but as time went on and no new information surfaced, Schwab abandoned that theory. If it was a local, someone would have heard something, but there was not one whisper of information.

Solving the robbery became Schwab's "obsession."

"I have a tendency to get more obsessed as a case goes on and not solved. So I would be watching everything; I would be looking for everything. I was checking other places where there may have been a robbery—if there was anything that was similar."

It would be five months before Schwab got her next solid lead—and it came to her when she least expected it.

"What really caused me to become obsessed was Dilworth [Minnesota] on August 17, 2007. There was a bank robbery there. I was up at the doctor's office." She was sitting in the waiting room. "I saw the bank robbery on KVLY-TV...and it was the same guy."

She had examined the grainy footage from the Devils Lake robbery over and over, until the robber's body shape and movements were burned into her brain. After seeing just a snippet of the Dilworth video on the news, "I knew it, just the way he walked, the way he looked...and I stood up, and I said, 'That's the guy!'"

The other people in the waiting room were shocked.

"I said, 'That's our bank robber!' And people, of course, are staring at me, and I sat back down."

Schwab called Dilworth to get a copy of the video.

"And I watched it and watched it and watched it. I watched it for years." She laughs. "I'd have it out trying to find something—and at that point, people here, too, would look at it and say, 'That's the same guy! That's the same guy!' And so I started checking into more places that might have had bank robberies."

An FBI agent indicated there were some similarities to robberies in Jackson, Minnesota, that occurred on July 18, 2006, and then, one in LeMars, Iowa, on August 4, 2006.

"And there was a bank robbery at Park River, too, during this span...I believe it probably is the same person," says Schwab.

Before Dilworth, there was also Canby, Minnesota, on May 11, 2007.

"I just kept online constantly. I'd just Google bank robberies, anywhere...and then I came up with one that looked very similar to ours that happened on January 4, 2008, in Duluth, Minnesota.

"Just looking at the way the person walked," Schwab says, he seemed to fit. But there was another tip in that footage. "He had this big watch on, and in our robbery, this guy had this big watch on his hand, and you could see that. Plus, he had kind of a lumbering walk, I thought, and the person in Dilworth had kind of a lumbering walk...just the body build or the movement, just reminded me very much of him."

Charlene, I knew, received just such a large watch among Jimmy's personal effects after his death. And Jimmy's walk, due to what he claimed was a logging injury, was pretty distinctive.

Schwab jokes she became so familiar with the suspect, "We could tell when he got a haircut!"

Schwab and the department's office manager would frequently discuss the case, sharing theories and going over the clues that convinced them it was all the same guy. One similarity they noticed again and again was a physical feature Schwab calls "man boobs"—fleshy pectorals, which appeared consistent in the footage and photos Schwab was amassing from various bank robberies in the region.

Next, Schwab became aware of some robberies in South Dakota. A bank in Redfield was robbed March 28, 2008. A month later, he struck at Watertown.

"I would call agencies, and call agencies. And I would get their photos or videos...and then Lisbon [North Dakota] had one on the eighteenth of June of 2008."

By that time, Schwab had collected information on ten robberies in four different states, but no one seemed to take her seriously.

After Lisbon, there was a robbery in Wahpeton, North Dakota on July 2, 2008. The surveillance tape from that robbery picked up the suspect on the sidewalk, where he came face-to-face with a bank customer, before heading inside, hopping a counter, and heading back out the way he came, with an empty soda pop carton full of money. Items of clothing found following a later robbery are an exact match.

Despite the fact a suspect with the same basic physical description seemed to be striking again and again—in similar small-to-medium-sized towns in the area—few of Schwab's peers were interested in listening to her theory about a serial bank bandit.

A robbery in Mandan, North Dakota, on October 15, 2008, Schwab believes, is another in the spree.

"I just didn't know who this person was, so I contacted all of these correctional facilities in Iowa, because he had done one there...I thought maybe he was a veteran...because it looked like his leg was messed up... just a wild-goose chase...I really knew nothing except what was on these videos."

Schwab figured the man had tattoos on his arms because he always wore long sleeves, even in the summer.

"I was just obsessing, just constantly looking, working on it all day long. People would come in and tease me...Every time there was a bank robbery, they'd tease me, like, 'Don't tell her there's another bank robbery because she'll start obsessing again.'"

After a robbery in Jamestown, North Dakota, on December 16, 2008, Schwab expected to get the same reaction she had in just about every other town. She would call different jurisdictions, trying to follow leads in the other cases, and more times than not, get brushed off because it was old news.

"I was getting frustrated because I thought this person was a serial bank robber and he was going to hurt someone eventually, because he seemed to be carrying a gun and using a gun quite a bit in these robberies."

Schwab feared, eventually, someone was going to get seriously hurt or killed.

"And it did seem like some agencies, the people I spoke with, at times, like FBI, that they weren't taking it seriously. Like, they didn't see the seriousness of the situation. I was thinking there should be some type of task force. Something."

The Jamestown police chief and the police in South Dakota were taking it seriously.

"We even had a meeting, in January 2009. A group of law enforcement came together, and we discussed it."

Though there were concerned officers, no one had much to go on, Schwab says. Many times, there was not even a description of a vehicle to look for, and a suspect who just walked away like nothing happened.

Though the TV airwaves are full of bandits who are given catchy names to interest the public in their cases in the hope it will eventually lead to a capture, no one ever named her suspect. The Soda Box Bandit was one name that would have fit, because several times, the robber used an empty cardboard soda or beer box to haul his loot. Schwab laughs at the suggestion, remembering that the robber used an empty Shasta box in the Wahpeton robbery.

"I was calling different places after that to see who actually carries Shasta anymore…because I thought, you don't see Shasta that often…so I was calling grocery stores."

On March 9, 2009, *the same bank* in Dilworth was robbed again, but Schwab couldn't know the robber probably got a huge kick out of watching the coverage on TV the next day—his birthday.

"It just seemed like he was so reckless," Schwab says.

Perhaps most frustrating to Schwab was the lack of interest by the FBI, even after the death of a bank robber in Williston, North Dakota.

"I suppose the FBI has to be careful, and they said they can't come out and say it," even if there was a good possibility Jimmy Krimm was the man behind all of these crimes.

Bill Rehder can understand Schwab's frustrations. The retired FBI agent calls it the "duck theory."

"If it waddles, quacks, and loves the water, it's a duck."

Rehder profiled dozens of Jimmy Krimms in his role as head of the bank robbery division in the bank robbery capitol of the nation: Los Angeles. A book about Rehder's career became my first primer on how bank bandits operate. When I call him on the phone to get his opinion on the Krimm case, he is clearly fascinated, just as he was when he was tracking robbers for the Bureau.

As Rehder sees it, "You have one guy. He's big. Takeover style, he goes behind the teller line."

Sometimes he carries an empty carton; sometimes he uses a note; sometimes he shows a gun; and sometimes he wears a mask. Other times, he's in sunglasses and a ball cap, but the consistent physical size and the general style of the robberies are all the same.

"It's not a huge leap of faith at all to say, 'Hey, these are all done by the same guy,'" Rehder says. "Somebody should have been able to put these together."

And Sue Schwab did, long before anyone else took any notice.

Rehder doesn't buy the FBI's excuse that the crimes can't be attributed to a dead man.

"I'd be looking at this guy," Rehder says. If there were other robberies, with the same MO, the same physical description, and a similar photo, "I'm solving the case."

Like Schwab, "I'd have been fascinated enough by the guy's lifestyle I would have jumped on it with both feet," Rehder says.

During his career, Rehder had no problem attributing crimes to a robber who couldn't be tried and convicted. But Rehder says you have to consider the priorities, once a serial bandit is off the street.

"The FBI doesn't have a big desire to solve these cases now. They're solving a 'paper case.'"

They know Krimm's spree is over, and they have plenty of active serial bank bandits to pay attention to. There are dozens of serial bandits operating in the United States at any given time. The FBI clearance rate for bank robbery is in the neighborhood of 80 percent, because when a robber is caught for one crime, typically, he is tied to many more.

"I'm sure they solved a bunch of robberies on him," Rehder speculates, but for one reason or another, the FBI doesn't care to make it public if they don't have to.

Rehder was known in his heyday in Los Angeles for giving bandits a catchy name that would intrigue TV stations enough they'd put a picture on the news.

A code name like the "Mountain Dew bandit" would have gotten the spree more publicity, Rehder says, but publicity isn't always seen as an asset by law enforcement.

Still, he says, "Given a little time, I would have come up with something," to get the public interested in the case in the hope someone might finger the culprit. "If he had a good picture and a good name, I could get it broadcast."

There is photographic evidence to suggest Jimmy Krimm robbed as many as sixteen banks between March 2006 and September 14, 2009, but to date, only a handful of cases have been officially closed.

I file a Freedom of Information Act request in the spring of 2010 seeking to identify closed bank robbery cases in which Krimm is named as a possible suspect. After months of waiting, initial document releases from the FBI contain less information than Schwab's files, though they do attribute to Krimm several more of the robberies she identified as part of his spree.

For Rehder, the answers are pretty obvious.

"It's all the same guy...It's highly unusual that you would have the same general physical description, similar photographs, the same general MO," and nearly all in a swath that intersects the states of North Dakota, South Dakota, Iowa, and Minnesota, and all, seemingly, coming to a close with the death of Jimmy Krimm in September 2009.

"This would seem to be an easy matter to put together, quite frankly. This is not rocket science," Rehder says, as long as someone is paying attention.

Unfortunately, "They're not paying attention to them in some parts of the country. The FBI is not even getting good reports from some local police departments as to whether a bank robbery has occurred."

And that's partly the FBI's fault.

"The Bureau has kind of pulled in its horns after 9/11," shifting its priorities to counterterrorism.

"Violent crime, in particular, is one of the lowest priority matters the Bureau works right now. Local PD and sheriffs can handle it," Rehder says. "The Bureau does go out and work some of them. Other parts of the country, not so much."

Even though, with Jimmy Krimm's death, Schwab knows there is little point in continuing her investigation, several pieces of information come to light after his death. It was a lot easier to trace his whereabouts once she had a name.

"He does have a very long record," she says. He was arrested twice for driving under the influence of alcohol during the span when his U.S. spree was occurring.

The first citation was in Becker County, Minnesota, near Detroit Lakes.

"He was released the day before our robbery. Luckily, the highway patrol down in that area, he actually had kept the video for whatever reason. So I have that."

Once again, someone has surprised me with evidence I could never have imagined existed. Just like Charlene handing me Jimmy's Michigan prison letters and Jim showing me Jimmy's last letters, Schwab is producing for me something so vital, so valuable, I can hardly believe it.

The video is a gold mine for Schwab, who tried for so long to get into the mind-set of Jimmy Krimm, and for his family, who had not seen him in sixteen years. For me, a person who has heard Jimmy's words only on paper or through other people's recollections, hearing and seeing him speak is a revelation.

It is about 7:00 PM, March 18, 2007, when a Minnesota Highway Patrol trooper stops a small maroon car for making a wide turn. The video lasts about fifty minutes, about twenty minutes of which contain images and audio of Jimmy Krimm answering the officer's questions and taking field sobriety tests.

He looks trim and fit, wearing jeans and a sweatshirt or long-sleeved T-shirt tucked in, with a ball cap on his head. He has a goatee. As the trooper is running the plates, information comes back on a Michigan warrant outstanding for James Edward Krimm. The trooper goes to the car and asks Jimmy about a previous stop when he was warned about clearing the warrant, but his answer is nondescript. Whatever the charge, the dispatcher tells the trooper Michigan is unwilling to extradite. (Schwab learns later it is for a car theft in 1994, in West Bloomfield, Michigan.)

Jimmy displays some paranoia early in his contact with the trooper, when the officer makes reference to Jimmy living in Dilworth.

"How do you know I live in Dilworth?" Jimmy asks, repeating the question more than once as the trooper attempts to proceed. Finally, the trooper motions back to his car, saying he has a computer.

Jimmy hands the trooper an instructional permit. He has no driver's license. The trooper opens the passenger door of the car and asks about an open container in the back seat.

"Why are you searching my car?" Jimmy asks.

"Do you have a problem with me searching your car?"

"Yes," says the ex-con, who once took a paralegal course. Jimmy mutters something about "improper search and seizure."

The trooper asks him to get out of the car and begins administering the horizontal gaze nystagmus test. In the test, the subject is asked to follow a pen or finger with his or her eyes. If the subject's eyes bounce at the sides as they follow, it is an indication of intoxication. You are not supposed to move your head. Jimmy moves his head.

Jimmy stumbles slightly as he follows the trooper to the front of the car to perform other field tests. The trooper asks him to do a heel-toe walk. Jimmy asks if he can put his coat on because it's cold.

He is polite, answering nearly every question with "Yessir" and "No, sir."

"Any questions?" the trooper asks before commencing the heel-toe test. Again, Jimmy complains of the cold.

"I'm kinda cold," Jimmy whines, and I read in his voice that he is trying to manipulate the officer. "It's kinda chilly. Can I put my coat on?"

The officer ignores the request, but Jimmy interrupts him again.

"I'm cold. I'm starting to shiver."

The trooper dismisses Jimmy's lament, telling him he won't be outside that long. It's not that cold.

Jimmy seems to do okay on the test. Next, he has to hold one foot up in the air for thirty seconds. Following that test, the trooper notices a pocket knife in a sheath on Jimmy's belt and tells Jimmy he is going to remove it and place it on the dashboard of the car. He lets Jimmy grab his coat out of the back seat and put it on.

"What's this?" the trooper asks, looking in the back seat again. He holds up some kind of aluminum can wrapped up in a plastic grocery sack. Jimmy says it's a can of oil. Then the trooper asks about a bottle under the passenger seat. He says it looks like a bottle of alcohol.

"That's what you thought when you pulled out that can of oil." Jimmy smirks.

The officer goes to his car and gets the breathalyzer device and asks Jimmy to take the test.

"I'd like to ask why first. Just because you asked, doesn't make it right," Jimmy says.

The trooper tells him he has probable cause to believe Jimmy is intoxicated, based on the other tests. The trooper, by this time, has asked Jimmy repeatedly if he has had anything to drink.

"No sir, no sir," Jimmy answers, again and again.

He blows a .137. Legal limit is .08. He's under arrest. As the trooper goes back to his car for something, Jimmy can be seen on camera, almost imperceptibly shaking his head. At this point, he looks across the road, looks at his car, and it's not hard to imagine he is sizing up his chances for flight.

"Were you drinking when I stopped you?" the trooper asks again, when he returns. Jimmy declines to answer any more questions. When the trooper comes with cuffs, Jimmy quickly places his hands behind his back—so quickly, it's as if the procedure is very familiar to him. The trooper tells him, "We'll cuff you up front so you can sit easier."

"Okay, that's cool," Jimmy says. After placing Jimmy in the patrol car, the trooper can be seen on camera searching Jimmy's car. He finds a mix of what appears to be Wild Turkey and Mountain Dew in a cup between the front seats.

He opens the trunk, which looks orderly. The trooper examines a black and grey backpack, zipping and unzipping all of its compartments.

"He's got a lot of stuff in here," the trooper comments. The contents include groceries and clothing. He notes there's a CD player and a scanner in the front of the car.

"The scanner? What's that about?" he asks Jimmy, when he returns to the patrol car.

"I use it for emergency weather reports."

"Why is it on a police channel when you're driving?"

Jimmy answers again that it's for weather.

The trooper asks if there is a large amount of money in the car or anything valuable Jimmy doesn't want to have towed. "No, sir. Not at all."

Then, Jimmy starts talking about all of the other "idiot" people driving around, complaining because he is getting pulled over for the second time in a month, "for nothing."

The trooper says he was pulled over because he made a wide turn. Jimmy says he was making a wide turn "out of respect" for the officer, because he wasn't sure which lane the officer was in.

"I wasn't speeding, swerving, and you still pulled me over. I don't understand it. I never will. I lived a long time in the United States of America. I've lived in Minnesota maybe six months. I've been stopped twice for nothing. I see these people driving like idiots, violating the speed laws—tailgating—cutting people off. It just kinda bothers me a little. You know what I'm talking about. You've been off duty and seen these people drive like idiots. I'm not one."

There is an edge in Jimmy's voice. He has to be annoyed he is getting arrested, and it's as if he can't stop himself from delivering some commentary. Rob's past comments about Jimmy having no filter between his mouth and his brain come to my mind. The trooper tells him he should write to his congressmen about the need for more officers on patrol.

"Yeah, you're right," Jimmy answers, but still he cannot let go of the fact he's been pulled over for some "funny" things.

"But you're not getting arrested for a funny thing now," the trooper tells him. "Drinking and driving—and you shouldn't be driving without a license."

"You're so right," Jimmy says. "I went and got a permit and had it in my mind to get a license."

The trooper tells him he won't be able to get his car out of the impound unless he has a licensed driver with him. The trooper then goes back out to the car to conduct a written inventory of the contents, noting the items previously mentioned, along with the scanner, which is picking up police chatter.

"You're not supposed to have that," the trooper can be heard saying to himself, outside the patrol car once more. The trooper can be seen on camera, walking back to his own car with a coffee mug and the alcohol he has collected from Jimmy's car.

Jimmy, inside the patrol car, can be heard to mutter, "This is bullshit."

When the trooper comes back to car with the scanner, he tells Jimmy, "This is playing back Becker County Police channels. You can't have that."

"Said who?" Jimmy asks.

"Said the State of Minnesota."

"Oh really? Even for emergency weather?" Jimmy asks.

"They give emergency weather bulletins on the radio, too."

"No, they don't, sir," Jimmy answers.

The trooper goes back outside. Jimmy sits in the car muttering about how much it will cost to get the car back. I can't help wondering what licensed driver he found to go with him the next day to retrieve the car. The arrest also explains the incident Jimmy mentioned to his dad, when he was picked up in Dilworth for an outstanding DUI warrant.

Another interesting tidbit Sue Schwab uncovered is a contact with her own dispatch, which occurred on December 1, 2008. Jimmy called the law enforcement center in Devils Lake to report an injured deer—proving the story he'd written on the back of a photo of an injured deer was true, after all. It also proves he was certain enough of not being fingered for the Devils Lake robbery, he wasn't worried about traveling in that area again.

Schwab's research also uncovered contacts with police in McCone County, Montana, on July 29, 2006, for misdemeanor theft—ten days after the Jackson, Minnesota, robbery—as well as an arrest in Idaho, on July 25, 2009, less than two months before Jimmy's death.

The Idaho incident would be Jimmy's last known contact with police before the Williston robbery. According to records from the Shoshone County Sheriff's Office, Jimmy was arrested for driving under the influence after terrorizing some people at a campground. Corporal Darius Dustin wrote in his report that he was contacted by people in a white Ford pickup who said a green car was chasing them, trying to run them off the road. Dustin located the green car and asked the occupant what he was doing.

> James E. Krimm informed me that he was sitting at his camp and the individuals in the Ford pickup drove by, flipping him off and calling him a "faggot." I asked Krimm if he felt it was appropriate to chase after the vehicle, and he informed me he does it a lot. Krimm informed that he chases people down to find out why they're treating him that way.

I can't help but flash on the reasons Jimmy would become enraged at being called a faggot. It had to remind Jimmy of Rob's concern years earlier that Jimmy's sexual advances were gay.

Dustin noticed the smell of alcohol on Jimmy. When asked if he'd been drinking, Jimmy said he had not. Later, when asked again, Jimmy admitted to having had "a few beers."

Dustin conducted field sobriety tests, taking grief from Jimmy, who said the officer was taking too much time.

Jimmy made several mistakes on the heel-toe test and on the one-legged test. He also made mistakes on a counting test.

"I informed Krimm I believed he was under the influence of alcohol and I needed him to submit to breath testing."

Jimmy then told Dustin he wanted to be placed in handcuffs because he wasn't free to leave. Dustin was only too happy to comply! At this point, the trooper began a fifteen-minute required wait time before he could administer the breath test. Jimmy wanted to know why he had to wait, and Dustin told him it was standard procedure.

"Krimm informed me he wasn't aware the waiting period was so long and requested to be removed from the handcuffs. Krimm had been cooperative so I removed the handcuffs."

Jimmy blew a .115 and a .133.

"I informed Krimm he was under arrest," and Jimmy placed his hands behind his back. A vehicle inventory turned up a cooler with a nearly empty bottle of Jim Beam inside.

"While awaiting tow, Krimm made numerous statements about chasing people down when they flip him off and call him a 'faggot.' I asked Krimm what he does when he catches the individuals, and he informed me that he makes them think about what they're calling him and why they're doing it. Krimm stated people usually change their statement… when they see a bigger guy with flame tattoos confront them."

I am fascinated. The exchange seems to suggest Jimmy has been called a faggot on numerous occasions. Like a murderer who can never wash the blood from his hands, Jimmy cannot escape what he did to his little brother. For some inexplicable reason, total strangers can see it on him. It had to have freaked Jimmy out just a little. Like, how could these people possibly know?

I also see the same old element of denial; each time the possibility of homosexuality is raised—just as when Harry raised it—Jimmy attempts to settle the dispute with aggression.

No matter how many years have passed, no matter how he has distanced himself from his family, no matter how far away he runs, Jimmy cannot escape the accusations, even if they are mere coincidence.

For the first time in my life, I come face-to-face with a notion that startles me. As a victim, I have never considered the aftermath for my abuser. Now, I am forced to see how an abuser's actions are just as damaging to himself.

Jimmy destroyed his own peace of mind when he abused his brother. He could never shake it, never forget. Each time someone taunted him, he was forced to remember what he did to Harry—like a song hitting a skip on an old vinyl record, wearing an ever-deeper groove each time it plays.

Rob takes small comfort in knowing that even if Jimmy didn't spend time in jail for raping him, he spent the rest of his life tormented by the hazing of strangers.

Ten days later, out on bond for the DUI, Jimmy contacted the towing company to find out the charges for getting his car out of the impound lot.

He was told it would cost $1,012, more than half of which was for storage. According to the towing company, Jimmy stated he would come in that day, August 5, 2009, to pay the fee and pick up his car, but he still had not arrived by closing time.

Jimmy's cell phone history filled in a few more gaps about his whereabouts in the last months of his life.

On April 23 and 24, 2009, Jimmy placed calls to an auto repair place in Sioux Falls, South Dakota, and to a manufactured home dealer. On April 30, he ordered pizza in Mitchell, South Dakota. That same day, he called a hobby shop in St. George, Utah, to see about ordering a part for one of his radio-controlled airplanes.

Then, on June 12, 2009, Jimmy ordered pizza in Williston, once again putting him in the vicinity of what will become his final bank robbery. But the Idaho DUI proves Jimmy could not have hung around Williston all summer. A call placed to a Greyhound bus depot in Idaho the day Jimmy told the impound yard he was coming to retrieve his car must not have provided the information he needed, because before the tow company opened the next day, Jimmy's car was gone.

The next time a trooper saw the green Mitsubishi up close, there would be a pistol hanging out the window—firing at him.

"Memorale (sic) day weekend 09. Pulled a four wheeler ATV off a kid who rolled it in front of my car in this picture...He said 'I can't breathe' Crash site behind my head on hill."

August 22, 2009

Hello!

Sorry these pictures took so long!
I've been busy fuckin' up this year. Bad camping trip!
Some people drove by my campsite and flipped me the bird, so I gladly chased them down—got them to stop in their white, Ford pick-up truck, then jumped out of my car to <u>Confront </u>them.
They saw me coming with my shirt off, and hit there gas flipin' the bird again!
Soooo...I get back in my car, to chase them down again, and a sheriff was on the side of the road sittin'.
These "clowns" stop at the Sheriff truck and told the cop "some guy is following me and I'm scared." He then "took off," allowing the Sheriff to hand me my second D.U.I. and do 10 days in Jail.
Now for some good news—IF there is such a thing for J.E. Krimm.

I saved a kids Life on "Memorial Day" when his 4 wheeler Rolled & pinned him under it. (He went over the handle bars.) It happened in front of my campsite (at 2 p.m.) his leg was pinned and he had the wind knocked outta him. (A.T.V. on top).

The thing was still running & leaking gas bad. I pulled his little leg outta the peg & frame And pulled it up off of him.

He layed there & said "I can't breath." His dad rolled up on his 4 wheeler and come a running saying "What happened!!??"

I told him, "He wrecked." Then his fat, stupid, wife (no pun intended) came up & Bumped Dad's Big Polaris sending it down at "US" (me & Dad & son) on the side of the hill. The stupid Bitch said nothing! But I saw what was coming.

I run up the hill on all fours like a dog—cause Father & Son with Daughter now (they all had separated 4 wheeler A.T.V) Did not see this coming at US!!

This was a **MONSTER** Polaris. And I Barely stoped it!!

The Fat Bitch just sat there and looked at me!

I turned the wheel of this thing, so IT was stable. Then went back down to assist Dad

Dad looks at me coming down the hill and says, "What was that All About? (I told himstory) But didn't say his wife hit it from behind and Almost Killed us All. (They were drunk) I was still sober—(5 days again) Then yep, you guessed it—off wagon.

(The Kid was 10 or 12 yrs old.)

Soooo…I tried to get on internet to say hi, but place was busy. So I write leter & tell Fart Jokes. (We all run from our Farts Sooner or Later!) □

Love Ya, J. Krimm (Jummers)

P.S. Kid walked away from Crash! We both smelled like Gas. Dad said "That's it for today!"

CHAPTER EIGHTEEN

Two Steps Back

September 14, 2009

"Krimm! Squadron commander wants to see you at 1500!"

The words jolted Rob. What had begun as a good day, a day when he was getting his hands dirty and feeling like he was "in the zone" suddenly turned into a moment when an eighteen-year military career felt tenuous and unsecure.

What now? The appointment was only a half hour away. Talk about short notice. It was like—bam!

They asked him if his "blues" were ready.

"Yeah, a half hour away at my house," Rob answered.

Just ABUs (the airman battle uniform), his everyday work clothes, would have to do.

Which incident did I fuck up royally? Rob wondered. It seemed sometimes like his whole career was one screwup after another. It had always been one step forward, two steps back. Somehow, he'd managed to hang on, as if a guardian angel had his back. This time was different. A second Article 15 in a six-month period would mean a hard bust. His record of infractions was already as thick as a phone book. After taking a peek, one guy said, "I could have separated four airmen with the amount of paperwork you have."

Having patient leadership was a blessing. But patience was wearing thin, and retirement was so close—February 1, 2011.

"We want to see you retire" was a phrase frequently uttered in Rob's presence.

If he could retire, he could go to school and pursue his dream career in computer programming and then go to work at Pixar Animation Studios. The dream even went so far as to include a wife, maybe even a couple of kids, waiting for him to come home after work.   But if getting a job at Pixar was a long shot, sometimes it seemed a happy and stable personal life would be even more difficult to attain. Rob hadn't had a lot of success with long-term relationships, and he worried whether he would make a good father and mentor to any kid.

What Rob had hoped to find in the military was an example, because he'd never had correct guidance. What he needed, even if he couldn't have articulated it fresh out of high school, was a force bigger than himself to illuminate a path. He wanted to be around people who did things the right way. After a certain period of time, after a certain amount of training, Rob believed that correctness would rub off. But it didn't exactly work out that way.

Sure, he was a good guy, an honest citizen, serving his country honorably. He paid his bills. But that elusive "correct" path turned out to contain a minefield of rules.

At least his current job, as an electronics troubleshooter, was a step toward computers. It involved working with the aircraft navigation and targeting system called LANTIRN (low altitude navigation targeting infrared for night). LANTIRN is old technology—1970s technology. A cell phone has more processing power than the FLIR—forward looking infrared.

The FLIR produces the kind of video you see on CNN when buildings are blown up. COD Modern Warfare 2 had a level with FLIR-type imaging so realistic it gave Rob chills when he played it on his X-Box 360.

Rob was also trained to repair the FLIR ball, the camera portion of the pod, which looks like an upside down R2-D2 from Star Wars, hitching a ride underneath a C130 gunship.

You could get in trouble for something as minor as using the wrong lug nut on a pod. It wasn't like anyone went around deliberately trying to mess one up, but the stakes were high. Pilots relied on this technology to help them bomb the right target. Though Rob never dropped those bombs, his work allowed that destruction to occur. As long as he did his job right, in theory, only the "bad guys" were going to get blown to bits.

His days spent troubleshooting the wiring in some piece of electronics, in portable bays set up inside of a military shop, had the feel of a military hospital—sterile and intense. But unlike a surgeon who had a nurse at hand to wipe the sweat from his brow, there was no one in that bay looking out for Rob except Rob. And what kind of surgeon had minders, following along to make sure the patient was healed properly? There was no equivalent of malpractice insurance covering Rob's butt, yet lives depended—or could be lost—as a result of his work.

Most of the rules seemed so hokey pokey, so arbitrary, so asinine. But Rob had to admit, he'd had a rash of major and minor screwups over the past few years. He'd grown so accustomed to responding to reprimands, he could cut and paste his answers. *That* did not fly well.

Rob settled into a chair outside the commander's office thinking about the ration of bad luck he'd had the past year. It all seemed to go back to the time, eleven months earlier, when he wrecked his car and injured his neck on the way to work. He'd refused an ambulance but later needed surgery. They gave him forty-five days' leave to recover.

Suddenly, Rob found himself thirty or forty pounds overweight. He'd had two serious reprimands—two Article 15s—in just six months, both aimed at forcing him, literally, to shape up or ship out. The fact he'd spent forty-five days lying around playing X-Box while recuperating from surgery seemed lost on the Air Force. Of course you're gonna gain some weight!

He didn't complete the paperwork *exactly* on time for his food log, and he missed an appointment for a review of his mandatory physical fitness orders, but he actually accomplished the harder part of the mission. He lost forty pounds, dropping from 265 to 225 pounds!

The Air Force didn't seem to care that he was now in top physical condition—that he had, in fact, "shaped up." All they cared about was the paperwork. Stupid shit.

And all it took was for one anal-retentive master sergeant to look at these transgressions and decide there was a problem. Suddenly, it's "Krimm's fucking up."

Things get blown all out of proportion, Rob thought. *Was the point that I did the paperwork or lost the weight?* It was so frustrating.

It was while sitting in the "waiting room" outside the commander's office that Rob overheard two guys talking, both master sergeants. The senior NCOs looked like mobster henchmen the way they huddled.

"What's up with Krimm?" the one guy asked the other, with a lift of the head toward where Rob was sitting.

Rob couldn't believe they would just talk about him when he was sitting right there, within earshot. Like, guys, am I invisible or what?

That was when the asshole who'd just come off four years of duty as a drill instructor answered, "Losin' a stripe."

Losing a stripe?

Suddenly, Rob felt like vomiting! *Losing a stripe?* Over some stupid food log or some missed appointment or using the wrong lug nut? Whichever infraction, each seemed as unlikely as the other. But before Rob could even attempt to digest what was now clearly going to be a very serious reprimand, the asshole, as if to justify his answer, added the word, "Finally."

What an asshole!

Finally? Really?

Finally? Is that what they think of me?

Wow.

Finally.

It was only a short time later when the commander's first sergeant came to summon Rob.

He stood up, suddenly dizzy like he was going to pass out.

"Are you okay?" the first sergeant asked.

"I am so worried right now," Rob said, not sure if a lack of circulation, holding his breath, or simply getting up too fast was to blame. It was as if he could hear his heart pounding in his ears, even though his heart was still in his chest and not in his head.

"You look pale," the first sergeant said. "Just take a minute."

"I'm really scared right now," Rob said.

"Just take a minute and breathe," he said.

It was no use putting it off. Time to square the shoulders and walk through the door toward a punishment he now expected but couldn't comprehend that he deserved.

It was a familiar feeling, though he hadn't experienced anything quite this intense in a very long time. It was obvious. He was about to be screwed.

Losing a stripe?

The only shame attached to this event would be a missing stripe on a uniform. As bad as that was, Rob couldn't help thinking back to tougher times making lasting scars, when he hadn't deserved any punishment at all.

This commander was one of the better ones he'd seen in his eighteen-plus-year career. He got out there with the troops at 0630 to run a couple miles and encourage them to run faster. He actually gave a shit! After all the Friday morning runs, facing him as a person, now it came down to this.

Rob gave two taps on the door.

"Enter," the commander's voice boomed from the other side.

Rob opened the door and closed it behind him, made a beeline to the commander's desk, and saluted.

"Staff Sergeant Krimm, reporting as ordered, sir!"

That was the last time Rob would introduce himself as such. He listened as the commander read the Article 15 word for word.

"After a thorough investigation, it was decided you were guilty of missing an appointment and failing to turn in your food log."

Heinous crimes! It actually sounded even more ridiculous out loud.

"It is my decision that you be held accountable for behavior non-becoming of an NCO...Reduction in grade."

Rob's whole world went into slow motion when he heard the last three words. Every pore in his body began to itch. He could have sworn he felt his hair turning grey right at that moment.

"Effective today, 15:20," the commander concluded, and with a swipe of his pen, the most humiliating episode of Rob's adult life was reduced to an exact moment—3:20 PM on a Monday afternoon.

Jimmy pulled into the town of Williston, with the late-afternoon sun over his shoulder. He'd grab a quick bite to eat somewhere before the job and lay in a few more supplies in case he got stuck out in the boonies after.

As he cruised to the intersection where two banks cowered, one on the west and one on the east, he made a right-hand turn down a street locals called "the Million-Dollar Way," which was a laugh. He heard someone say it got that name for the cost of paving it "back in the day." You'd have to call it the $50-Million-Dollar Way if you wanted to repave it now.

Jimmy was running low on cash. He figured he had maybe $800 left from his last job. He had a little more cash stashed in a storage unit, but the last time he'd brought some of that cash into a bank, the teller gave him a look. The bills, he had to admit, had a bit of an odor. Musty. Like they'd been unearthed instead of earned. Well, that was true enough. He hadn't earned them, and they had been underground a while.

Jimmy pulled into a McDonald's, negotiated the drive-through lane, and placed his order: a Big Mac, fries, and a tall iced coffee. After all these years, eating at McDonald's was still a treat. It was a luxury when he was a kid, so a chance to eat fast food still seemed like a special occasion.

There was no sense tempting fate—or conversation—by eating inside. People in North Dakota were too damn friendly. It was annoying. Bunch of inbred Scandinavians, mostly. They acted like everyone was family. If two lifelong North Dakotans met at any spot in the state, they were bound to discover some relation or acquaintance in common. Jimmy had seen it happen in more than one bar over the years. No one was likely to know the people in the circles where he spent most of his life. Jimmy was not native, not friendly, and not interested in making small talk with some nosey Norwegian. Even worse were the real cowboys who looked down on a guy without manure on his boots. Rig hands, what some people called "oil field trash," he could stand, but even talking to someone like that was annoying. They assumed he must have a job in the oil field, or want one. He wouldn't have minded giving it a try, but with his record and mandatory drug tests, there wasn't much point in applying. Besides, he didn't have a driver's license, and that, too, was a must.

Anyway, he already had a job he was good at.

After getting his food, he pulled into a parking space to have his lunch. *Look at me,* he thought, *big bad bank robber, with my heart-attack sandwich and an iced coffee.* The days when he'd deprived himself of coffee and grease were long in the past, as were the days when he'd spend hours pumping iron. Huge biceps and a barrel chest only served to announce "joint body" to every cop in kingdom come. Any cop or con could recognize the type from a mile off. And brawn was not necessary in his line of work. All the muscle he needed came in a little package that shot 9-mm ammo.

Now the joint body included a bit of belly. But he had been cutting back lately. It wasn't just for his health. Who wanted to be the bank robber they described on the news as six feet three inches and 330 pounds? He'd never been that heavy. But he'd actually lost about forty pounds in the past six months, living on what he liked to think of as the "Jack Daniels diet." The diet contained plenty of protein in the form of meat cooked on an open flame, but there were no "good carbs" because they all came from alcohol. He'd learned all about good carbs and bad carbs in the joint. Prison libraries were full of self-improvement shit like that.

Jimmy rolled down the window, enjoying the late-afternoon air. It was a pretty day, even if it was an ugly town—kind of dirty, in a wholesome way. Williston, hell, any town in North Dakota, was pretty much lacking in any kind of extras. There was no such thing as landscaping. It was all concrete and pavement—or plain old dirt.

He could almost convince himself he was back in his hometown of Taylor, Michigan, if not for the prairie visible to the north. In Williston, as in South Detroit, ugly chain stores and dowdy mom-and-pop shops stretched for block after block, with a car dealer or fast-food joint thrown in here or there. This "Million-Dollar Way" might just as easily be Telegraph Road back home, except Telegraph stretched across many more miles.

Home. Jimmy almost snorted coffee through his nose at the thought. Taylor was a pit in a way a town like Williston could never be. Or at least, it had been the last time he was there. The biggest difference was the people. North Dakotans were easy pickin's. They tended not to have the kind of street smarts that come from having a welfare project in your backyard and crack down every alley.

Finishing his sandwich, Jimmy looked up the block. Huh, he could see the American State Bank sign to the north. He hadn't even planned that. He'd already scoped out the whole area on his last trip through here. And just as he'd remembered, it was a sweet set-up. Easy.

There were several shop-type buildings to the south of the bank. He could park unnoticed and out of sight of the bank's drive-up window, walk to the entry in seconds, do the job, then disappear around the other side of the building, get back into his car, and drive off unseen.

It was a system he'd perfected in a dozen other robberies. It was almost foolproof. He wouldn't even bother with the mask—his sunglasses would be disguise enough. His shades were like a good-luck charm. He'd bought them shortly after getting out of jail in Canada and worn them for his first bank robbery back in the States. Sure, they were a little worse for wear, but it was nothing a little JB Weld couldn't fix.

Besides, it was actually a little hot out. No sense getting all sweated up with a mask. For what? Hell, he was half-tempted to smile for the cameras, strike a pose, even. The FBI had no clue. They never even came close to catching him. He wasn't even nervous anymore.

Robbing banks, at first, was a thrill ride unlike the best roller coaster a Sandusky, Ohio, amusement park could offer when he was a kid. Better even than the big hill he and his brother used to scream down on their bikes when they were little. Man, what a rush!

"Slam on your brakes!" he called out, and Harry's tires made a mark that covered the distance it would take to pass twenty-five yards full of old people, fists shaking.

"Hey, you damn fucker, stop!" one old guy yelled at them, mad about skid marks on the pavement in front of his driveway.

What was it with old people and swearing anyway? Old people didn't even swear right. They asked to be laughed at, cursing like that.

Then, as now, Jimmy didn't stop for anybody. But something told him Harry was still taking orders. He probably made a whole damn career out of the military. Well, good for him. Hell, Harry might be giving orders by now. For all Jimmy knew, his brother could be a general or something. Fucking Harry. He thought again of his brother adopting the name "Rob." It made him laugh every damn time he thought of it. He was no Rob. What a hoot!

It seemed to Rob like the worst kind of nightmare imaginable. Everything he'd worked for taken away with a few drops of ink on a piece of paper—not to mention the $600 that would be missing from his bank account each month since the reduction in grade came with a corresponding drop in pay.

I'm going to wake up. This can't be real, Rob thought.

"Dismissed!" the commander said.

Rob made the salute, as required, delivering the expected words along with the gesture.

"Good afternoon, sir," Rob said, as the commander returned his salute.

As Rob left the commander's office, he couldn't shake the desire for time to run backward. If he could only do it over. But there were no do-overs in the military. There was no pause button and certainly no ability to rewind the sands of time.

Sure, the commander was unenthusiastic about taking a stripe from a guy with less than two years to go before retirement. But what else was he gonna do?

Rob actually had shown up at the appointment he was getting demoted over, but because he didn't print out the certificate from the online coursework, as required, they'd turned him away and wouldn't let him check in. It was reported to the commander as a no-show. Rob explained the circumstances in his written answer to the charge, but it didn't make any difference.

It was just so frustrating! Air Force doctors had diagnosed him with attention deficit disorder and depression. And it was Air Force doctors who'd prescribed the drugs he took every day to deal with those challenges. The Air Force might be the most forgiving of the military branches when it came to emotional health issues, but there was a limit.

The Air Force knew the disconnect Rob had with practical applications—getting to work on time, turning in paperwork as expected, following the rules, but the medications were supposed to take care of the problem.

It was an effort every day for Rob just to fulfill the simple requirements of following Air Force rules, but no one was going to give him a medal for doing the minimum, no matter how difficult. He knew that. It just didn't seem right not to have some acknowledgment of how hard he tried.

There never seemed to be anyone standing there to notice all the days Rob did show up on time, had his paperwork done, followed the rules. And after eighteen-and-a-half years in the military, Rob knew there never would be. He'd long since stopped hoping for any kind of break or recognition of his daily struggle just to be average.

He worked at it, being average. The Air Force might be forgiving of mental disturbances—like, they never took away his security clearance after the breakdown that led to him going on the meds—but the Air Force also held people to a higher standard. Little mistakes were elevated. And the same standards applied to all. But, as usual, he was blindsided. It always seemed that just when he had himself convinced he was in the groove, reality slapped him upside the head.

Like, forgetting to check his e-mail and discovering a summons to an appointment a day after it was scheduled—that was the incident that caused his second Article 15. That time, he hadn't even shown up.

It wasn't like his job was one where he was able to sit in front of a computer screen all day. It had been a busy week, and there was no time for the computer. The satisfaction Rob felt all that week, getting down and dirty working on the pods, disappeared when he finally did check his e-mail.

That was part of the problem with ADD. Once he got into a zone, he felt like he was flying, rolling with every punch, handling every bump with agility until, *blam*, major roadblock. An e-mail he found on a Thursday, which was from three days earlier, commanded him to report in two days for an appointment about a food log he'd failed to turn in.

Don't let this be true, Rob thought, staring at the words on the screen, commanding him to report to an appointment he'd already missed.

That time, too, he found himself wishing time could move backward. Back to the moment, three days earlier, when he'd been busy in the shop and that e-mail had appeared in his inbox. If he could only have walked into one of the offices in the shop, logged on to a computer, clicked a few buttons, found the e-mail, and gone to the appointment, he wouldn't be walking out of his squadron commander's office now as a senior airmen instead of a staff sergeant.

It really seemed that simple—and that arbitrary.

If they only knew how much he wanted to do a great job. If they could only see how disappointed he was in himself, wanting to do a great job and falling short time after time. They might be disappointed in him, but no more disappointed than he was in himself.

What was crazy was that he kept setting himself up for these failures, kept reenlisting, knowing the military would always demand a little more than he was able to give.

One step forward, two steps back.

Also frustrating to Rob was the feeling he hadn't always been this way. He used to be able to juggle more. He'd worked delivering pizzas all through high school, marched in countless parades, and played in the band during every football game. His leadership skills back then were such he'd been elected drum major.

It was Rob who wound up calling everyone in the drum section at 8:00 AM on a Saturday morning to remind them of a parade and ask them if they needed a ride and whether they had their instrument with them.

That one simple act, taking the initiative to phone the fifteen people in his section, meant the drum line was always fully functional. Sometimes, so many instruments were missing from other sections all the band could do was march to the cadence of the drummers Rob summoned.

Rob always thought the military would be the place that would recognize and reward that type of effort, but the rewards and recognition never came. You didn't get rewards and recognition for doing what was expected, and the times Rob had gone above and beyond, no one seemed to notice.

Rob was used to those moments, like in the commander's office, when he knew the punishment would be doled out. But just once, just once, he'd like to have a moment before that awful moment of humiliation, when someone gave him credit for how hard he tried. Just once, he'd like someone to recognize he wasn't anything like his brother, Jimmy—always taking, never giving back.

It was time. After finishing his lunch and dropping into a grocery store that very conveniently had a liquor store on the side, Jimmy stocked his cooler and then drove the few blocks toward the bank.

He pulled up in the alley between a welding shop and a Pepsi distributor to park his car. His little Mitsubishi might look like a piece of shit, and he might not have the certificate to prove it, but Jimmy knew how to tune an engine and his Mitsubishi ran like a fucking Jap rocket.

With a quick check in his visor mirror, Jimmy liked what he saw. The mirrored sunglasses hid his eyes, reflecting only the mirror back at him, which was reflected again in the mirror of the glasses, on and on, into oblivion. Good.

He didn't need to rehearse what to say—not like when he'd been a kid, practicing a party store holdup with Harry as his audience. Only the reward was the same. Cash-money-spew. Now there was no home and no one to "go home" to. Lately, he'd been in touch with his dad, but even that connection was disappointing. He couldn't tell his dad how he really made his living, as badly as he wanted to tell someone, anyone.

He'd done this so many times now; he could rob a bank with his eyes closed. It was so predictable. First, there'd be the shock of the people—that anyone would have the balls to just walk in, open the latch of the gate to get behind the teller line, and pull a gun. Then there'd be some fat-ass manager. You could actually see these people second-guessing themselves. They'd ask if he needed any help. *Hell no, not unless you want to give me the money out of your wallet, too!*

Next, there'd be someone who was either too stupid or too afraid to comply with his simple directions. Even those types didn't rattle him anymore. All he had to do was walk in and get on the clock. Two minutes, in and out. That was the drill.

He grabbed an empty cardboard soda box out of the back seat. This was his own signature move. It might seem odd to carry a soda box into a bank, but it certainly wasn't threatening, and he'd much rather stow his gun in a soda box than in his pants.

CHAPTER NINETEEN

Tellers

September 14, 2009

The events of September 14, 2009, shattered the faith of employees who believed their bank could never be robbed.

There had never been a bank robbery in Williston, North Dakota.

Angie Pierce, twenty-three, began working for Williston's American State Bank just a few months before moving to the north branch in July 2009. The single mother was born and raised in Williston. Diagnosed with depression as a teenager, she didn't let it stop her from entering the workforce as a fifteen-year-old, caring for the elderly at a nursing home or serving food at a chain restaurant. A job as a bank teller was a step up, providing better hours and a nicer working environment.

"No more uniform, no more scrubs," she tells me. "It was a great opportunity."

I meet Pierce in her modest home in a quiet Williston neighborhood about four months after the robbery.

She was working the nine-to-six shift on September 14, 2009.

"It was just, nothing out of the ordinary."

Lisa Barbula was another young teller on the line. She was just at her first anniversary with the bank, having moved from the main bank to the north branch the same month as Pierce.

The north branch was located on one of the busiest intersections on the outskirts of town, with later hours to accommodate the working customer who needed to make a quick stop on the way home. Barbula believes it's no accident this branch would become a target for a bank robber.

"I think a lot of it has to do with our location," Barbula says. "He knows there's going to be less staff out here."

I talk with Barbula and the branch manager, Elaine Fixen, in the break room at the branch after closing time one evening, a few weeks after interviewing Pierce. Two other bank officials listen in.

Fixen is relatively new in her job, too, though she had worked for the bank for fourteen years. Promoted to branch manager just a few weeks before the robbery, she takes her supervisory role seriously but regards her tellers as family.

"I couldn't protect them," Fixen says. "And so many of the tellers were so new at the job."

Coming off a week's vacation, Fixen should have been out the door at 4:30 PM, but she was playing catch-up with the paperwork piled on her desk.

At 4:55 PM, Pierce was leaving her teller station to help a childhood friend who had come into the bank for a cash advance. That was when she noticed a "nice-looking guy" enter the bank.

Barbula was at her teller station, helping another customer.

"I just looked at him and made sure one of the other girls was going to help him and then went back to my customer."

No one thought anything of the cardboard soda carton the guy carried.

"You know, that should have been our first clue, but the things people bring coin in." Barbula laughs, shaking her head. "We had a guy, not too far before that, bring in coin in an old, like, one of those clamshell containers that had a flashlight in it? He dumped all his coin in it, duct-taped it up, and brought it in."

"I figured it was change," agrees Pierce, "because people come in with the absolute weirdest things full of change."

Before anyone realized his intentions, the robber was behind the teller line. Pierce, who had her back to the gate, turned when she heard the latch.

"Obviously, he was experienced with them because starting as a new teller, you have no idea how to open that door. It's something that you either fiddle with or somebody tells you how to get back there, and he obviously knew," says Pierce.

Barbula at first thought the man must have a legitimate reason for being inside the gate. Fixen rose from her desk out in the lobby to ask, "Sir, can I help you?"

"He was a nice, clean-cut man," says Fixen, "and that's why I asked him, because we don't let anybody back there unless we know what's going on."

That was about the time she noticed the gun. Whether it was pointed directly at her didn't matter.

"He just told me to sit down, and all I did was observe what he did with the tellers, and just you know, do what he said—just like, everything got taken away from me. The control was just gone."

"I don't know who this guy is," says Pierce, all she knew was suddenly he was saying, "Gimme your money."

The man walked quickly to the far end of the teller line to make his demands.

"He's saying, 'Gimme your money. Take it out. Set it on the counter,'" recalls Pierce. "And obviously, everybody's in shock, at first, so he said, 'This is real.'"

"We stayed calm because I think we were all in shock," echoes Fixen. "Just do what he wants. Give him what he wants and get him out of here."

The pregnant teller next to Barbula was visibly upset.

"She started crying, and then he came over to my window and told me to get my money out. He started tapping his gun on the counter."

"That's when I'm starting to go, shit, I'm gonna die," says Pierce. "Like, I have a mouth on me, and I just kept telling myself, 'Keep your mouth shut. Keep your mouth shut.'"

Pierce was away from her drawer, and the robber said, "Don't move," so she didn't. "I don't have any money where I am."

At this point, the robber noticed Pierce was not moving. She told herself to record details.

"The first thing I noticed was a Pall Mall work shirt type of thing: 99 percent sure he was wearing boots, not cowboy boots, but like, worker boots, and he was wearing a hat. And he was wearing sunglasses. And the sunglasses were the reflective sunglasses, so they were the multicolored—you'd see yourself."

"This guy works on a rig," Barbula remembers thinking. The booming Bakken oil play had brought all kinds of new people to town in recent years—men from Texas and Oklahoma and Wyoming—all attracted by the chance of making $25 an hour or more working on the floor of an oil rig.

"A new face is nothing to us," Barbula says, because it seemed there was another new face every day.

"They say life passes before your eyes," Pierce interjects, but when the robber pointed his gun at her, "All I could see was an image of my daughter over the front of him. It was so weird, so I just keep paying attention to him, and he's pointing it at me, saying, 'Give me your money.'"

But standing where she was, on the opposite end of the line from her own station, she gave him a universal gesture of emptiness, arms out, palms up.

"I don't have any money," she told him.

The other girls were incredulous that Pierce offered any resistance, however passive.

"Angie!" one of them declared, "Just *do* it."

"And they all told me afterwards, even some of the upper management in the bank, said they were surprised that I didn't get shot," Pierce recounts. "I wasn't subtle about it, because at this time, I am not frightened from this man at all. I am not frightened for my life; I'm looking at you, like, 'You're crazy.' And when he first looked at me and said, 'Give me your money,' I smiled and almost started laughing."

A self-described adrenaline junkie, Pierce isn't sure to what she should attribute her moxie in the face of what appears to be a loaded weapon.

"I wasn't crying. I was just like, 'Screw you, dude. I don't have nothing here.' And he said, 'Go.' I don't remember him saying anything else, he just said, 'Go get it.'"

Pierce returned to her teller station, removed the money from her cash drawer, "and he came and swiped it into the box."

Barbula noticed how calm the bank robber was. He appeared unfazed by Pierce's momentary resistance.

"You knew right away it wasn't his first time he had done it—he knew exactly what he was doing," she says. "He didn't rush, and he wasn't shaky; his voice was very steady; he was very calm. He was *nice* about it," Barbula says.

"The only time he really even talked directly is when he went over to the girl sitting directly next to me—and he kept tapping his gun," says Pierce.

At each station, the tap-tap of the gun on the counter was a prompt, containing a menace that haunts Pierce months later.

"At first, when I could never sleep, that's what I'd always hear when I laid down, was the two taps of the gun," she says, recreating the staccato sound with her finger.

Barbula was stunned by a slight break in the bank robber's composure when one of the tellers began to weep.

"She didn't know what to do, and he took the time to reassure her that he wasn't going to hurt anybody," Barbula says. "It was almost like he was making a point that he didn't really want to be doing this to us, but he was going to do it anyway. It was weird. He was kind of contradicting himself."

Barbula's voice softens as she tries to imitate his tone in speaking to the hysterical girl.

"'I'm not going to hurt anybody. It'll be okay. Everything's going to be okay. I'm not going to hurt you guys, just do what I'm asking you to do.'"

"He could tell she was getting pretty hysterical," Pierce agrees. "And he said, 'Don't worry, I'm not going to hurt anybody.' He was so calm."

It was almost as if, Pierce says, he was *relaxed*. But there was no indication he was drunk or on drugs.

"He had a smell," she says. "At first, I thought maybe it was alcohol, but then I didn't think it was."

The closest Pierce can come to pinpointing the odor is what might be described as "road smell"—not the smell of a man working hard all day on the oil rigs, more like a man cooped up in a car.

The robber's size was not particularly intimidating to these young women, though they would report him as six feet three inches tall, and 230 pounds.

"Nope, not at all." Pierce shrugs. "He was just an average built guy...I mean he was not fat, but he was not skinny."

Pierce says he didn't fit the stereotypical description of a bank robber.

"I think it's a mental image from TV, that the people who do that are rough and gruff, creepy looking and not even only from TV—he didn't have that gun to hurt anybody."

Pierce bases that assumption on his demeanor but also on what she heard about the robber after his death.

"If he wanted to hurt somebody, he would have come in there yelling. He would have came in there with authority, if he was there to prove he was better and he was going to hurt you. But he didn't. He came in there, and this gun is just for you to listen—this is so you don't call the cops while I'm here. But I didn't feel deep down inside like he was going to harm us because he was such an average, like, not attractive, but nice-looking guy."

She never saw his finger on the trigger of the gun.

Robbing the north branch of American State Bank was just a job to this guy, she says.

"He was in there because that's what he does. He wanted money. I think also, if he was ready to hurt us, when I got lippy with him, he would have shot me, but he didn't. When Elaine started walking over there, he would have shot at the ceiling to tell her to shut up. You know? He could have shot one of the customers for us to believe he was there and this was the deal."

Pierce doesn't believe he would have fired the gun unless physically threatened.

"He was swinging it around, like, when he was walking back and forth, he had his gun, but he wasn't pointing it right at anybody."

The gesture, she says, was more like someone accustomed to always having a cigarette in his hand, "just very nonchalant."

Yet, her anger at the thought of him comforting the hysterical teller is palpable. She thinks to herself, *I want to punch you in the face, like, don't hurt anybody, just please don't hurt anybody—and just get out*, and, *I can't believe this is happening to me.* I was thinking that the whole time, *I can't believe this is happening and not only to me, but in Williston, North Dakota.*"

The fact that there was no demand for money from the vault, Barbula says, is just a further indication of the robber's discipline.

"He knew to get the small stuff and go and hit up the next one; otherwise it increases his chances of getting caught."

As the robber left the building, his parting words astonished tellers.

"He shook his gun up in the air, like, 'Look at me,'" Pierce says. "Then he said, 'Now sit tight and wait for the FBI because you know they're coming. *Thank you.*'"

Pierce isn't sure how to categorize the statement. There is the hint of a smile around the robber's lips at the mention of the FBI. She wouldn't describe the thanks as sincere. Barbula has a word for it.

"It was very genuine, and I mean it was after he assured us he wasn't going to hurt anybody, you know: 'Everybody just sit tight, wait for the FBI to come. Thank you,'" she says in a level tone, imitating the robber's voice once again.

The bank's security camera recorded the total length of the robbery. The bandit was out the door and seen crossing in front of the outside window in under two minutes.

"He wasn't running; he wasn't walking fast. He was walking at a completely normal pace," Pierce says.

Fixen asks, "If you were trying to get away, wouldn't you run away?"

Pierce suspects the robber wanted to get caught.

Adrenaline junkie that she is, Pierce believes the thrill for this robber was gone. It wasn't fun anymore. After walking into a bank time after time, meeting virtually no resistance inside and never coming close to a confrontation with police, Pierce believes the bandit did everything he could to tempt fate. She sees that in his actions at her bank, compared to some others he robbed wearing a mask.

"He didn't care anymore. He was waiting to get caught."

Robbing banks no longer provided a thrill for him.

"He gave up on himself a long time ago. He just wanted to know how long he could go."

Whether colored by the lens of her own depression or perhaps because of the added insight her experience lends, Pierce sees in the robber a man with little to live for.

"He didn't have a job—to him, he had no family, because if you have a family, you love your family and you keep in contact with your family, you bend over backwards for your family, and he didn't," Pierce says. "And even before you know all that, it adds up after you figure it all out, after you learn everything about him. He did it for fun. It wasn't like he was going in there because his kid needed diapers."

Pierce believes robbing banks was a decision the robber made, never realizing until later how it would isolate him, how impossible it would become to have a normal life.

"If he was not waiting to get caught and he was not doing it for fun, he would have had a home, he would have been, you know, a regular at that restaurant down the street—and he wasn't."

Pierce cannot fathom such a solitary existence, but she can put herself in the shoes of the robber's mother.

"Knowing that your child has scarred that many people? And it's not physical, it's all mental, and I think that's the worst kind of pain there is."

While his victims have to live with the trauma of a terrifying event, Pierce says, his mother has a much heavier burden.

"She has to go to bed every night thinking of her son being screwed up and what did she do wrong? She didn't do anything wrong...If she would have been standing there, he probably would have done it to her, too. For a mother to have to live with that, I think, is worse than probably all of us put together."

After the robber exited the bank, "The friend I was helping was like, can I go out there?" Pierce says.

His girlfriend had been outside with a four-year-old child, waiting in the car.

"So I said, go out there and make sure they're okay, which, technically, legally, you are not supposed to leave," says Pierce, but she couldn't deny him.

After determining that his girlfriend and child were okay, he poked his head around the corner of the bank building, spotting the green sedan that was the robber's getaway car. Without that detail, police would have had no idea who they were looking for.

Inside the bank, tellers and customers alike were falling apart.

"And we were so pissed, because in Williston, you can be anywhere in less than ten minutes—and something like this, why are they not here? Why are they not here?"

Pierce credits depression medication with helping her to remain calm in the wake of the hysteria following the robbery.

"Because afterwards, as they're losing it, as I'm breaking down, I'm grabbing the robbery stuff, the robbery packet, and I'm handing it out, 'You get over here. You fill this out. You shut up.'"

The employees are later commended for their actions in helping to put together an immediate physical description in the minutes following the robbery.

Pierce says, "All the girls, we all agreed that while he was there, it was nothing we were taught. We were not thinking, *Okay, what did the book tell you on page 3 of what to do?*...It was street smarts."

Pierce takes each day since the robbery one at a time. She is moving on with life. Four months after the robbery, she has recently quit working at the bank. She is moving to another town and preparing to enter college. Each day since September 14, 2009, "You just wake up that morning, and hopefully, that's not the first thing you think about...I'm just hoping that someday down the road, I'll go a week, a couple days, without something happening."

Tending bar part-time for a relative while waiting to move to a new town, Pierce has yet to find peace.

"I'll never close alone again," Pierce says, following a recent flashback when she was alone in the bar with three late customers. "I was absolutely terrified. I was practically in tears when I was closing because it's an older building so you hear noises. I was down on my knees, stocking the cooler, and I see somebody staring in at me, which, after I was done hyperventilating—it was my own reflection."

It's a scar Pierce says may never heal.

"For you to get your adrenaline rush of getting out of that bank or getting out of that gas station and going to another, even if it's at the gas station for 50 bucks, even if they catch you ten minutes later, you have still emotionally hurt that person—and they have never done anything to you."

Fixen, too, continues to have impacts from the bank robbery. Above all, she has lost trust in her own safety.

"I feel like I can't go anywhere, constantly looking over my shoulder. I live by myself, and I just have a fear, walking from my car to my house that somebody is going to be around. To see someone with a gun, even on TV, I can't watch. To know your life was in front of you, scares the crap out of you…just because of somebody's stupid decisions…ruining how many lives? Just because he wants to do something that he thinks is important? But it's not."

Fixen has nightmares of the robbery.

"Just seeing him walk around and having lost control. If he were to use the gun, I couldn't do anything," she says, breaking down at the thought.

Her feelings of hatred, a veiled rage, shake her voice, even months later. She is angry.

"Look at how many lives he affected in our bank, let alone how many other banks, their feelings, and they probably didn't have a gun pointed at them, but it's still the same. You go through the same emotional trauma, you deal with it, but yet you're traumatized for the rest of your life."

Fixen struggles with her feelings toward the robber and toward the many assumptions she had about her own safety.

"Always, in my banking career has been a thought in my mind, what if it happened? How would I handle it? And then it's just like, no, it's not going to happen. We're just a tiny town. You don't even worry about it, and I guess the shock is still within me. We're just a tiny town; why did it happen to us?"

CHAPTER TWENTY

Just Sleep

September 14, 2009

A first sergeant graciously supplied Rob with a copy of the disciplinary paperwork and the advice to look on the bright side.

"You still have your career," he said.

It was pretty tough to be appreciative. It was bad enough to have stayed in the military for eighteen-and-a-half years without attaining another stripe, but to actually lose one? To have to go back to his shop and face people who minutes ago were his subordinates? To have to tell his mom, at some point in the future, that her "good" son had failed so miserably?

There was no "bright" side Rob could see, only the need to go to the "stitch witch" and have his staff sergeant's chevrons removed from his uniform.

He got into his car and couldn't help thinking of the $377-a-month payments that yesterday had seemed like no sweat for the fulfillment of the lifelong dream of owning a hot Mustang. How was he going to pay his bills now?

Rob glanced at the gas station on base as he rolled by, thinking of the gas he was burning every day on a thirty-mile commute. Next, he thought of another type of fuel: vodka—a half bottle of it, still at home. That was one purchase he wouldn't have to make on the way.

Stopping at the little sewing shop just outside the main gate was a necessity. The sign read, "SEW-What." It seemed a trite title for a place where uniforms were altered no less exactly than the lives of airmen receiving a promotion. Far fewer, Rob realized, had occasion to visit the place for the reason he did.

As he entered, an Asian lady called out, "Just a minute," and Rob took off his shirt, laying it on the counter. With his face looking about as dull as his military-issue T-shirt, Rob asked if she had any old patches. She directed him to a five-gallon bucket filled with a random assortment of old stripes tossed aside by other guys, happy guys, thrilled to be trading up.

Just one more indignity, Rob thought, digging through the cast offs of a bunch of guys who would never have need of airman insignia again.

Finding a matching pair of the correct patches, Rob asked, "How much are these?"

"Free!" she said.

Well, that's something, anyway, Rob thought. At least he didn't have to pay extra for the humiliation of having to wear them.

"I need these sewn on," Rob told the woman. "Can you do them while I wait?"

The woman paused a moment, taking in the meaning behind some guy needing lesser insignia sewn on.

"You wait here?" she asked.

Rob nodded.

Five minutes later, she returned.

She pointed out the tan line where the old stripe used to be, not to mention the odd thread still poking out around the outline of the old and larger staff sergeant patch, now replaced with the smaller, used patches Rob had pulled from the bucket.

It wasn't as if he didn't need a new uniform soon anyway. This one would have to do for a few days at least.

He thanked the lady for putting a rush on the job. It wasn't her fault. He left the shop, throwing the shirt beside him in the car.

It was halfway into the robbery before Jimmy woke up enough to realize something was different this time.

Up until the point when one of the tellers went all hysterical, it had all gone, if not like clockwork, pretty predictably.

The bank manager, a heavyset lady, had risen from her seat across the lobby to ask him if he needed help when she saw him cross behind the teller line. He told her to sit down, and she did. A couple of the tellers froze, like some always did, when he first made his demand. A couple of taps of his gun barrel on the counter was enough to get them moving.

And sure enough, there had to be an adrenaline junkie at this bank— a young gal whose eyes had the brilliance of excitement as he faced her. She wasn't moving, wasn't getting her money.

What gave her the gumption? You really had to wonder. Most people were just sheep. They did as they were told—but not this girl. Something made the prospect of a loaded weapon seem as harmless as a cigarette to her. He told her to move, and still, she stood there.

"I haven't got any money," she said, arms stretched out. She was almost, not quite, smiling. Did she think this was a joke?

"Go," he said, gesturing with the gun. "Go get it."

Her name was Angie, he learned.

"Angie, just *do* it!" one of the other girls told her.

And she moved then, over to her drawer, opened it, and put the money out on the counter as he tapped the barrel twice more, giving her a little incentive to hurry it up.

Just then, the teller next to her really started to lose it. It sucked to see someone so upset. Another teller was obviously pregnant. *Shit! That's all I need,* he thought, *to cause some girl to abort right here on the bank floor.*

These girls didn't get it. How could they? They'd never been robbed before. He wasn't going to hurt anyone. The gun was just his ticket to the money. He'd never hurt anyone in any of his bank jobs. There was no time to hurt anyone. In and out. Two minutes.

Shit, she is really gonna lose it, Jimmy thought. It was just like that time in Grande Prairie, when the teller fainted. That day had not ended well. And he'd had seven years to think about how he should have just walked out that time, empty-handed.

Didn't they train these girls? Didn't they tell them as long as they did what they were told, no one got hurt? Hell, he might be a lot of things, but he didn't want some chick to lose her baby! And another teller was ratcheting up the emotion for all of them by crying. He had to say something.

"I'm not going to hurt anybody. It'll be okay," he murmured to the hysterical one, as gently as he could without getting all smarmy about it. "I'm not going to hurt you guys; just do what I'm asking you to do."

That seemed to do the trick. They got the job done, quickly and pretty efficiently, despite the few dramatic moments when the one girl defied him. Hell, these girls were all pretty young. They did good. They got through it just fine.

It made him feel a sense of kinship. Pride, even. He might be the one robbing the bank, but their cooperation made it all possible. And from the looks of it, this was gonna be a damn nice haul. Not his best, but enough to last a while.

After giving them the standard warning about sitting tight until the cops came, he couldn't resist speaking again.

"Thank you," he said, and he walked out the door.

This job was over. History.

The faces of the tellers, the shock written all over them, the tears of relief after his departure, the frantic calls that must be placed to the police and the main bank, none of these were images Jimmy could witness or even needed to imagine. He hadn't hurt anybody. What was the big deal? *They'll be fine,* he told himself. They did a good job. It was over—in the past.

Rob's commute home was long and straight. Popping a DVD into the dash-mounted player, he thought again just how much his car payments were gonna hurt in the future. The DVD player was standard issue in his dream car. *May as well enjoy the luxury as long as I'm paying for it,* Rob thought.

Soon enough, the show and the ride home were over. Time, he realized, eighteen-and-a-half years, had whizzed by in a blink—as fast as a single episode of a television show or one drive home. And all he had to show for it, Rob realized, as he got out of the car, grabbing his shirt from where he'd tossed it, was a uniform with a tan mark left behind where sergeant's stripes ought to have been.

Once indoors, he resisted the urge to fix a drink before getting his PT gear ready for a morning run the next day. That chore complete, he found the half-full bottle of vodka and mixed it with some orange Gatorade. He had every intention, this night, of drinking himself into oblivion.

Finally. Sheesh. That still stung. Bad. Like an invisible punch in the nose.

Settling on the couch, Rob transported himself to a place where ammo is infinite and the bad guys to shoot, unlimited. Hooking up for an online session of Horde would do nicely, under the circumstances. In between levels, Rob munched on some nachos he'd fixed himself and poured himself another drink.

The embarrassment. The humiliation. He cringed just at the thought of people referring to him as "Airman Krimm." He'd prefer simply "Krimm," with nothing in front of it.

Might as well take his meds early. Let the pills kick in so he could get some sleep and take his mind off what a disorganized mess his life had become. He felt so low he wasn't even capable of hurting himself, unless you counted the names he beat himself with—failure, douche bag, shit bird. Yeah, all of those, and more.

With the pill bottle in hand, Rob thought only briefly of swallowing a handful of the tablets, but he couldn't even accomplish that. He couldn't do that to the person who would have to find his lifeless body when he didn't show up for work the next day or to his mother, or anyone else.

As bad as his life had ever been as a kid, no matter how much any physical punishment hurt, despite being absolutely trapped in a house with a brother who was no better than an animal, Rob never once thought of killing himself. Not once. And compared to the horrors of his childhood, what was this demotion? Just one more submission, that was all. It sucked to have to submit; it made him physically ill, in fact, to even think of it. But then, as now, what choice did he have?

Standing up to the Air Force and beating a demotion was no more likely than standing up to a brother who was a foot taller and a hundred pounds heavier. If a drill sergeant told you to drop and give him twenty, or if your big brother met you at the door after school with a wooden paddle in his hand, you did as you were told.

Returning to the online game session, Rob and his group of fellow gamers wound up beating the horde, advancing to level 50 in a deserted town. Normally, an achievement like that would be cause for celebration. He might even be moved to raise the remote in a one-armed fist pump. But not this time.

Jimmy felt like he was in his worst nightmare and, in fact, had imagined just such a scenario many times. But nothing like the fuck-ups of this day had ever occurred in the past—well, not unless you counted the time he got drunk in a stolen car, fell asleep eating a pizza, and got sent to prison for five years.

Since leaving the bank in Williston five hours earlier, Jimmy had been chased, shot at, chased some more, lost, chased again, lost again, and now there was a fucking airplane spotlighting him.

Two of them were flying around up there, in fact.

Why the hell should he be surprised? He'd always known this day was coming, and he'd never been afraid, because the way out had become so obvious. Shoot the cops, or shoot yourself. Either way, you're dead. There was no way he was going back to prison, and no way they weren't going to send him away for the rest of his life now that he'd shot at a cop.

He'd known about the road construction west of Williston. It hadn't worried him in the least, because he figured he'd be long gone before anyone in Montana knew about a bank robbery twenty-odd miles across the border.

Besides, heading toward road construction would seem to the cops like the absolute least likely direction of travel, right? What bank robber would let himself get stuck in a line of vehicles following a pilot car? *Only a dumb robber,* Jimmy thought, and as it turned out, *he was that guy.* His plan was to do something so stupid it would be the perfect cover, but in the end, it just turned out to *be* stupid.

Someone had spotted the car leaving the alley behind the bank. His scanner told him they knew it was a green four-door, but they were looking for a Pontiac or a Taurus, not a Mitsubishi, so he wasn't all that worried.

Not to mention, the police were notoriously poor about communicating across state lines.

It just figured the wait at the road project was taking lots longer heading west.

When a Montana trooper rolled past him and gave him a look, Jimmy waited only long enough to see the guy turn around before he pulled out of the line of cars, sped ahead, and turned into a farmstead.

Shit! He was excited now. No more sleepwalking through this day.

After being chased through a pasture and back out on to the highway, Jimmy found himself headed in the wrong direction, back toward the road construction. *Shit! Dumbass.* That was the way back to Williston. There was nothing to do but turn around and face this guy.

Jimmy floored it, putting enough distance between his car and the trooper's so he'd have time enough to turn around.

He felt like he was in a movie—one where the bad guy shoots at the cop and gets away. There was no time to form a definite intention. That cop just needed to be stopped.

"Pop, pop, pop, pop," Jimmy fired at the trooper's car as he met it.

Shit! What was he doing? Shooting at a cop? Stupid, stupid, stupid. Bank robbery was one thing, but shooting at a cop? There was no getting a break on that kind of rap. Besides, Jimmy was tired of running.

He looked in his rearview mirror to see the trooper making a U-turn. It was kill or be killed, or be captured. You roll the dice, you take your chances. Hell, his whole life was nothing but a crapshoot. He could live like a king for months on this haul. Or he could wind up dead.

If he didn't stop that trooper, every cop in a hundred-mile radius would be shooting first and asking questions of people driving green cars later.

Jimmy flipped a U-turn of his own, but then the trooper stopped, and for a split second, it looked like maybe he was hurt. It wasn't until he saw the high-powered rifle come out of the cop car in the hands of the trooper that Jimmy realized who was going to be the loser in this face-off. These were the highest stakes ever. He might be tired of running, but his pistol was no match for a rifle.

Jimmy changed directions yet again, away from the patrolman. Just then, there came a sound like the "peenk" of metal piercing metal, and a hole appeared in the console, just above the glove compartment, across from Jimmy. *That fucker is shooting at me!* The adrenaline now rushed so furiously Jimmy swore he was hearing his own heart beating. That shot had missed him by inches! Just a little to the left, and it would already be over.

He'd gotten away, finally, only to get lost and come upon three more cops a couple of hours later, back on the North Dakota side, near a town called Grenora.

Once again, he managed to elude them, but his avenue of escape—a wheat field—provided such good cover he didn't see the rock pile until it was too late to avoid getting hung up. He'd had to hike to a nearby farm and steal a pickup.

Now, after running into yet another cop and considering, if only briefly, shooting at him, Jimmy had to admit he was stuck. Once those planes spotted him, there was no longer any point in running. Still, he kept moving, working up his nerve.

On top of the vodka, the pills were kicking in, and in just a few more minutes, Rob knew, he could escape the horde, the Air Force, and all of the thoughts about what a terrible year it had been—first the car accident, then the breakup with Carol, then getting evicted, neck surgery, all the trouble with food logs, having to lose weight, and now this. He was thirty-eight-fucking years old, and his life stank like a college freshmen who comes home broke and hungover after dropping out of school.

He could not have imagined how much a little piece of cloth on a uniform could mean to him. He did not want to believe his dignity could be stripped away as easily as snipping a few threads off a patch. And for what? No fucking reason! It might as well have been for wiping his ass wrong as missing an appointment he actually showed up for.

Finally, Rob just wanted to pass out. If the Fates wanted to fuck with him, he had to admit, this was about as low a blow as they could deliver. On top of every other setback in Rob's life over the past year, this demotion was the last straw. Maybe now, finally, his luck would change.

Rob read the clock showing it was past 11:00 PM as a sleepy peace settled over his brain. He entered a state of consciousness where nothing mattered—not the demotion, not having to get up the next day for work, not living, not dying. Just sleep.

With two airplanes overhead and headlights closing in on his location from three directions, his stolen pickup stuck in the mud, Jimmy got out of the vehicle, ready, if not exactly willing, to carry out an action he'd never rehearsed physically, though he'd pictured it many times.

He wouldn't have to worry anymore about how he was going to make a living or how he might die, because he was taking control. Death, he figured, was like sleep. Just pull the trigger. Just sleep.

CHAPTER TWENTY-ONE

The Chase

September 14, 2009

Montana Highway Patrol trooper Rick Kessner wasn't looking for any trophies. With twenty-nine years in law enforcement, the fifty-five-year-old could retire anytime, joining his father, brother, brother-in-law, and an uncle, all career lawmen.

"Since 1966, in our immediate family, we've been tied up with law enforcement," Kessner tells me.

In twenty-nine years, Kessner has been in physical altercations with drivers, had the hood of his patrol car stomped nearly to the dashboard, and even had his weapon out a time or two. But he's never had to fire on a suspect. If he ever doubted he could, that doubt disappeared the day he crossed paths with Jimmy Krimm.

Kessner was on routine patrol near his northeastern Montana home of Culbertson late in the afternoon of September 14, 2009, when he heard a bulletin to be on the lookout for a suspect who'd robbed a bank in Williston, North Dakota. All Kessner had for a description was a white male in a green car, maybe a Pontiac, North Dakota plates, unknown direction of travel.

"I went east, and I made it about seven or eight miles," Kessner says. "I noticed a string of cars coming at me."

A major road construction project was slowing traffic. The third vehicle in the line was a green passenger car.

"So I slowed down, and I looked at him. He looked at me as we went past, and it had North Dakota plates. It was a green car, a white male."

There was no room to turn around until the queue of cars had passed. Once Kessner turned around, "I started passing all the vehicles. No lights, no sirens, no nothing, because I was just going to get a license plate on it."

He was not the only one out of line. The man in the green car was passing people, too. Even though the action was suspicious, Kessner still couldn't be sure this was the guy, but doubt faded as the vehicle pulled into a farmstead, about five miles east of Culbertson. The car headed for a tree line.

"I get around the trees, and he's already down through the pasture at a high rate of speed."

By then, Kessner knew he was chasing a bank robber.

"He goes through a fence line, right through the gate, doesn't stop to open it up, so I slow up so I can get through the gate without grabbing the barbwire, and then we end up all through the back country there. It's probably a mile, mile and a half, and then we're going back toward the main house."

The green car plowed through another gate and then screamed through a playground near the farmhouse before getting back onto the highway.

"That's when I turned on my lights and siren," Kessner says. He also engaged the in-car video system that would record events from that point on. Kessner shows me the video, playing it for me on the computer in his patrol car a few months later.

I see the green car begin to outdistance Kessner.

"It's a fast little car. And he just pulls away from me," Kessner says.

On the computer screen, Jimmy's car is becoming a tiny dot in the distance as I watch. He is getting away.

A few miles down the road, the green car slows and turns around, coming back toward Kessner! It doesn't make any sense. Clearly, the patrol car is no match for the Mitsubishi, so why turn around?

Kessner quickly calculates his options.

"I'm thinking to myself, *Should I hit him head-on?* No, because I might get trapped in my car. *Should I sideswipe him?* No, because I could still get trapped in my car."

If he was going to take action, it had to be quick and decisive. But there was no time. All he could hope to do was make himself a moving target.

"I'm crouching down in my seat, and he comes at me, and he slows down, and he's dragging a whole bunch of barbwire and fence posts." Kessner laughs. "And I key in on that for just a split second."

But something else caught Kessner's eye.

"I see the pistol come out, and I see it start to bounce...and I lay down in the seat and I hear, *pop, pop, pop, pop*...four rounds. And I just accelerated at the same time that I laid down in the seat."

I see the pistol too, there on the screen, and I can't believe it. It is like watching a movie. *That's Jimmy,* I tell myself—Charlene's son—sticking his arm out the window of a car holding a gun, shooting at a cop! I could just hear Rob's pronouncement, *"Dumbass!"*

One round struck Kessner's bumper; another caught a tire. Two more hit the pavement.

As Rob points out, "He was aiming for the engine compartment or the tire," not someone's head.

Charlene, too, cannot believe Jimmy would try to kill someone, no matter the other crimes he committed. Even after I tell her I saw the video myself, she has a hard time accepting it.

Perhaps it's natural for his family members, even an abused brother, to have a hard time believing Jimmy intended to kill someone. After everything I've learned about Jimmy, it's hard for me to believe, too, much as I understand how Kessner must feel.

With the robber past him, Kessner peered over the dash in time to miss a delineator pole on the shoulder of the road.

"I'm down in the ditch again, and I come back, and I do a U-turn to go back after him."

As Kessner was making the turn, he looked up to the sinking realization the robber was now turning around, too, heading back for a second pass. His intention was not just to disable the car, Kessner believes, but to take him out.

Had Jimmy practiced such a scenario? I wonder. The same way he'd practiced holdups as a kid, pulling a gun out of his sweatshirt in front of his little brother? But his actions just don't add up. There is not one single report anywhere to indicate the use of deadly force on Jimmy's part. Not in any of the robberies he committed in the United States or in Canada. There is not even the mention of a raised voice. How do you go from calm and cool to suddenly shooting at a cop?

Then again, there is only one other time I know of that Jimmy came in such close contact with a cop following a robbery. It was thirteen years earlier, the day his Canadian spree came to an end. He had to be scared shitless. So when he's in the clear, why does he turn back toward trouble, let alone face it head-on?

"I figure I'm probably the only law officer who's ever confronted him so soon after one of his robberies, and he just didn't know what to do with that. He had to try to eliminate the threat," Kessner says.

With over $20,000 in the car, Jimmy had strong motivation to do whatever was necessary to get away. Instead, it looks as if he is trying to pick a fight. Did he have hopes of going out in a blaze of glory? Was he *hoping* the trooper would return his fire?

Rob has another theory, and as crazy as it sounds to me at first, I know Rob understands what his brother is capable of, perhaps better than anyone else.

What if, Rob theorizes, Jimmy was worried the trooper needed help?

I think of the deer in the ditch near Devils Lake and the kid pinned under an ATV, and I wonder. Could Jimmy have turned around to see if the trooper needed assistance? Could he have realized in the split seconds after he shot at the patrol car, that he didn't want a murder on his hands?

It is a stretch for Rob to attribute a trait like mercy to a man who showed him none. And yet, as crazy as it sounds, it's just crazy enough to be possible. Thinking back to some of the convoluted logic on display when Jimmy talked with troopers in Minnesota and Montana, frankly, I wouldn't put anything past him. Could he actually have thought, somehow, that after shooting at a cop, he could undo it by coming to his aid if he were hurt?

As Jimmy's car approached him a second time, Kessner already had his assault rifle out and unlocked. Jumping out of the patrol car, he took aim at the green car.

"And he's, I estimate, 250 feet away to 300 feet, and he turns around and does another U-turn, down in the ditch and starts to leave. And it's still going through my mind, *he's going to kill somebody; he's tried to kill me twice, so, okay*. I shot at him three times."

Kessner had no idea at the time just how close he came to knocking out the robber with one of those shots. A bullet that struck the suspect's trunk came to rest in the dashboard of the Mitsubishi, missing Jimmy by inches.

The pursuit resumed, but a bullet hole in one of Kessner's tires soon caused him to pull over.

"I could hear my left front tire going *wop, wop, wop*," but at 105 or 110 miles per hour, the tire finally blew.

Looking back, Kessner felt lucky.

"My feeling is he was trying to kill me," Kessner says.

The attempt at a second pass sealed that belief.

"That was what was the deciding factor for me," says Kessner. "He was trying to kill me so he could get away. And I couldn't let that happen. I had to try to stop him. When he saw that high-powered rifle, boy, he was turning tail. Because the pistol, yeah, it might have hit the car, but the accuracy isn't there, not the accuracy with the assault rifle."

Kessner's take is the obvious one. But there are at least two other possibilities. Did Jimmy simply lose his nerve? Was he having second thoughts about forcing a showdown? Was he contemplating "suicide by cop," hoping for someone else to put him out of his misery and then chickening out? Why on earth would he attempt a second pass unless he was willing to accept the consequence he might be the one who died?

In the end, Jimmy did back down. He *did* chicken out—either because he didn't want to kill someone, or because he didn't want to die.

Under Rob's scenario, once Jimmy knew the trooper was ambulatory, any sudden pang of mercy was moot. If the trooper wasn't going to die, Jimmy didn't have to worry about having killed someone, so he turned around and sped off.

Kessner spent the next six hours involved in the manhunt for the bank robber, but missed the final showdown about a dozen miles inside the North Dakota border.

"It's frustrating," Kessner says, but he has a souvenir by which to remember the case.

"I went back and found the tire. The tire is mine," Kessner says, the bullet hole obvious in the sidewall.

He plans to make a clock out of it and hang it in his garage.

When Divide County Sheriff Lauren Throntveit first heard the bulletin about a bank robbery in Williston, sixty-eight miles to the south of the county seat of Crosby, he figured, *What are the odds he's going to be here?*

Throntveit's laugh after the fact belies the seriousness with which local officers took the bulletin. Throntveit has been enforcing the law for three decades. Now, in his second term as the elected sheriff, he'd grown up in the county, like two of his three deputies. Prior to his election as sheriff, he was Crosby's police chief for nearly twenty years. I have been calling him nearly every Monday morning for the past ten years to collect crime news for *The Journal*.

By and large, the rural population of Divide County is honest, friendly, and hardworking. Armed altercations with bank bandits are unheard of, and with the exception of an armed standoff with a man on a farmstead a few years earlier, the need for deadly force is virtually nonexistent.

I sit down with Throntveit and Chief Deputy Rob Melby one day in December, at the law enforcement center that used to be the sheriff's residence and jail, built in 1917.

After hearing the bulletin about a bank robber, Throntveit dispatched Deputy Brent Gunderson to the town of Grenora, just a few miles over the Divide County line, in Williams County. Melby abandoned a day off to join Gunderson and a U.S. Border Patrol agent at the stakeout.

"I said, 'Well, if anything comes up, just call me,'" Throntveit says, "but what don't we have down in that area? Cell phone service. And radio service isn't very good either."

An hour went by.

"You assume he's going to be out of the area, or lost, and in Divide County."

Located in the extreme northwest corner of North Dakota, Divide County is something of a dead end. A bank robber wouldn't be likely to be able to cross into Canada legally, and a growing amount of border surveillance since 9/11, in the form of unmanned cameras and aerial surveys, have lately made it more difficult to try to cross illegally. No major highway cuts through the county. There is virtually no traffic, no towns of any size, and no chance of getting lost in a crowd.

"Why would you head *this* way?" Throntveit wondered aloud.

Roosevelt County Sheriff's sergeant Jason Fredericks is a ten-year police veteran who lives in Poplar, Montana, thirty-three miles west of Culbertson, the town where Kessner is based. Fredericks was coaching Little League football that afternoon, as part of a program sponsored by the sheriff's office.

"And I got a call from one of my reserve deputies who ended up being the one with me that night, saying, 'What's going on? I just heard Highway Patrolman Rick Kessner say, 'Shots fired.'"

Fredericks called his dispatcher and learned of the manhunt for a bank robber.

"I'm still in shorts and sandals," Fredericks says. He threw on a sheriff's T-shirt, grabbed his duty belt and a bulletproof vest, and headed for Culbertson, picking up reservist Cam Friede along the way. "We kind of drove the back roads for a while, until eventually, our entire office got there—several more highway patrolmen and several officers from the Ft. Peck tribes."

When Roosevelt County Sheriff Freedom Crawford arrived, a briefing was set up in the small town of McCabe, north of Culbertson.

"All we know is he went north on a gravel road, just east of Culbertson."

Across the border in North Dakota, the Divide County deputies had yet to hear about Kessner's run-in. In fact, for a couple of hours, the stakeout near Grenora appeared to be a bust. Communication difficulties heightened the impression not much was going on.

"You've got two different states chasing the same guy, but they can't talk to each other," says Throntveit. "It becomes a major problem."

It was specifically for the possibility of picking up some radio traffic from Montana that the officers headed to Grenora in the first place. They certainly didn't expect to cross paths with the suspect forty-six miles from Williston, when he had had enough time to travel a couple hundred miles.

Not hearing anything that sounded like they could be of assistance. "We were about ready to leave Grenora, too. It was starting to get dark," Melby says.

That was when the approach of a car caught his eye.

"This car comes up from the south, and I'm like, 'Hey, guys, that's a dark green car.'"

But it was not a Ford Taurus or a Pontiac Grand Am as bulletins had indicated. It was a Mitsubishi. Melby wasn't deterred by the lack of an exact match. He'd sat at a lonely intersection for hours. He figured they might as well stop the car and see who was inside.

"We all jumped in our vehicles to take off, and the car sat at the intersection. It hesitated, indicating indecision about its direction of travel.

"Like, what should I do? You know, the wheels go kind of like this," Melby indicates, first turning one way and then the other. "All of a sudden, it took off and went east."

With three police vehicles now in pursuit, the car turned north, just on the eastern edge of the remote prairie town, which is surrounded by miles and miles of grain fields.

"I was probably an eighth of a mile behind him at the beginning, but you know, we have SUVs and he had that car."

By the time Melby crested the first hill out of town, "He was probably a good half a mile to three quarters of a mile ahead of me. And by the time, you know, we got further down the road, he lost us."

When deputies reached an intersection—one road cut back into Montana to the west; another continued north toward the all-but-abandoned town of Alkabo—they couldn't be sure which path to take. It was at this juncture the paved road ended.

"There was a little bit of dust, so we were trying to figure out which way did he go?"

It was soon clear no one else had the robber in sight or in custody. It had to be him. Officers from three counties and two different states headed toward the location.

"At that time, they'd already gotten the plane up, too," says Throntveit.

"In the meantime, we're looking for him; we're running back and forth," Melby says, on roads dotted here and there with farmsteads.

"The initial three of us, we split up."

It looked once again like the suspect was home free—a needle in the proverbial haystack—only in his case, it was more like a fish swimming in a sea of wheat.

"He started driving through wheat fields—standing wheat fields—with the car."

By now, Fredericks and the other Roosevelt County deputies had spent hours knocking on farmhouse doors, widening their circle all the way to the North Dakota line.

"Our biggest fear, on the Montana portion of it, was him getting to a farmyard and taking someone hostage."

Fredericks found most of the rural residents were already aware there was a manhunt in their neighborhood.

"A lot of the farmers and the people in the towns, they have scanners, and they do listen to it. I probably went to a dozen, dozen and a half houses, and I think only one person hadn't heard of it...There was people out there, retired law enforcement guys, out there in their own vehicles."

These "helpers" were mostly armed, as were the farmers holed up in their homes.

"There were actually several we talked to that said, 'Oh, I got the shotgun right here.' You know, good ol' northeastern Montana! They're well prepared." Fredericks chuckles.

It was during this patrol that Montana deputies received word the subject had been spotted near the state line.

"I was probably the farthest away when they spotted him," Fredericks says. He sped about forty miles to Dagmar, Montana, "And we sat there for oh, an hour, hour and a half."

"All of a sudden we get a call," Melby says. "'We just had a pickup stolen right out of our yard,' a black pickup."

Melby was frantic to get the information broadcast quickly so other agencies would know about the stolen pickup.

That the information got out at all was a fluke. Cec Raaum, who called in the theft, actually placed two calls before she got anyone to stop long enough to realize her call was connected to the two-state manhunt.

Cec and her husband, Jerry, and Jerry's brother, Ronell, were sitting down to a late supper on the farm six miles south of Westby, Montana, when they noticed taillights leaving the yard. It was harvesttime, and the family worked late, only stopping to eat when it grew dark—and dark came late in the neighborhood that time of year, about 9:20 PM, North Dakota time.

"We stepped outside to see our 1994 black Nissan pickup driving away with no headlights on and not a sign of another vehicle," Cec told the *Westby Border News*.

Unaware of the bank robbery or manhunt, Cec called the sheriff's office and was told everyone was busy. Not satisfied, she placed a second call, this time to the North Dakota statewide emergency number.

Sheriff Throntveit is not surprised there was confusion that night. Besides officers in two states and four counties on either side of the border involved in a manhunt for a bank robber, officers in the Raaum's county seat of Plentywood were dealing with a guy who pulled a gun at a local motel.

"I mean, it was crazy," says Throntveit, especially considering armed holdups are so rare in the area.

"In the meantime," Melby says, "I talked to the highway patrolman, who would have been Chris Pulver from Stanley."

It was Pulver who let Divide County lawmen know the robber had shot at Kessner.

"Which certainly changes the status of this chase," says Throntveit.

The drama, he says, ratcheted up a notch, "From 'Let's try stop him' to 'Let's just do whatever it takes and stop him.'"

After what happened to Kessner, Pulver knew he, too, was a target. He sat at the intersection of ND5 and Divide Co. 5, just west of an old Air Force radar station, five miles west of the town of Fortuna. He was ready to stop any vehicle matching the description of the stolen pickup. This was about a half hour after my kids were getting home from the volleyball game, about a mile away, as the crow flies, from my house.

The now-abandoned air base opened in 1951 as a safety net to alert the military in case Russian bombers ever attempted to fly over the polar cap to attack America during the Cold War. Decommissioned in the early 1980s, the site today stands as a relic of a threat long since eradicated— but posing a new threat should an outlaw choose the site as a place to hole up or hide out. The radar base is closer to our farm than any of our neighbors. I don't feel so foolish, suddenly, for having armed myself and my children that night.

Pulver was unfamiliar with the area, seeing it for the first time, in the dark.

Around 10:10 PM, Pulver saw a vehicle approach from the direction of Westby, Montana, on ND 5. It was a maroon SUV, nothing suspicious. Pulver watched the SUV roll past him, and he watched a second or two as the vehicle's taillights traveled up the hill to the east. Pulver looked west again and within moments turned his gaze east once more—once again in the direction of travel of the SUV.

"Now there are two sets of taillights," Pulver says, and no place but the base, or cross-country, for a vehicle to come from.

Pulver pulled onto the highway to check out both vehicles. As he caught up to the second set of taillights, he smelled the distinct odor of burning grass on a catalytic converter.

"I knew someone had been doing some off-roading," he says, by that smell alone. Figuring there was no other way for the dark-colored pickup to have gotten on the highway but to have driven cross-country, and based on the location where Pulver first spotted the taillights, the subject had to have literally come off the prairie right under his nose.

Knowing what Kessner had faced when he approached, "I wasn't going to try to stop him until I had backup."

With the suspect truck traveling only about forty-five miles per hour, Pulver did nothing to indicate he was in a law enforcement vehicle. He used no siren, no lights, but it soon became obvious the suspect had a scanner. Why else would he pull over to the shoulder of the road as soon as Pulver called in the plate?

"He came around and came back toward me," Pulver says.

Suddenly, Pulver found himself faced with the same moment of truth Kessner had faced five hours earlier. The only difference, Pulver believes, was that the suspect couldn't fire because he wasn't absolutely sure, in the dark, whether the blinding headlights he faced were those of a patrol car.

"It was pitch-black dark," Pulver says.

But once again, Jimmy's actions are hard for me to understand. To me, he looks like a man tired of running. Once again, he planted himself in a position where confrontation and death are very likely consequences. And this time, even after he has to know the other car contained a cop, he didn't shoot. Pulver never even saw a gun.

Once the pickup rolled past Pulver, "He actually pulled over and stopped again on the right shoulder," before plunging into a ditch on the south side of the highway.

The prairie trail Pulver describes is just over the hill from my mother-in-law's place. No wonder she had five cop cars in her driveway that night!

I wonder at Jimmy's state of mind at this point. What on earth can he be thinking, setting out cross-country in unfamiliar terrain, in the dark? Does he still believe escape is possible? Or is he merely looking for the right place, the right excuse, to stop running once and for all?

Unable to follow in his cruiser through the broken terrain, "I was amazed at just how much off-roading he was able to do," Pulver says.

At the time, "I thought it was a local because he was doing such a good job driving off trail."

Though Pulver was locked out of the chase, now the noose could be tightened. Two airplanes were flying overhead, and officers from two states were screaming toward the tiny town of Fortuna.

"Chris calls it in, and everybody's spread out, and they're trying to get over there," says Melby, who, along with Border Patrol Agent Ross Eriksmoen, were the two closest to the location where the suspect left the roadway. Sheriff Throntveit was headed there, too.

"Again, the communication problem is, we still don't know *there are how many Roosevelt County people driving around in our county?* Which becomes a bad thing, because, ultimately, you're chasing taillights that shouldn't be chased," Throntveit says.

The airplanes evened the playing field, giving the lawmen an overwhelming advantage. Through a process of lights-on, lights-off signaling from the police below, the pilots were able to determine which vehicle was the robber's. They could track his every move on infrared camera.

Now there was little need for the police on the ground to chase. The spree was over, even if the bandit didn't know it yet.

"Everybody kind of stops. You slow down. You gotta slow down," says Throntveit. "There aren't many schools that teach you what to do out in the middle of nowhere."

The night of September 14, 2009, provided a crash course.

Knowing the suspect had already shot at a cop, and with a dozen lawmen now closing in, "Either he's going to stop and do this," Throntveit says, his hands up in the air, "real quick-like, or he's gonna get it—I mean, you don't have a choice."

The possibility of getting shot by the suspect was not the only risk, however.

"The thing everybody kind of forgets about is the dangers involved, at these high speeds, at night, on gravel roads."

Throntveit hit a deer even as he was pulling out of Crosby that night.

"I think two deer or three deer were hit that night. And you're driving 100 miles an hour, you hit one, and there's a chance you ain't gonna make it," he says in all seriousness, adding with a laugh, "Where was that damn deer when I needed him?"

In truth, not long after heading off-road from ND 5, the robber narrowly missed two deer in his path. The infrared camera overhead in one of the planes recorded it. Months later, I watch the last twenty minutes of Jimmy's life roll by like OJ's white Ford Bronco on a California freeway—from above.

The system used in the police planes is the same type of FLIR (forward looking infrared radar) system used on U.S. Air Force planes to verify targets. It is the same kind of system Rob Krimm services at an Air Force base in North Carolina.

"The airplane is saying, 'I think we got him. I think we got him. Keep hitting your lights so we can figure out who he is,'" Melby says.

Throntveit adds, "The circle was getting smaller. Of course, the airplane was right on top of him."

I watch on the video, seeing Jimmy drive out of a field onto a gravel road, coming to a complete stop just past an intersection. He backs up to the intersection, and sits there for several seconds, seemingly undecided. There is the suggestion of him crouching down in the seat, leaning forward, and looking up through his windshield at the planes overhead, perhaps realizing at that exact moment, his escape is unlikely, even if there are no police in sight on the ground.

He meanders this way and that, on gravel one minute, entering another wheat field the next. By this time, I am sure, Jimmy can see his way out; he's just looking for the right place, the right opportunity, or some fated obstacle to force his hand. He can't do it until something or someone forces him to stop.

"Once he got down in that area, everybody is closing in more; everybody is trying to get in here, and now he's out in this field, and we're kind of pushing him in here," says Melby, anticipating the final showdown.

"He's already shot at us. Unless he's screaming, and you can hear him saying, 'I give up! I give up!' We aren't gonna ask him to give up. Cruel reality," Throntveit says. "I mean, he's escalated that. He's already robbed a bank with a gun, shot at cops, outrun cops. He's pushed it to the ultimate limit."

Without a direct request, it is unusual for Montana deputies to cross the state line into North Dakota.

"I don't know that they requested us," Fredericks says, "but I just barely got into Grenora and Sheriff Crawford said, 'They spotted him. He's out in the middle of a field.'"

Fredericks was in unfamiliar territory.

"From there, I can't tell you where I was. I know I headed north on the highway—and I was trying to get to some town he was telling me—but I was able to follow the plane in the air to get to it."

Once Fredericks, accompanied by Friede, began following the plane, finding the bandit was easy. The two Montana lawmen were traveling north on a gravel road, south of Fortuna, when they saw headlights coming directly at them.

"And we come over a couple of hills, and the headlights were gone. I come by a dirt road, and my reserve happened to look over and see taillights to the east of us so we stopped and backed up and headed down a gravel road. And as we got closer, the vehicle, the lights, we could see he picked up speed, so at that point, we were pretty positive we had the vehicle."

Fredericks knew the suspect was now in a pickup.

"At one point, we were looking for three different kinds of green car. We had anywhere from a Taurus to a Grand Am to a Mitsubishi," he says. "Fairly quickly, we got the report that he had taken a black Nissan pickup, and we went over some oil ditches and through some tall grass and finally ended up in a wheat field, and at that point, I finally recognized the writing on the tailgate. It said 'Nissan'...one occupant...we went around in circles for I don't know how long."

Fredericks backed off, following the pickup at a distance of one hundred yards or more, running without emergency lights or siren.

"At one point, we're going through a field, and I see headlights coming at us, and I see headlights coming to the side of us. And I was relieved at that point. I thought, *Here's our help.*"

But Fredericks' relief was short-lived.

As quickly as help appeared, "Everybody was gone again. It was just us and him, and I'm looking at the reserve like, 'Where'd those headlights go? Where's our help?'"

A short time later, Fredericks crested a hill and saw the black Nissan hit the bottom, coming to a stop.

"I came down the hill, parked probably sixty yards away from him, seventy, maybe."

Seeing the reverse lights of the truck blink on and off, on and off, Fredericks realized the suspect vehicle was stuck.

"'Get ready, because it's going to go down right now,'" Fredericks told Friede, who was armed with a twelve-gauge shotgun. Fredericks had a .223.

"The door came open. He stepped right out next to his vehicle. At that point, I opened my door, and the grass was probably six feet tall where we were parked. So both of us had to stand on the floorboard of the vehicle. And at that point, I started giving commands."

Fredericks called out, "Show me your hands," and the suspect raised his hands.

Watching on the FLIR recording, I am amazed how closely this scene mirrors the picture I had in my head all along—of a man, hands up in a flood of light, surrounded by a bunch of police, guns drawn. In my mind's eye, the scene plays out in Technicolor, like a movie. But this is real, in shocking infrared. I am about to witness Jimmy's last stand—his final choice.

"To me," Fredericks says, "It looked like he raised his hands over his head. We thought, *Shit, this is going to be easy. He's going to give up*—because it looked like his hands are above his head—but then a shot fired."

CHAPTER TWENTY-TWO

Chase Ends

September 14, 2009

At the flash of a single gunshot, Roosevelt County Deputy Jason Fredericks and Reserve Deputy Cam Friede open fire.

"They see a flash of gunfire, and, of course, they think they're getting shot at," says Divide County Deputy Rob Melby. "Rightfully so."

"I engaged nine rounds at the suspect," says Fredericks, "and I think my reserve deputy fired three or four rounds of .00 buck."

The suspect disappeared from view in the tall grass. The deputies didn't know if they had shot the man, killed him, or if he was merely hiding. It was pitch-black across the countryside, with only headlights to pierce the gloom.

"We didn't know at that point," Fredericks says. "It's racing through your mind, *Did you shoot him? God I hope not.* I always ask myself, could I do it? Well, I proved I could do it, but do I want to do it? No, I never want to deal with that."

Realizing there was no return fire, "I got back on the radio and advised Sheriff Crawford that shots had been fired," says Fredericks, "and we backed up to the top of the hill, and we just kind of scanned the area."

Word was relayed from the airplane that the suspect appeared to have shot himself.

Believing the threat was now neutralized, Fredericks and Friede drove toward the suspect vehicle.

"And we seen another vehicle pulling in, and they pulled up parallel to us. And they got out and started advancing, so we got out and started advancing," says Fredericks.

Divide County Deputy Rob Melby heard the same report from the plane as Fredericks.

"I was coming down the hill, and as we get down there, the airplane is like, 'He's down,'" says Melby. "So at that point in time…we get down there a ways, I mean, this grass was as tall as us—slough grass, bullrushes."

"When you're in there, you're up to your nose," adds Divide County Sheriff Lauren Throntveit. "We were going to try to clear the scene because we didn't know if he was still alive or what he was doing, we didn't know."

Fredericks, Friede, and a Sheridan County deputy were walking in on foot, too.

"You can't see nothing," Fredericks says. "I'm telling you, we're in six feet of grass, five feet of grass."

"I mean, the stuff is like this," Melby says, hand up to his neck, "and you're trying to see, and we keep working our way in there."

As officers from three different agencies approach the suspect vehicle, "You can see the door is open and he's not sitting there," says Fredericks.

All of the officers had guns drawn.

"There he is," Fredericks called out, and everybody halted their advance for a moment.

Seeing no movement, the approach resumed, and Fredericks heard a sound from the suspect.

"We walked up to him as he took his last breath is what I believe," says Fredericks. "But it was definitely a fatal gunshot wound. I never heard him say a word, nothing."

The officers noticed the suspect's weapon had fallen on the ground, between his legs.

"I'm thinking, *Should I grab it? Should I not grab it?* and the under-sheriff from Sheridan County, he's like, 'He ain't in no shape to get it.'"

"You know, it was to the point where there was nothing we were going to do for him," says Melby.

Nonetheless, Melby went back to his vehicle to retrieve his first-responder bag.

Looking back, several weeks later, "I thought for sure he was firing at us," Fredericks says, but he is relieved he didn't kill Jimmy Krimm. "There was definitely a sense of relief that he took his own life, and sure, you wish you could talk him out of it, but there just wasn't time for that."

"I certainly don't wish death on anybody," Fredericks adds. "If there was more time and the circumstances were right, I would have loved to have a chance to talk him out of it...I guess I always wonder why? What's so bad...that you take your own life? I really don't think there was anything we could have done different, should have done different, that would have changed the outcome. The fact of the matter is, he was either going to get away, or his life was ending—and he wasn't giving up."

The infrared video from the plane shows Jimmy getting out of the pickup to stand beside it. He raises his gun hand in a gesture of futility and lets it fall. Next, he raises his left arm. It looks for the world to me like he is flipping the bird—to the officers, to life, to nothing in particular. A split second later, he raises his gun arm again and points the barrel at his temple. There is a flash, and his body falls.

I am shocked by what I am seeing. I feel like a witness at an execution. Knowing that these events transpired four miles from my house, as I sat with a pistol, my kids also armed, is surreal. But I also feel, as I watch the video, as if I am riding with Jimmy. I feel the adrenaline. I feel the panic—that feeling of being trapped.

I can almost put myself in his place—thinking of all the ways he must have felt the world failed him. How even when he tried to do something good—like rescue a kid pinned beneath an ATV—he got nothing but a hard time from the people who should have been thanking him. What was he thinking about? His mom? That she will suddenly feel sorry for all the ways he imagined she wronged him? Is he thinking his death will be a great way of "getting back" at her for telling him he'd never amount to a darn? As twisted as Jimmy's sense of right and wrong has always been, has he somehow managed to convince himself his brother betrayed him? What about Paula or Shelly or the baby he briefly believed was his, only to be told no, he was not a father after all? Was he thinking of his own abuser, whoever that person was?

Was he mad at God? Or was he just tired of running? Was his suicide just the ultimate act of selfishness, not caring, as usual, how his actions affected other people?

Or was it just a spur of the moment decision—not even a conscious choice? *Just an automatic reaction.* I think back to Charlene telling me about the television commercial that suggested to her she could find peace with the firing of her pistol. I think, too, about her friends' decision to take her bullets away. Just as there was no one to protect a bank from someone like Jimmy, there was no one to take *his* bullets away. No one to save Jimmy from himself.

Bill Rehder is surprised to hear Jimmy Krimm shot himself. The retired FBI agent and expert on bank bandits hasn't seen too many cases come to that end.

"It's rare," he says, "unless there's a whole bunch of other stuff going on. We just don't have that."

Given the outcome and based on his vast experience with serial bank bandits, Rehder has no doubt what was going through Jimmy's mind at the end.

"His plan was if he ever got caught, he was gonna kill himself. I think that was all part of the plan. He's forty-two. Why screw around?"

By killing himself, Rehder says, "He gets a bigger exit from life." And with over $20,000 taken in his last robbery, "He went out on a high note."

Rehder sees in Jimmy the kind of guy who "always wanted to be 'somebody' and never wound up being anybody."

Jimmy, he says, sounds like the "classic serial bank bandit" who starts out young—stealing candy bars, doing his first holdups of mom-and-pop–type stores, and then graduating to car theft and going to jail.

"Things always get worse because we learn more criminal activity from the other guys inside—they've got nothing to do but sit around and talk about their crimes," Rehder says.

Rehder accurately pegs Jimmy's progression from a note-passing robber to a takeover bandit, even before I have collected all of the news clippings from the Canadian spree. Spending seven years in a Canadian jail had to have put Jimmy in contact with people who suggested a more lucrative method of robbing banks, and his later robberies reflected his ability to put that method into action.

"Bank robbery still has this aura about it," Rehder says, appealing to characters like Jimmy—with low self-esteem, no skills, and something to prove. Bank robbery is a crime committed in broad daylight, usually, with many witnesses.

"There's a cachet about it. People who do it have got some balls. You gotta have some balls to do one of these," Rehder says, and that's part of the allure. As a bank robber, Jimmy got to be "the *man*."

"You put it all on the line for the two minutes in the bank. It's exciting."

To Rehder, "This guy is interesting because he's one of the lone-wolf bandits who didn't let anyone in on his life," and though he left plenty of clues for his family, it does not appear he ever told anyone, straight out, what he was up to.

A North Dakota Bureau of Criminal Investigation agent called in to document the death scene provides a clue to local officers, almost immediately, about why Jimmy Krimm wouldn't want to be taken alive.

"He told us that this was probably their suspect in seven to ten other robberies in North Dakota," says Fredericks, who adds, nothing surprises him.

It's just another example, he says, of someone making a bad choice, based on a flawed belief system—thinking you can get away with murder, or with robbing a bank.

"It catches everyone eventually."

Roosevelt County Sheriff Freedom Crawford sees the same dynamic.

"People make their own choices in this life. Everyone has freedom— their own free will and their own choice what to do with this life," he says.

"I think he thought, well, this is the end...because he doesn't want to go back to prison, and he can't get out of it," says Throntveit.

His deputy agrees.

"I'm sure he could hear the airplane up there."

"And he shoots himself, which is the best thing he's ever done in his entire life. I'm sure it is, based on what he's done. All he's been is a criminal," says Throntveit.

When he got his car hung up on some rocks in a wheat field, Jimmy abandoned all of his equipment and personal possessions except his gun, a scanner, and the money.

Left behind was a tent, some food, a cook-stove and some firewood, says Throntveit. Police also recovered several photographs, including self-portraits Jimmy took on the road. A few appear to be "trophies" celebrating a heist, alone, in some remote campground.

"It didn't seem like he had any friends," says Melby.

These photographs provide the FBI with some of the only clues about where Jimmy spent the last five years of his life.

"Some of the pictures they kept are of backgrounds to see if you can place him somewhere in another town and figure out maybe if they can find a house or an apartment," says Throntveit.

Also in the car, were four pieces of false identification later tied to a farm burglary across the state, just days before the Williston robbery. An identification card found in Krimm's name shows an address of Valley City, North Dakota, but officers find nothing there. Later, I will go to the address and find the address does not exist. There is nothing nearby, but a dingy little drive-up sort of motel converted into an apartment. I can find no one to verify whether Jimmy actually lived there.

In the days following Krimm's death, police learn of four other vehicles registered in his name. Soon, one of those vehicles turns up in a storage unit in Valley City, but there is no other evidence recovered.

"He had bank accounts in various banks in North Dakota and Minnesota," says Throntveit.

One teller, at a bank in Moorhead, Minnesota, told the FBI Krimm regularly made withdrawals of $1,500 or so. He always seemed to be driving a different car. He would hang around longer than most customers to chat, but the teller described his demeanor as "unusual." She got the impression he had an attitude like it was "him against the world." He even made a statement that he had been pulled over by police so many times, the next time he got pulled over, he wasn't going to stop. He once made an inquiry about whether the vault at the bank had enough money to cover a check of $10,000 if he wanted to cash one.

Throntveit said a teller at one bank said Jimmy deposited money that smelled "musty," leading to speculation some of his loot from past bank jobs may have been buried.

Charlene received two bank savings registers among Jimmy's personal effects, from the FBI, after this death. They show a high balance of over $11,000 in one of the accounts, a few months after Jimmy's big haul in the LeMars, Iowa robbery, on August 4, 2006.

Jimmy opened his account at the State Bank of Hawley, Minnesota, in October 2006, with a deposit of $3,000. By November, regular deposits had swelled the balance to $11,686. Pretty good for a guy who only just completed a year-long prison sentence five months earlier!

He drew down the Hawley account over the winter. By March 10, 2007, the balance was down to $431.37. On March 20, 2007 he robbed the bank in Devils Lake ($3,904); in April, he is believed to have hit Park

River; and in May, he robbed the bank in Canby ($3,900). In June, it was Weyburn, Saskatchewan ($1,100). Then, on August 17, 2007, he robbed a bank in Dilworth, Minnesota, netting $22,470. Jimmy's total pay since getting out of prison the year before — over $81,000! Not bad for a high school dropout.

In September 2007, Jimmy started making deposits again: $1,945 on Sept. 25; $2,000 on Oct. 17; $1,150 on Oct. 22; and $2,200 on Oct. 26. To a teller, it might appear as if he were a working guy, depositing his weekly pay. A series of withdrawals followed, through November 2007. Then, *one day* after a robbery in Duluth, Minnesota, on Jan. 4, 2008, Jimmy made a deposit of $2,200! By Jan. 16, his balance was down to $165. But "payday" came again on Jan. 30, when he deposited $2,560.

On March 28, 2008, a bank in Redfield, South Dakota was robbed. The *next day,* Jimmy deposited $1,500 in his account in Hawley, four hours away. Similarly, *three days* after a bank in Watertown, South Dakota was robbed, Jimmy deposited $430 in his Hawley account. A few days after that, he deposited another $1,000.

By May 29, Jimmy's account was down to just $36.29. On June 18, a bank is robbed in Lisbon, North Dakota; on July 2, a robber strikes at Wahpeton, North Dakota; and on Oct. 10, in Mandan, North Dakota. A few weeks later, Jimmy abandons his Hawley account in favor of a new one in Moorhead, Minnesota, just across the bridge from Fargo, North Dakota.

He opened that account with a deposit of $300 in November 2008. Within a month of a Jamestown, North Dakota robbery, which netted around $8,000, Jimmy deposited a total of $4,150 into the bank in Moorhead. By March 2, 2009 he was broke again — with just $93.42 showing on his register. He needed a quick solution. After all, his forty-second birthday was coming up. Just three miles away from his Moorhead bank, the bank in Dilworth, Minnesota beckoned once again. The day before his birthday, on March 9, 2009, he robbed that bank for the second time in 18 months. Over the next few weeks, he made deposits in his Moorhead account totalling over $10,000!

It was enough to carry him almost through his last summer. In all, Jimmy had deposited over $48,000 in his own bank accounts over a period of three years, but his total take from the spree was closer to $150,000.

By Aug. 14, 2009, however, his balance had been drawn down to just $83.84. A month later, with his $21,000 haul from the Williston robbery stuffed into a back pack, he was dead.

Given the fact it appears Jimmy was living out of his car at the time of his death, Bill Rehder doubts he left anything of value behind. Even though Jimmy kept some of his money in banks, he spent most of it as fast as he got it. If he ever did keep any money in a storage unit somewhere, I can't help thinking of the elation of the manager who unlocked that unit once the rent ran out. How likely is it that anyone finding such a cache would report it?

Throntveit wouldn't be surprised if Jimmy's transient lifestyle allowed him to prey on children, given the fact he abused his brother for so long.

"You don't have to go to the moon to see monsters. They walk amongst us every day. They're monsters. The only good thing he ever did in his life is he shot himself. So nobody got shot or had to shoot him. The last thing I want to do is shoot somebody, but at that time, I knew he was going to end up dead, one way or the other, because he's escalated the situation up so far, the outcome was basically written on the wall."

Throntveit doesn't understand the public's thirst for thrills and chills. He gets all he needs at work.

"Why watch a horror movie? I've sat with all kinds of them. And they're monsters, and they are the scariest people in the world."

Anyone who would prey upon a child, as far as Throntveit is concerned, is beyond redemption.

"You're a monster, drive a stake through his heart...It's almost like they're carrying some sort of bacteria with them," says Throntveit, who has been on the job long enough to be arresting the grandchildren of some of these perpetrators. "They're just as bad as serial killers, except they let their victims live."

It seems almost like a never-ending cycle, in which a child, once victimized, is predisposed to becoming a predator. But Throntveit knows not all victims follow that path. Sometimes, they go the opposite direction, haunted by monsters every step of the way.

Williston Police Detective Mark Hanson can imagine that Jimmy must have been very desperate to get away on the night of September 14, 2009. But he has difficulty trying to put himself into the mind-set of a bank robber.

"He obviously thinks of things different than what I consider normal people would think of. Normal people would not do that [rob a bank]."

Hanson was busy in the aftermath of the robbery.

"After everything I could do here, interviewing witnesses and customers, I went home," he says. Later in the evening, when he heard the suspect was back on the North Dakota side of the border, Hanson knew what must have happened.

"The luck had run out for him that day. If he would have just stayed where he was and just spent the night, he probably would have been better off," Hanson says.

Knowing everything he knows now, Hanson believes Jimmy was as comfortable walking into a bank to demand money as walking into a grocery store and picking out purchases.

"He does this for a living…And he's done it for some time…it is within his comfort zone because he is able to accomplish this task. The first few he did he was probably pretty nervous, but after that, he knows, 'Hey, they're not giving me any grief; this is a cakewalk,' you know? 'I just walk in, tell them to give me the money, show the gun, don't have to hurt anybody, they give me the money, I leave. They don't catch me. Move on.' And it got comfortable for him."

Not that it takes a lot of smarts to rob a bank.

"It really doesn't," Hanson says. "You learn what the employees will do," and you learn that in smaller Midwestern cities like Williston, bank guards are virtually unheard of.

But Hanson says it would be a mistake to believe that an armed holdup is easy for witnesses to get over.

"I don't care if you have a little five-foot-one-inch man that's forty pounds, you pull out a gun…That's a threatening gesture and threatening visual situation for those people to see that. They don't know this man from Adam. They don't know what he's going to do."

Even though tellers related that Jimmy was calm during the robbery, they were terrified.

"I think the worst part for those employees came later, when they started thinking about how close they could have come to dying."

It is a relief for Hanson to know Jimmy Krimm can't victimize anyone else. Though no one was ever killed or injured during any of Jimmy's robberies, Hanson believes that has more to do with the other people involved.

"Would he hurt a bank employee? Back him into a corner, I think he would. I don't think he wants to. Law enforcement, I don't know if he really gives it a second thought…When somebody has got the courage to take a gun and shoot at a police officer, you don't have a lot of sympathy, or you lose it if you had any…He lowered himself enough to aim a gun and shoot at a law enforcement officer, and that really bothers me."

Having searched long and hard to determine Jimmy's next of kin, Hanson remarks, again, on the oddity of a forty-two-year-old man with seemingly no connection to anyone. It's not something he's seen very often in his thirty-two years on the job.

"I don't know if there ever was a woman or children in his life. His mother, I know, would really like the answer to that question."

Even if there was a relationship, if it was outside the immediate region, "They might not hear about this."

Though Hanson understands the possibility many criminals may start out as victims, to him, it's still no excuse.

"Sometimes I sympathize; sometimes people make their own bed. Most people make their own bed…He had control over what type of life he had. And…that choice is something that every human being gets to have. Some make good choices, and some make bad. I know there's a lot of bad people in this world because the prisons are full of them. And after I'm sitting here thinking about this, I get information a bank was just robbed in Riverton, Wyoming. It's just *As the World Turns*. It's just going to keep on going."

For Devils Lake Police Detective Sue Schwab, the death of Jimmy Krimm brings closure to a case that haunts her but also raises questions about the effectiveness of law enforcement.

After requesting a photo from the Williston Police Department, "I looked at this guy, and I said, 'Yeah, that's him,'" Schwab recalls. "We just knew it right away."

Schwab was frustrated, however, when the FBI would not close their Devils Lake file.

"They told me officially, 'We don't close this,' but I said, 'That's the same guy; that's our guy. I'm gonna close ours.'"

Schwab says she was told to do as she saw fit, so after several months, she got the okay from her police chief to close her file.

"I said, 'I'm closing this, because this is our guy,'" even though the FBI cautioned her that if another suspect was identified later, it could hurt the case.

"No," she says, "this guy is dead."

It frustrates Schwab that Jimmy Krimm had so many contacts with police over the years, to no avail.

"He wasn't a person that never came to the attention of law enforcement. He obviously had been arrested for other crimes in addition to other things he didn't get caught for...It's disconcerting. It's just, here he was; he just fit right in—just melted into wherever he was."

She's glad her case is closed, but there's also a sense of loss. There's no arrest, no trial, and no end to the questioning.

"He was such a mystery to me. I think that's why I was so obsessed. We just couldn't seem to get this guy."

Some questions will never be answered.

"I am just wondering why? What was in his mind that he did this? What caused him to commit his first bank robbery? I would just like to ask him, *Where did you go?*

"He was an enigma."

Schwab knows the victim tellers will be asking themselves those sorts of questions for a long time, too.

"The first thing that happens is their security is gone, their basic security of just walking on the streets; it's now been violated, and they feel that something has been taken away from them...It's hard to gain that trust back...You're always going to be watching and looking for this to happen again."

After the Williston robbery, teller Lisa Barbula found herself with an intense curiosity about Jimmy Krimm.

"I was on the Internet constantly. I wanted to know who he was, where he was from," she says. "I just wanted to know everything I could. I just wanted to know, why?"

Time and knowledge have begun to dim her hatred for the man who victimized her.

"I don't know if I hate him anymore, because I did for a long time, but for me, I'm just, I don't want to hear any more about it. I don't want people to bring him up. I don't want to get comments about the robbery still. I'm ready to be done with it."

But some customers can't resist mentioning it.

"It was very frustrating for me, and I was very angry for a long time about it. Not just at him, but at the people who would come in and just have the audacity to come in and just bring it up. You know, nonchalantly be all, 'So you guys had a little excitement?'"

"We had a customer two weeks ago that just brought it up," says Branch Manager Elaine Fixen, nearly four months after the robbery. "And it's just like, it's done, let us move on, let us forget about it."

"I actually had an altercation with a customer who said something," Barbula relates. "It was, like, three days after the robbery. And she came in and said how sorry she felt for him and for his family, and it's really hard because people don't realize. They think no one got shot, nothing happened, so what's the big deal?"

The reality escapes people who have not been faced with a similar trauma, Barbula says.

"He never made me feel like he was going to shoot somebody, but he made me feel, had somebody done something that he didn't like, he would have. And if he wasn't going to, he wouldn't have brought the gun in."

Barbula and Fixen feel certain the gun was loaded when Jimmy robbed the bank. They base that assertion on the knowledge he shot at a highway patrolman just a half hour later.

"If he's going to shoot at a cop, he wouldn't hesitate to shoot at us," Barbula says.

Now, "I look at everybody different, whether it's a customer whose been coming in here since I worked here. Even if it's somebody I know... And you know, it's just you don't trust anybody anymore. You can't."

The realization that Jimmy Krimm might have entered the bank on a previous occasion to learn the layout introduces a new fear and also some regret.

"Some of the girls that were here said they'd possibly seen him before. That maybe he looked familiar, maybe he'd been in the bank before. And that makes you think, what if we had paid attention? And you know, done some of the things they always tell you to do?" Barbula says.

Might engaging a new face in the bank have prevented a robbery? Barbula wonders.

"Would he have second-guessed himself? I mean, you don't trust anyone anymore. Someone who walks up and just wants a roll of quarters, maybe they are going to do laundry, maybe they're scoping out your bank."

Barbula has thought about what she would say if she could have faced him in court.

"I'd want to make it very clear to him that he was just, you know, worthless. What did he do in his life that made anything better for anybody? He didn't even bring joy to his own parents. And I do have a lot of anger towards him, and maybe I do think worse of him because of what I went through…that what he did was horrible. I don't think he thought of how it affected everybody."

Barbula was mad when she first learned the robber took his own life, because he would never be brought to justice, "but the more I think about it, he would have went to jail for a while, and he would have got out and done the same thing again. And then it got to the point where I was—hate to say it—happy. *He's gone; he's not going to hurt anybody else. His family is not going to have to deal with him anymore.* It sounds horrible, but when you're a person like that and all you do is create horrible things in life, he just, to me, he was worthless, and for him to be gone, it's better that way."

Fixen, too, will never face Jimmy Krimm in court, but she's left with a feeling she has fulfilled the role intended for her—helping put a stop to a spree that might have victimized many more innocent people.

"God used us as his tool to stop it," she says. "And that's one of the questions us girls had. Why? Why us?"

Fixen's faith tells her it was planned that way.

"God used us as his tool because he was tired of it, and he knew we were strong enough that we could handle it, that we could do the job and get it accomplished."

Fixen is very familiar with the concept of angels watching over people.

"How many times have I said there were angels and God watching over us that day? So many times."

But she can't forgive.

"I hate him. I just hate him," she says, and that's a heavy cross for a Christian to bear.

Schwab admits it was anticlimactic when she finally learned her suspect was dead.

"I just lived this case for so long. I wanted to find out so bad. Sometimes I'd put things away for awhile," but even in her off time, she searched.

She was so obsessed, at one point, she thought she found her suspect while off duty at the North Dakota State Fair. But after looking into the individual pretty extensively, she had to conclude he was not the guy.

"I'm glad he's caught," she says. "I just feel, did we do enough?"

Almost to a person, the cops and victims take Jimmy's death as something understandable—something justified. It is something they are glad about, or at least, relieved by. Jimmy's death gives his victims some peace of mind, and for the cops, it contains the satisfaction that at least one "monster" is off the streets.

Having read his letters, having met his mother and his brother, it is hard for me to believe he was 100 percent bad, 100 percent without anything like a conscience. I started out wondering if Jimmy was truly a "bad" guy or just a lost one. At first, I saw his suicide as the chicken way out—the ultimate selfish act. But as time goes on, and whether he intended it or not, his decision—to take himself out instead of hurting someone else—smacks to me of Jimmy finally making the best choice for everyone but himself.

It's a shame the FBI is not pursuing bank robbery cases the way they once were, says Bill Rehder. Bank robbery is declining nationally. Bandit barriers, access control units, digital photography, dye packs, and tracker packs have "dampened the allure."

But these technological advancements, to some degree, are also responsible for an increase of robberies in rural areas.

"Robberies around smaller towns are increasing," Rehder says. Jimmy Krimm is not alone in having figured out that small-town banks in rural areas are more vulnerable.

"They have less technological advancement because of cost, and there's nothing to justify it," or at least there wasn't, until recently.

"As long as banks continue to have money, there are going to be robberies," Rehder says.

There will always be someone like Jimmy Krimm, who is willing to put everything on the line to take that money.

Jimmy may have started out stealing candy bars, Rehder says, but "so did John Dillinger."

Detective Sue Schwab (above) holds the files she amassed as a spree of bank robberies unfolded in North Dakota, including one at Wahpeton (left) and at Mandan, below. The hulking figure with the lumbering walk used an empty soda box to carry off his loot from several of the crimes. Schwab suspected the man had tattoos because he always kept his arms covered, even in the summer.

IN ACCOUNT WITH

James E. Krimm   No. 617217

This book is accepted and all deposits are made subject to the Rules and Regulations, now and/or hereafter adopted by the Bank, governing deposits made in the Savings Department.

No payment can be made or money withdrawn without presentation of the book.

DATE	INTEREST OR INITIALS	WITHDRAWALS	DEPOSITS	BALANCE
10-13-06	Opening deposit			3,000.00
10-27-06	Depost			1,500.00
10-30-06				500.00
10-30-06				1,700.00
11-03-06				800.00
11-06-06				1,000.00
11-10-06				1,180.00
				10,680.00
11-17-06			1,000.00	11,680.00
11-27-06		1,800.00		9,880.00
12-09-06		1,000.00		8,880.00
12-18-06		2,000.00		

IT'S NOT WHAT YOU EARN—IT'S WHAT YOU SAVE

Jimmy kept at least two bank accounts. One of those was opened at a bank in Hawley, Minnesota, a little more than two months after his huge haul at LeMars, Iowa. He deposits a total of $11,680 over a period of a few weeks, then just as rapidly draws the balance down. Another account, opened in Moorhead, Minnesota, is located just three miles from a Dilworth, Minnesota bank he robbed twice.

An Internet screen capture from a news story about the Williston robbery (above); Montana Trooper Rick Kessner (right) believes Jimmy Krimm intended to kill him when he fired four shots at his patrol vehicle.

Divide County Deputy Rob Melby and Sheriff Lauren Throntveit (above) were among the officers who closed in on the robber after he abandoned his Mitsubishi (left) and stole a pickup from a nearby farmyard.

Inside the stolen pickup, police find a backpack stuffed with $21,000 in bills from the Williston robbery (above); Roosevelt County Deputy Jason Fredericks at first thought the suspect was going to surrender. He believes Jimmy took his last breath as officers approached the location where he fell.

Jimmy's childhood sweetheart, Paula Almas with Charlene (above), following a memorial service for Jimmy; Charlene's house in Taylor, Michigan (right); Rob, Cecile and Charlene (below), November 5, 2009, after the service for Jimmy.

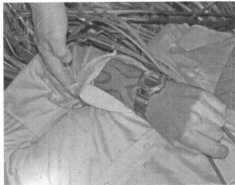

Rob and Charlene support the publication of a photo of Jimmy's death scene because it so starkly illustrates the consequences of his life choices. At left, a glimpse of the full sleeve flame tattoos emblazoned on each of his arms.

PART FOUR

CHAPTER TWENTY-THREE

This Works, Too

Rob Krimm is no longer haunted by monsters. His brother's death is a relief.

"I was actually happy about it," he tells me. "I was elated—like Christmas-type happiness. He's dead? Party in the street. Drinks on me!"

However, he concedes, "Many forks went off of the happiness."

One fork leads him to wonder what life would have been like with a brother who was a positive force in his life.

"He used to be someone I looked up to as we grew up. I remember standing on a milk crate to be as tall as he was one time, looking over the counter at a fireworks stand, amazed at all I had been missing…As I replay these moments in my life, I get a glimpse of the person 'Jimmy,' gettin' some fireworks, gonna explode some stuff. Excitement!"

Before his brother's death, he couldn't see Jimmy, the person, only Jimmy, the abuser.

"It's all been about anger and being pissed off. Now I'm thinking differently. It's a new way of thinking for me. Everything that was, is now 'has been'…I literally feel a little bit smarter for not having him in my head. It's like one less thing I have to worry about."

Rob no longer fears for his own safety, or for the safety of his mother.

"I was always worried that he would show up at my ma's house and hurt her, because now that she's a senior citizen and all, it would be real easy for him to dominate or be an authority over her. She would be helpless to do anything to protect herself."

Now, instead of constant worry, "there just is this empty spot there. That's what is so weird. No longer do we have to worry about this impending disaster that might someday happen. It's just this emptiness that's left behind—a part of the sky is missing, and you look at it and go, 'Oh, that's nothing.'"

Rob understands the cliché of having a weight lifted.

"The relief that I have that he's gone is like a warehouse in my brain that's opened up. I'm free from all that bitterness and hate...I don't have to see him or deal with him. I don't have to carry it anymore."

Not everyone understands his reaction.

Charlene called Rob at work with the news Jimmy was dead. She didn't want him to be alone when he found out, and in the end, Rob is glad she did it that way.

"It did feel good to get it off my chest, just to say something to the oncoming shift, just to tell somebody and let anybody know," Rob says. "I'm like, 'You guys will not believe what just happened,' and they had no idea. 'My brother just robbed a bank, ran for five fucking hours in stolen cars, and then shot himself in the head.' And they're all just like quiet... I am the master of awkward silences...My brother was dead, and I was happy about this moment in my life."

Stunned, one co-worker finally said, "I'm sorry,"

Rob told him, "Don't be."

It's not unlike the exchange of the master sergeants when Rob was demoted. Their declaration that Rob was "finally" getting what he deserved—losing a stripe—was the same as Rob's own reaction to his brother's death: finally.

Finally, Jimmy got caught. Finally, Jimmy got what he had coming. Finally, Jimmy can't hurt anyone.

"I feel guilty that I didn't talk about it sooner. I felt guilty that I let him get away with it, you know?"

At first, Rob had a hard time looking at photos of his brother.

"I shudder. It's like, I look at it, and I go, 'Aw fuck,' and then I force myself to look at it. Because he's gone. To me, it's like looking in a mirror...something I see and some part of looking at that picture is like looking in a mirror. He just makes me so mad."

One day, Rob had a photo of his brother on his computer screen at work.

"I stared at it, thinking, *You fucking dumbass.* I'm at work sitting there in my uniform, guys at work are passing by not taking notice...Until I ask one of them, 'Does this guy look familiar?' To my relief, he's like, 'He looks a little familiar, but he doesn't look a thing like you.'"

It is the answer Rob needs to hear at the time.

In another conversation, with one of his supervisors, the man said if it was his brother, he would be totally distraught.

"Under normal circumstances, I would understand that," Rob says. "I didn't really have normal circumstances...Part of the reason I am taking all of these meds is because of him."

When Charlene broke the news about Jimmy, Rob couldn't tell his mother about his own crisis on the very same evening.

"I just couldn't drop that on her at that time," he says, and so, once again, he was left to deal with his own hurts privately, without the support of a parent.

"She's so proud of me," Rob says, "and I'm like, 'Why are you proud of me?'"

Weeks later, she learned she could have lost both of her sons on September 14, 2009. It is a thought almost too horrible for Charlene to comprehend.

Learning that Jimmy may have saved a boy's life before he died causes more tears. Charlene sees at least the possibility there was still some goodness in her oldest son, no matter the mountain of other evidence to the contrary.

Jimmy's death tells Rob something about his own life that was difficult for him to see while his brother was alive.

"It's like I'm learning from him from the grave. Here at my worst point in life—where I'm demoted—he comes up to prove to me I've still got it all going for me; that's what he showed to me. I've got a job. I'm a loyal citizen—just being a regular Joe loyal fucking citizen. So he's taught me at least that lesson, and he didn't even have to say a word.

"Compared to my brother," Rob says, "I've got the entire world on my side, going my way. I look at my life and all my accomplishments that I've done just in the past eighteen years, what I've had to overcome, just to get ahead in life. And all of a sudden, I feel like a rock star by comparison! No exaggeration. I really feel so successful just by being who I am."

Jimmy's death has provided Rob with perspective on his own disappointments in life.

"I set a high standard for myself, and oftentimes, I don't reach it, but I still have that goal up there that I want to reach, and it's often a high expectation for myself. I get very disappointed when I don't reach it."

Now he sees, "you don't have to shoot so high that it's unattainable."

Rob finds himself trying to understand how a kid goes from stealing Heath candy bars from the corner store to being a serial bank robber, even though he witnessed the beginning of that transformation. When it came to candy bars, "he could never be satisfied with just one," Rob says. "And it was just so petty. It wasn't worth it."

Robbing a bank may not be petty, but the compulsion, apparently, is the same. Rob sees a gradual progression in Jimmy's crimes—from one candy bar to several, to a grocery sack full of whatever he could walk out of a store carrying, to robbing party stores at gunpoint, to stealing cars and breaking into people's homes. Bank robbery was the obvious next step.

But what if Jimmy was given short shrift—by an abuser who was never brought to justice, by a school that failed to recognize ADD, and a prison system that failed to provide the tools of reform?

"I find myself discovering things about him that were blinded by my hate—his human side that actually laughed. Now, knowing my own thoughts were skewed by my own anger, I find myself diving further into the abyss of my memories trying to capture—I don't even know what," Rob says.

"All I really know of him is the abuse. I've never known the person 'Jim.' He was either drunk and blacked out or abusing me. He'd come home so drunk that he would wake up the next morning and ask me what happened, and I was like, 'You were stabbing the toilet seat with a knife.'

"And he's like, 'I was doing that?'

"'Yeah, you were laying on the bathroom floor drunk.'"

Slowly, memories of Jimmy are coming back that have nothing to do with abuse.

"As we're going over moments, I briefly remember human aspects that might have been positive. I just wish I knew of more when I got to spend time, and he was decent. I guess I blocked out all the times that just didn't make up for the abuse."

Now, small moments that were forgotten gain clarity.

"I do remember times," like listening to a new Ozzy Osbourne album. "We came home, sitting there on his bed. We just sort of jammed out to Ozzy Oz's new album."

When Rob recalls those brief moments, "I get to see the person instead of just an asshole."

Rob sees a gradual progression in his brother's aggression too; he was not just a monster hatched whole and let loose on society.

"He sort of developed into the serial criminal, possibly by the need to survive," Rob says, acting out with abuse as a result of the abuse inflicted upon him, stealing cars and robbing banks because of his inability to learn the skills he needed to attain money and possessions legally.

"Was it his abuse that made him slow in the brain, because it did me—and perhaps that's what happened to him. He had to block out so much shit that it took a lot of brain power to block it out. There's not a whole lot left for being a fully functioning person. That's where Straterra works in my life. Those brain receptors and neurons are firing off like they should, like they're supposed to be."

And yet, Rob finds no excuse for his brother's actions, even if he is better able today to understand them.

"I think it's based on decisions. I think he made certain decisions based on laziness, and if he had made other decisions, he could have worked harder at it and gotten certified in something. When I got into the Marine Corps to play drums, they didn't automatically go, 'Bada bing, bada boom, you're a drummer.' No. They said, basically, 'You suck as a drummer, and you're going to have to work at it,' so I worked at it… But he was never willing to put that effort in there, to say, 'All right, I failed the test; now what do I have to do to pass it?'"

Rob remembers instances like that in his own life when, faced with a choice of learning or failing, he at least kept trying. Anytime knowledge stood in the way of attaining a goal, "I would have been like, 'Give me the book. How much does it cost?' and read the book, and, and, just, you know, committed the book to memory and taken the test again, and how often can you retest? I would have been all over that, but he just made shitty decisions. Like, let me decide whether I want to be a good citizen or a bum, a vagabond, and literally bum money off of people on the streets," or become an abuser and a bank robber.

Rob believes Jimmy knew right from wrong and chose wrong.

"We were both exposed to almost exactly the same thing," Rob says, including childhood sexual abuse, an absent father, a mother who worked three jobs to make ends meet, and an environment where young people were almost destined to fall into substance abuse and crime.

Even as a kid, Rob says, "I knew what was right. I knew what he was doing was the opposite of right."

Recalling those fireworks that were so exciting to Jimmy as a kid, Rob suspects the excitement was a motivator for Jimmy when it came to robbing banks.

"It was the 'thrill of the chill,'" Rob says, as much as the necessity borne of having no other means of support that motivated Jimmy to rob. "This is like a Vegas rush when you win the jackpot! So, he's pretty arrogant and very confident at this point—sitting there in his car stuffing his pockets with cold hard cash. This to me sounds like he was feeling so confident that he felt almost indestructible. Knowing this feeling myself, I know that having overconfidence in yourself is dangerous... Being demoted, that's just humiliating. I never thought that would happen to me."

Just as Jimmy never thought he would have to pay for his crimes.

And what happens when the thrill is gone?

"No mask in the bank. He went in there, got the goods, and walked out! This was so common to him that it must have been like brushing his teeth."

Isolated from everyone because of his criminal exploits, what could Jimmy have to live for once robbing banks became as common to him as shopping at the corner store?

"It just makes me wonder. Was he just trying to have fun and then got addicted to it?"

Another theory Rob has is that Jimmy was taking a "victory lap" of sorts that night, when he stumbled upon the officers near Grenora.

"He ditched his plan just like he ditched everything else in his life. Everybody knows you make a plan and you stick to it, but it's never that easy, is it? Confidence through the roof—he felt safe again. This was just a common thing to him. So he's like, 'Skip it; let's go back home.' Already brushed his teeth for the day, so to speak."

Not that Rob wishes his brother would have gotten away, "but I ask myself what if I was in the same position? Would I be blinded by my confidence? Having stars in my eyes with all this money in my possession? I'm not sure exactly but one thing is for sure...you ditch the car! Hole up in a bunker or sleeping bag. Whatever is available. Making a fire is questionable because it would draw attention to you. See? There I go again. I'm trying to figure out the best way to do something, whatever it is I do. He, on the other hand, was not healthy, and I don't know that he had much of a thought process…But this approach would have made him successful at whatever he did, and he was not."

Was it, as when Jimmy stole from his mom, just about the money?

"Money is power, and the more money you have the more power you have," Rob says. "I would like to have power, so I can give more power to other people," but it's not likely Jimmy would have looked at it that way.

"If it was money or power, it would be spent within a day and a half, so the general desires are the same, but what you do with them if you were to attain them is what makes us people."

Rob struggles with the possibility of whether Jimmy could feel remorse for the things he did.

Jimmy made an apology of sorts, after learning Rob planned to join the Marine Corps.

One of his letters said: "I know I don't write you, but sometimes I don't know what to say for myself."

Rob can read a lot into that one line today, written from inside a Michigan prison two decades ago.

"It was an acknowledgement that he knew he was fucked up; he doesn't know what to say for himself and doesn't want to dwell on it. That's the most of an apology I'm ever going to get—like he knew he was a fuckup, he just didn't know why or how to fix it."

Rob wonders at the thoughts and emotions behind his brother's words, because he knows his own limitations when it comes to expressing himself on paper.

"I can hear Mozart, and it's like sunshine, high-definition TV for me, but all that comes out is one sentence. And that one sentence doesn't do all that justice. And that's a constant dilemma with me. As if, he _knew_, you know, sort of reflecting on all that he's done. Maybe he was just hoping that I would drop the whole subject and never reveal any of it. Maybe that one sentence was a whole story in his mind, and he wasn't able to get that story out on paper, and that's all that came of it."

When Rob heard the words to the Johnny Cash song "Hurt," played at his brother's memorial service two months after Jimmy's death, his reaction surprised him.

"I'm like, what the fuck am I crying for? Something inside of me is touched. It's touched. I find myself caring about reform in the prisons. Why? This would presuppose that I cared about my abuser. That really confuses me."

The initial happiness and relief he feels, hearing of his brother's death, is a fluid state, washing up many thoughts, many feelings.

"Turns out, happiness is a complicated emotion. Turns out there was this floodgate opened up in my brain, but as I sort through repressed memories, I'm seeing a glimpse of a person who was confused at best. Sometimes generous and giving," even if the only gifts he could give were stolen from someone else.

Dealing with Jimmy's death has been a process.

"I finally realized, on some small level, why my mom cried over his death. This delayed reaction was like a small detonator, activating a Mount Vesuvius of tears. Where was this coming from? I guess, deep inside, all my anger turned into tears, washing away my guilt—the guilt of being a victim."

Rob takes in the knowledge that his brother was once prescribed an antidepressant and wonders at a system that would require Jimmy to be off psychotropic drugs before he could advance to a training facility where he might obtain the skills necessary to survive in a free society.

"That's just a disservice to sit there and say they want to reform people. They have to do the wrong thing is what it seems like, to deny reform in order to make it through a day to get to a better prison—those were the high hopes for him."

Rob sees hints of intellect, indications of ambition, however misplaced, in the letters Jimmy wrote from prison.

"Maybe medication enabled him to write and remember and learn. They say, 'get healthy,' but they only want you to *be* healthy; they're not going to sit there and help you be healthy. Knowing all that now, it's like—it's contradictive. There should be, like, steps—medication, then you should be able to work. Instead, it's just the opposite."

That his brother, who had trouble passing an engine tune-up class, actually attempted to take a paralegal course astounds Rob.

"He did a lot of brain work trying to learn the legal system and trying to outsmart the system. That's actually intelligent. There's some glimpse of intellect to actually get that far."

That they both faced the worst day of their life on the same day seems to Rob like some kind of karmic justice.

"We have a foundation of similarities, like it or not—like twins that would sense on the same day that something with the other one had gone wrong."

The very fact Rob made it through that day and Jimmy didn't is due in part, Rob says, to the fact Jimmy abused him. Compared to almost daily sexual violation and beatings as a kid, a demotion in rank is hard, but not worth dying over.

"If there ever was a time that I would have actually gone through with it, like killing myself, it would have been on that same day he killed himself. I made it through the toughest part of my life, and he couldn't.

"And while at times, it feels like it's tough to carry on and wake up every morning and go to the same old job, it's just a little bit longer, and I'll have my pension. It's tough just to do the same mundane thing over and over, but I made it through the toughest part, and I'm going to be successful. And I'm going to be a young man, and I'm going to be able to get a new career and go to college and meet people and make a new life."

Those are benefits Rob earned during the same amount of time Jimmy spent making a career as a criminal. All the while Jimmy was stealing, Rob was working for the things he and Jimmy could only dream of as kids, like owning a Ford Mustang, the ultimate dream car they both coveted.

It seems to Rob almost as if this showdown, in which two brothers faced their own personal worst day, was orchestrated by some universal force.

"In the bigger picture of things, I think the forces that be needed to take a life. And whenever it was realized that I was just going to be depressed, go to sleep, they're like, 'Okay, then Jimmy has to kill himself.'"

Unlike Charlene, who grew up with a strong Christian background that laid a foundation for the Gnostic beliefs she now embraces, Rob doesn't have a strong feeling about the identity of a single all-knowing, all-seeing God who metes out justice. He is open to the possibility of many gods, many spirits, each with an agenda.

So what force was at work that day, September 14, 2009?

"Death. Death as a spirit," Rob says. "If there was a spirit that goes around collecting souls, death needs a soul, and he got one...And it's just something bigger than us that's orchestrating all this, and death obviously needed a soul that day. And I seriously think that if I ever was going to kill myself, it would have been that day, and I didn't. So death gave up on me and focused on Jimmy.

"Now I'm free to live, because they got a Krimm. They took their life that they needed, and they got him, and now I'm free to carry on. And that's why it's just like a weight lifted off my shoulders. I feel very light, light-hearted, light in thought, that I made it."

What would Rob do if he could face Jimmy one more time? On the day of Jimmy's memorial service, it's not something Rob dwelled on.

"Besides fighting back the desire to punch him? No, I never really acted out what I would say to him because I don't know what the fuck I would say to him. He's not forgiven. He's got his day, and that's it. He got what he deserved. And that's what I really wanted to say to him—all the shit he did to me is going to come back on him threefold—and the fact that he's gone, it just proves that."

Rob always believed Jimmy would have his day of judgment—that Jimmy would face conviction for what he did to his little brother. Rob always pictured the judgment coming in a courtroom—certainly not in a slough filled with reeds up to a tall man's neck, with cops all around, guns drawn, and an airplane flying overhead to capture on an infrared camera the delivery of a self-inflicted death sentence.

Late in December 2009, Rob knows I have seen the FLIR footage, and he wants to see it, too. I want to provide that for him, even though I have conflicting emotions about it. If it were my abuser, wouldn't I want to see it? Wouldn't I want the proof? Wouldn't I like to see the life snuffed out of someone who hurt me so horribly? Still, I feel a little like the Grim Reaper, delivering such a dark package to someone whose welfare I care about. And I would never forgive myself if seeing that footage caused Rob harm.

I make a copy of the DVD, and I send it to Rob, making him promise not to watch it alone. What I really want is for him to watch it with me on the phone. If he is upset, I want to be there for him. At the same time, the journalist in me has her own agenda. She wants to hear his reaction as it occurs, not as he remembers it later.

Technical difficulties make it impossible for us to watch it together, and Rob decides he will watch it at work. This does not sound like a good idea to me, but at least he won't be alone. He plans to ask his friend, Ronnie, to watch it with him. In fact, he winds up watching it with Ronnie and a half dozen other airmen in his shop—airmen for whom FLIR video is nothing unique. They are used to seeing this kind of footage, only it's usually produced on a plane making a bombing run and ends with a building blowing up.

"What's this?" various people ask as they walk into the bay where the DVD plays.

"'It's police video of my brother shooting himself,'" Rob tells them, slightly annoyed. "Now shut up!"

This news generates even more questions, forcing Rob to give a quick overview of the story. He has the description reduced to a well rehearsed script by now.

He tells them, "My brother robbed a bank, then ran for five fucking hours, stole a car, and now he's surrounded by cops, and he kills himself."

Hearing about this episode later, it seems to me as if Rob was as mesmerized by the fact he watched his brother's final moments on the same technology he services as he was about witnessing Jimmy's actual death. It is just further closure, he says. No big deal, even anticlimactic, months after the fact.

"It was like, 'Well, that wasn't bad at all.' It's not Hollywood. It's just like 'that's it.' The plane just kept circling around. I could just hear the pilot after he went down saying, 'Subject's down. Cease fire. Subject's down.'"

If anything, there is a celebratory aspect to having witnessed his brother's death.

"It was just satisfying—very empowering. I felt lucky to be the one who survives...like I got to shoot him—almost like having the ultimate revenge without having to commit a crime...That's kind of what Hollywood does. You put yourself in the Terminator's position. You're the eye in the sky, looking down on this whole thing, and it's like justice is served."

I am relieved that Rob sees the experience as positive. I have no way of knowing if this is healthy for him, from a psychological standpoint, but it sure seems to be.

"It was very nice to have that little bit of closure even though it's something so morbid," he tells me, and I understand what he means, even though the FLIR of Jimmy's death amounts to a snuff film. We survivors seem to have some ability, because of our abuse experiences, to disassociate ourselves and view hard realities with clinical detachment. We can't change that about ourselves anymore than we can change our past. It just *is*.

Rob believes Jimmy was probably drunk by the time he pulled the trigger, based on information from the autopsy that Jimmy's blood alcohol level was .04—four days after his death.

"Decisions made on alcohol do not end up good, and that's one of those decisions. You make big, bold decisions when you're drunk," Rob says.

This decision was permanent.

"He was drunk, and he just did it."

The fact Jimmy was forty-two, was a vagabond, and seemingly had no one in his life plays into the decision-making process, Rob says.

"He's just living off of other people's money. He's a homeless person—with cars and money."

We both agree it might be wise to keep the video from Charlene, at least for a while. It is one thing for a brother to watch his abuser blow his brains out; quite another for a mother to watch her son die, the heat from his body making an infrared outline on the ground, until, as the minutes tick by, the glow gradually fades, and you see what it means to watch someone's life drain away.

The aftermath strikes Rob as vividly as it does me—seeing the bright infrared images of the heat-filled police bodies advancing to the spot where Jimmy's form is "ghosting away."

Though this justice is different than Rob always envisioned, "This works, too."

CHAPTER TWENTY-FOUR

Connections

Charlene believes in a lot of things some people might dismiss as "New Age" or "mystical" or "supernatural," and not everyone is comfortable with some of these ideas. I've grown more comfortable with them, because I've seen the beauty in how we found each other. Charlene believes everything happens for a reason, exactly as it was meant to happen, all for the enrichment of our souls.

That I could have desired the chance to tell a story using my particular gifts and background and that such a story could, literally, drop into my backyard, is miracle enough. But there have been so many miracles, so many coincidences, so many instances of serendipitous connection, so much cooperation on the part of almost everyone from whom I've sought information, it almost defies belief.

Each of us, Charlene, Rob, and I, have experienced weird little happenstances since Jimmy's death. For instance, I've always been one to pick up pennies. I've never been able to turn my back on that saying, "See a penny, pick it up, and you'll know you'll have good luck." I pick up coins right side and wrong side; it makes no difference to me. But in the course of writing this book, over a period of roughly eight months, I have picked up *dozens* of pennies, nickels, dimes, and quarters. I know because after a while, I started putting them in a little dish on my kitchen counter. They currently number forty-two. And even as I sit here, having just risen to count them, I have to shake my head. The fact the number forty-two is significant—Jimmy's age at the time of his death—you can say is just an odd coincidence. But things like that have happened over and over. Coins have suddenly popped up out of nowhere with dates that have significance, as have coins of types with which I can reason a relationship.

For instance, the day I am setting out for a trip to North Carolina, in March 2010, to meet Rob's dad, I run across the street from *The Journal* to go get some money from the bank. A snowbank that had accumulated on the curb in front of the office is finally melting. I don't notice anything when I leave to go across the street to the bank, but when I come back, retracing exactly the same steps I took moments earlier, I find three pennies. Judging from their appearance, they have been buried beneath the snow all winter. One is a wheat penny, one Canadian, and one a regular old U.S. penny.

What does it mean? Charlene believes it means whatever I want it to mean, and here's the significance I give the discovery: The wheat penny represented Jim Krimm, who I was about to meet. Wheat pennies are older pennies, and he's an older person. The Canadian penny was me, because I live so close to Canada. And the other penny was Rob, from the United States.

Think I'm crazy? How about this? I am sitting in my farm home, talking to Charlene about some aspect of Jimmy's case. I stare aimlessly, not really focusing on anything in particular, until I get up to say goodbye and hang up the phone. That's when I notice, not three feet from where I have been sitting for two hours, another relatively rare wheat penny—this one dated 1944. Charlene says that one should have been a 1943, her birth year, but in 1943, pennies were made of steel and that would have been a tough one to manufacture "out of thin air."

It's crazy, I know. But you can't top this last example. I am walking through the Divide County Courthouse one day and want to pitch an empty soda can in the trash. I toss my can into the trash, and it makes a "tink" sound—aluminum, connecting through the plastic of the trashcan liner with the metal of the trash can. I don't know what makes me look, but inside that trash can are a dozen bright, shiny pennies! In the bottom of an otherwise empty trash can!

It got to the point where I just chuckled each time I found another coin. Somewhere, someone was getting a huge kick out of this.

I open my cell phone, and a penny drops into my lap. I step out of the car at a gas station to find two pennies on the ground. I remove a stack of papers on my desk at work, and there is a single penny beneath the pile. I could go on and on. You get the idea.

And it's happened to Rob, too. You can say it's just because we're paying more attention, but never, in any eight-month period of my life have I serendipitously "found" forty-two coins in my path. Never. And I didn't even start setting them aside until after the bonanza at the courthouse.

At first, I thought of them as pennies from heaven, and in a way, they are. It's not that I think they're materializing out of thin air, but I have come to believe an event as innocuous as finding a penny in your path can be orchestrated by a force that is bigger than what we can comprehend. For me, that higher power is the one I know as God. Other people may recognize it as some other "spirit" or "guide." The point, for me, has been to recognize that in some way, we are all connected, our lives intersecting in ways both profound and mundane. And sometimes, even in the most mundane of events, like one person dropping a penny and someone else finding it, *the curtain veiling the universe of things unknowable is drawn back to whisper of things we cannot understand.*

As you might imagine, I haven't gone around Crosby sharing with everyone my amazing ability to attract stray coins. I get the fact that, sometimes, a person can get carried away with ascribing too much meaning to some random coincidence.

By early June 2010, I had grown quite accustomed to discovering "connections" and "coincidences" in the process of researching Jimmy's story. The first coincidence I knew of, that the robber was from Michigan, state of my birth, was quickly followed by learning Charlene's maiden name was Crosby—county seat of Divide County, where Jimmy died.

From the very first conversation I had with Rob, it has been as if he is telling me my own story, "killing me softly, with his song," as the old Roberta Flack song goes.

Both of our dads served in the Air Force and were largely absent from our lives. We each discovered gifts; for me it was writing, and for Rob it was playing the drums, as an almost direct response to our abuse. We both married high school sweethearts and saw those relationships disintegrate under the emotional baggage we carried from our childhoods.

Just like Rob, I moved out of the house before my high school graduation and was estranged from my mother for a period. Like him, I almost didn't graduate from high school, in part because I was exhausted from working a full-time job in a restaurant. While he played in the band at high school sporting events, I led cheers at them.

Like Rob, I enlisted in the military right out of high school, but through a series of issues, including the fact I forged my mother's signature on the paperwork (I was only seventeen), I never actually entered the service. And yet, despite our respective fits and starts as young people,

Rob and I basically turned out "okay." We dealt as best we could with the reverberations of abuse, and all the issues that come up in relationships as a result of those traumatic experiences.

We share a similar sense of humor. We are both, basically, loners, never mind that we can talk your ear off in a one-on-one conversation.

We're both Lutheran. I was baptized as a baby, and Rob was confirmed in Julie's church before they were married. Though we both identify ourselves with a traditional Protestant religion, we are both also open to the possibility of some alternative spiritual *something* that flies in the face of traditional dogma.

In yet another strange coincidence, when Rob was in Arizona at the same time I was visiting my mom in May 2010, we laughed over the odds of her mobile home park in Apache Junction being located on the same street as the school he hoped to attend after his retirement, albeit, twenty miles away in Tempe.

After so many months and so many coincidences, I accept them all with a shrug of the shoulders, but also with the feeling I am fulfilling one of the chores Charlene would say I "charted" in my life before I was born.

In the midst of this amazing story, my marriage fell apart. Examining a subject as intense as the sexual abuse of another human being required me to dig deeper into my own past than I'd expected to need to. I'd come into this project thinking I was going to be the teacher, helping a younger victim find closure. Yet somehow, I became the student. I thought I was "done with all that." The truth is, I will never be done.

I like the analogy a counselor once shared with me. She said dealing with abuse is a lifelong process, like peeling an onion. Each time, it will produce tears. Each time I deal with it again, she said, I will peel off another layer. I might never reach the "core," but with each peeling, that onion grows a little smaller, a little less bitter. I might come back to it at various times in my life, she said—like when my children reach the age I was when I was abused or when some other event in my life echoes something from my past.

Shortly after I return from my trip to Arizona, early in June 2010, I uncover a detail about Jimmy Krimm that shakes me to my core and, frankly, creeps the hell out of me.

This book is nearly written. All that remains is to wait out the slow wheels of bureaucratic red tape to obtain the release of as many of Jimmy's public records as possible. Without him here to tell us everywhere he went, all we have are his letters, public records, and news reports to illuminate his path.

The FBI, after promising me in October 2009 that all would be wrapped up in a neat little bow once they concluded their investigation, in March 2010, tell me they will not release the locations of banks they believe Jimmy robbed because the crimes can never be proven in court. Never mind that tack throws a monkey wrench into my research, it also was going to leave a whole bunch of teller-victims twisting in the wind with no closure. I file a Freedom of Information/Privacy Act request, seeking records pertaining to closed cases with Jimmy as a possible suspect. I'm still waiting for more documents, but fortunately, photos from bank surveillance cameras don't lie.

Photos from robbery after robbery match Jimmy's physical description. Identical pieces of clothing are found in his car after his death. That the FBI still refuses to attribute more crimes to him speaks as much to the FBI's desire to shield the public from the true prevalence of serial bank robbery, as to their own impotence in catching a robber as prolific and brazen as Jimmy.

We help the police in Weyburn, Canada, close their 2007 case when I stumble upon a YouTube video with a picture of Jimmy robbing a bank! Charlene provides Inspector Russ Chartrand of the Weyburn Police Service with the positive ID he needs to close his case once and for all. It is satisfying to add "international crime solvers" to our internal list of accomplishments, because that is the only reward involved!

Next, we try to get Jimmy's Canadian prison records but learn Canadian law prevents their release for twenty years.

It meant more sleuthing on my part, on both sides of the border. Notorious as the North Dakota Bureau of Criminal Investigation is about not releasing information, I need to cover all the bases. I am surprised when I contact the BCI in June 2010 and learn, yes, they will now release their files on the Krimm case, because their investigation is over.

The file only ties Jimmy to the Williston robbery and the one in Wahpeton in July 2008, but within that file is a connection that, literally, rocks my world.

I have been examining the files for what must have been a couple of hours before I find it. It is hard looking at the death-scene photos, knowing that Rob and Charlene will insist on seeing those images. I also watch video of the Wahpeton robbery from about seventeen different camera angles before finally settling in to read the investigator's report on the Williston robbery.

These are details I already know inside and out. I have interviewed many of the police officers, as well as the tellers. It is pretty unlikely I am going to find some new piece of information I haven't come across previously, so I am really just scanning the material, looking for something out of place or different than the story I already know so well.

Then, starting at the bottom of page 6 of the report, are the words that take my breath away.

> Upon searching through the decedent's wallet which was taken from the rear jean's pocket of James Krimm's person, S/A (special agent)(REDACTED) discovered four (4) items of identification bearing the name of Raymond Wehrman.

Wehrman? What the hell? W-E-H-R-M-A-N. My last name.
What?
To say I am shocked doesn't begin to cover it.
Jimmy died with my last name *in his wallet*? How was that possible? And how was it possible that no one, not one of the investigators I'd interviewed over the many months previous, had ever brought up the fact, that, "Oh, by the way, that robber you're writing the book about? He had four pieces of identification with your last name on him when he died."
And he'd practically been on his way to my house that night!
I look at the words again and again on the computer screen, still not believing what I am seeing, but there it is, in black and white.
I'd spent whole days reading Jimmy's letters, cataloging them, considering them; I'd spent eight months tracking his robberies, calling newspapers and radio stations, cop shops and courts; I'd spent hours more on the Internet, looking for other robberies committed by a familiar hulking figure. Rob once said I knew more about his brother than he did, and when it came to Jimmy's life after leaving Michigan, I guess I probably did. Of all the names in the world, and Wehrman is not a common one,

how on earth could Jimmy have wound up with my name on his body the night he died?

Just for a reality check, I tell my boss, Steve, about my discovery. Steve is not one to ascribe voodoo meaning to innocuous bits of information, but even he has to admit, this is weird. Beyond the pale. Cue the *Twilight Zone* music.

I feel sick. I have always wondered whether Jimmy could have visited Crosby before his death. Knowing that he roamed the highways aimlessly, how could he resist visiting a town with the same name as his mother's family? And there's still an unsolved bank burglary fifteen miles down the road from Crosby, in Noonan, North Dakota. Even though it doesn't fit Jimmy's usual modus operandi, evidence places him in this part of the state on either side of that crime.

And then there was the Weyburn robbery, sixty miles straight north of my home. I remember hearing about that robbery, in June 2007, and feeling a little vulnerable. A robber fleeing from Weyburn and intent on crossing the border illegally could easily have passed by my place!

We live on a road that has, for years, acted like a superhighway for people wanting to cross the border illegally. Jimmy could have driven right past our mailbox and seen the name "Wehrman." He could have read my name on countless bylines in *The Journal* over the past several years, news junkie that he seemed to be. He could have seen my picture or television advertisements when I ran for office in the summer of 2008. I came in contact with thousands of people during my legislative campaign, knocking on about 2,200 doors in our district. Could I have met him face-to-face?

Any of these are possibilities, however unlikely.

And who the heck is Raymond Wehrman? Is he related to my husband's family? The BCI report said Jimmy obtained the items in a home burglary hundreds of miles from my house, three days before his death.

I am reassured by the fact he broke into someone else's home, and not mine. But the fact he obtained these documents just days before his death spooks me even more. Had he known, somehow, that the Wehrman name was recognized in the Williston area, and it might be useful to claim that identity if pulled over after a robbery?

It didn't bother me at all to carry his ashes home to his mother, but the possibility Jimmy Krimm could have been stalking me or aware of me in any fashion scared the hell out of me. If he could break into one Wehrman household, why not mine?

I think of our unlocked doors while we were away at work and school day after day, year after year. Jimmy could have examined every corner of our home any day of the week. He wouldn't have found much of value, but who knows his mind-set? He'd once broken into a home in Utah and taken shampoo and shaving cream. Who is to say he didn't make a practice of breaking and entering, for whatever odd kicks?

After living with this mystery for several days, I simply have to know more. I call the number for Raymond Wehrman in Sentinel Butte, North Dakota.

Raymond's wife, Jeanne, answers the phone, and I tell her I am a reporter from Crosby, researching a book on the bank robber, James Edward Krimm. I deliberately withhold my name because I don't want to freak her out with the obvious connection. But we talk just a few seconds before she asks me, "Is your last name Wehrman?"

I apologize for not introducing myself earlier. She understands why I didn't.

Jeanne and her husband, Raymond, have been aware of this strange coincidence since shortly after Jimmy's death. A friend had mailed them a copy of *The Journal*'s initial coverage of the bank robber's death, and the first thing they noticed was the name of the reporter—Cecile *Wehrman*. They had remarked on what a coincidence it was but never thought of contacting me. We are no relation.

Jeanne tells me they were away from home on Friday, September 11, 2009, for a doctor's appointment. They'd been preparing for an estate sale because they were retiring from ranching. But no auction sale signs had yet been posted that might point Jimmy to their house or tip him off to the fact there could be any valuable items inside. Nothing about their home, she says, is ostentatious. Plus, she adds, "We live off a main road on a dead end. You cannot go any place from here."

Jeanne feels, somehow, someone Jimmy came in contact with had to have some knowledge of their upcoming sale. And she has the feeling, unexplainable, that a woman may have helped him with the robbery.

"He only took the good jewelry," she says, including pieces of Black Hills gold and some highly identifiable heirlooms, including a hand-carved rose quartz bracelet and earring set. He found the various identification cards in an old wallet of Raymond's, and they would have been of no use to him since Raymond is sixty-seven and dark haired.

But of all the things he took, Jeanne laughs, the thing that makes her the maddest is that he turned back their bedspread and took a matching pillowcase, ruining the set.

After Jimmy's death, police told the Wehrmans they found Raymond's identification, along with a pawn ticket from Fargo, dated the day after their robbery, but none of the items he took from their house. Nor did police find any of the Wehrmans' property in a storage unit that held one of Jimmy's cars in Valley City.

The Wehrmans were thankful, at least, to know the man who burglarized their home would not be coming back.

"The good news was they found the guy who robbed us. The bad news was they never found any of our stuff," Jeanne says.

Jeanne is intrigued to learn more about Jimmy's background and gain a little more closure after such a violation.

"I really had a hard time sleeping in the bedroom that night, just thinking someone had been in my house," she says.

I can sympathize. The idea that Jimmy could have rifled through my jewelry box or laid a hand on my pillowcase chills me to the bone. But I feel a little better having talked to Jeanne. Maybe it is just a weird coincidence, after all.

I call Rob to relay Jeanne's story. He still can't believe it, either. There just seemed no end to the strange connections we were discovering, but this one, to me, seems almost sinister. It doesn't help when someone close to me uses the term "the devil's handiwork" to describe it. I don't actually believe that, but still, it is creepy.

I get off the phone with Rob, having sat in a parking lot at a mall talking with him for about an hour.

I leave my car and take about six steps across the parking lot before a wave of vertigo sweeps over me. The next thing I know, I am lying on the pavement with concerned onlookers insisting I go to the emergency room. Nothing like this has ever happened to me before. This thing about my name being on Jimmy's body has literally knocked me off my feet!

At the emergency room, the doctor ascribes the episode to panic. Gee, you think?

I spend several more anxiety-filled days before I grow tired of feeling victimized by Jimmy Krimm. I put behind me any crazy notions about Jimmy having some intent to harm me or know me or to deliberately connect himself to me or my family in any way.

Instead, I decide to see my name on his person as confirmation I am the one meant to tell his story. I don't understand how this is possible, but I accept that it is so.

Knowing that Rob and Charlene have nothing to gain from holding their lives up to scrutiny, not all of which will be kind, I have plowed forward from the beginning, sure in the belief we are all on the path we are meant to explore. And Jimmy led us to it.

I have such mixed feelings toward him: fear, anger, disgust, amusement, curiosity, sadness—and at the end, gratitude, for all the ways learning his story has enriched my life.

Somehow, being exposed to his story has allowed me to approach true forgiveness. The very idea that an abuser is hurting himself as much, if not more, than he is hurting his victim is one I am not sure I could have learned any other way. It's a lot to chew on and swallow. Little bites are required.

It still all comes down to wrong choices, yet, in addition to the gratitude, I feel that Jimmy's life and death has brought me so far in my own journey toward wholeness, I also feel pity. I can pity Jimmy. I can pity my stepdad. The hell that must have been inside of their hearts and minds because of how they hurt others is staggering to me. Maybe I am giving them more credit than they deserve—maybe they were so immersed in their sickness they had no conscience, no remorse, no concern, but I can pity that, too. What a shame for any human to be so lost.

I can't help thinking, *There but for the grace of God go I.*

On August 14, 2010, Jimmy's "green monster" is auctioned at a county surplus sale. As I approach the car, some of the same sheriff's deputies involved in the chase the night he died are trying to jump-start the battery to prove the engine still runs. The car is basically trashed. The bumper hangs askew on the front passenger side. Trooper Kessner's bullet has torn a path through the trunk, through the back seat, and through the passenger seat, leaving a nick just above the glove compartment. Police never did find the slug.

As the engine of the car turns over, music begins blaring from the car stereo.

"What was he listening to?" someone hollers out.

That is a question I most definitely would like answered, so I hustle over to Divide County Deputy Brent Gunderson to find out. Instead of answering the question, he pushes eject and hands me the CD out of the car's player.

I expect to see an artist like Alan Jackson or Montgomery Gentry, but the CD Gunderson hands me is Ozzy Osbourne's *Black Rain*.

A smile spreads over my face, as I think of two young brothers in Michigan, sharing a rare moment of camaraderie, listening to an Ozzy album their mom bought them.

Gunderson walks away, leaving me with the CD and a chance to survey the detritus left behind in a bank robber's getaway car. A sheet of medicated corn treatment discs lies on the back seat on one side; on the other, an armful of firewood. Three empty cans of Diet Mountain Dew have exploded on the floor of the back seat while the car sat all winter in the county shop yard.

Opening the front door again, to get a picture of the bullet hole, I find a penny lying in the middle of the passenger side floor. I pick it up. That one is Rob's, I decide. I look across the middle console, and there is another one! I pick that penny up, too. That one is mine. Last, I spy a third penny, on the floor of the driver's side. This penny is Jimmy's. I will give it to Charlene.

Rob points out something I haven't considered, when I tell him how I helped myself to the coins out of Jimmy's car.

"People think pennies have no value," he says, but real copper pennies, the older ones, are actually worth more than their face value today. Even these common pennies are worth their weight in gold to me!

People keep asking me if I am going to bid on the car. It is tempting. I know how Jimmy loved that car, but as the deputies put it, the car "has issues." I know from Jimmy's own letters what some of those issues are. Besides carrying a bullet hole, it has a bad transmission. If I did buy it, I'd have to do the same thing Jimmy did with his extra cars—rent a storage unit for it.

It sold for $75 to a dealer who planned to salvage it for scrap and parts.

I have no illusions about what kind of man Jimmy Krimm was. He was an abuser, a criminal, and a drunk. It is not my place to forgive him for what he did to Rob. I could not blame Rob if he never found the ability to forgive his brother. The likelihood that Jimmy was victimized at some point too does nothing to diminish the hurt he inflicted on others. I have no doubt that in life, if we had crossed paths, there is a real possibility he would have found a way to victimize me, too.

But with his death, I can be amazed by how many good things Jimmy set in motion. Charlene shared with me in our very first phone conversation her belief that sometimes, people are put on this earth to teach us lessons we need to learn. Jimmy has taught me so many, and by extension, through contact with Rob and Charlene, through finally recognizing the ways abuse was still impacting my own life, I have literally been set free.

I look at Jimmy's mug shot today, and I can still see that unmistakable *something* that clued me in to the notion his story was about abuse. I can still see my stepfather in Jimmy's visage. But now that I have realized some larger purpose to having been abused, I don't have to feel bad about it anymore.

By sharing a story in which the choices of two men led to such different outcomes, I get to help other survivors consider their own choices. I get to help people see that while there may never be an end to the survivor's tunnel, there is light in that tunnel. You just have to choose it.

If you make the right choices—if you face what happened to you and work through it—you break the chain of abuse. Living well, rising above it, keeping yourself open and vulnerable to love no matter how you've been hurt in the past, this is the way to healing.

I am not that little abused girl anymore. But I am so proud of what she's overcome. And I like the woman she turned out to be.

Though it no longer causes me panic, I still consider it beyond strange that Jimmy easily could have wound up at my house the night he died. If he did know the way to Skjermo Lake and if he did know a prairie trail north of there led straight into Canada, his contact with North Dakota Highway Patrolman Chris Pulver prevented him from making the turn that would have taken him right past my house.

Pulver was already behind Jimmy's stolen pickup when he rolled past the turn, and it was less than a half mile from my mother-in-law's place that Jimmy turned off-road again, to his final destination, though not his final resting place.

CHAPTER TWENTY-FIVE

Ashes to Ashes

Charlene believes Jimmy would want his story told. She bases that belief as much on the son she knew as on an incident which occurred at the first church service she attended following his death.

A developmentally disabled man came up to her and said, "Your son is here, and he's watching over you."

Charlene acknowledged what he said, and the man walked away.

"And it wasn't but another minute, he came back and he said, 'Your son is here, and he wants me to tell you that he's glad you're telling his story.'"

The incident goes hand in hand with Charlene's whole belief system, that whatever we experience, we experience for God.

"Whatever happens to us and however we experience it, our soul is growing and we're continually trying to improve and perfect our soul or trying to be better and better. And when we come into life, we plan with God, all the angels...we plan our whole life."

In some cases, failure, tragedy, and even abuse are part of the plan, as a means of allowing other people to fulfill lessons they have chosen to deal with, before their lives began. That's a difficult notion for any abuse survivor or crime victim to swallow. Why would anyone choose to be hurt? But once you consider victimization from this viewpoint, it is empowering. If we chose it, we chose it to learn from it. Abuse becomes not something someone *inflicted* upon us, but something we *endured* because we wanted to understand the suffering of others. There is nobility in that choice, and sacrifice. Only a strong soul would choose such a difficult path. That's not the weakness of a victim; that's the courage of a conqueror!

If, as children, it was our choice not to tell on our abuser, but to endure the punishment for the lessons it would provide us, we no longer have to feel bad for having remained silent. What if, in telling, we found something even worse than the hell we already knew and were surviving?

It is only in the aftermath, when lessons have to be incorporated, that we face a fork in the road. We either choose to overcome, or we don't. If abuse is a lesson you choose, *not* incorporating those lessons into your life would mean you suffered for nothing. Once you look at it that way, there's no way you aren't going to strive as hard as possible to triumph over it.

Charlene has already seen much good come out of sharing Jimmy's story and her own lessons derived from it.

"People that have talked to me about this have just said, 'Thank you for bringing this up.'"

Charlene carries the lessons she has learned from parenting Jimmy into her job as a lunchroom aide at a local elementary school, hoping, always, to make a difference in some child's life.

She also believes, "There are a lot of parents this will touch," because they have children who are troubled.

Growing up, there was a girl Charlene knew who seemed to have the perfect life, the perfect house. It was the picture of this girl's life Charlene always held up as the example for herself. But since sharing her own tragedy, she came into contact with this old friend and learned her reality is very different than Charlene imagined.

"She has a daughter that she hasn't seen in a long time either. Even the 'perfect' person, even the perfect family, is going to have something."

Jim Krimm shared a favorite analogy with me—one that Rob has heard him utter in the past and one he also wrote down in a letter to Jimmy.

"Every pancake has two sides," is how Jim puts it.

It can be burned on one side and perfectly cooked on the other. His point, that no one is all good or all bad, goes hand in hand with his overarching desire that people remember his son wasn't just some "bad guy," but a living, breathing human with hurts and challenges, thoughts and feelings—the same as his victims.

I look at it this way—and I hope his victims will—that in his failure to deal with whatever it was that set him on a path of destruction, Jimmy gave us an opportunity to learn from his darkness and choose light.

Coming home to Michigan for Jimmy's memorial service, Rob was reminded of an earlier trip home, when he'd been in the Marine Corps for about five years. A drill instructor in boot camp told his young soldiers that one day they would realize the benefit of all of the opportunities offered in the military because they would go home to their old neighborhoods and see for themselves that life for those people back home had not changed or improved.

For Rob, that day came in a supermarket when he saw the man who inspired him to learn to play drums working at the deli counter. This was the guy who had been such a great drummer a young Harry would stop in the parking lot of an apartment complex just to hear him play.

It was an odd encounter—Rob was seeing someone with obvious talent working a menial job, while his drumming had been the launch pad for a whole career. There, in the grocery store, the stoner drummer and the Marine Corps drummer recognized each other and exchanged greetings. Rob learned his former drumming idol was still trying to make a career in music and was doing some gigs with a local country band.

If not for getting out of Taylor and joining the military, Rob imagines he might never have moved beyond working at the local pizzeria. Instead of playing Carnegie Hall with the Marine Corps Band, he might still be living at home with his mother, having never had the resources to get out on his own and make a better life. He might never have seen so much of the world, from duty station to duty station, across the United States, to Korea and England and back to the States again.

He might never have been exposed to the counseling and medications that changed his life.

No one in his youth recognized the challenges he had in school as anything other than a failure to apply himself. If they saw him sleeping in class, they thought he was being lazy.

"They didn't realize what a drain it was to sit there and read a paragraph," Rob says.

Given Jimmy's challenges in school—he dropped out as a senior, but with the credits of a freshmen—it is quite possible he, too, had ADD. And as Rob knows, just because someone doesn't do well in school doesn't mean they lack intelligence, ideas, or words.

"They've been in here the whole time," Rob says. He just couldn't get the words out. And neither could Jimmy.

Yet, he tried—in a couple hundred letters to his mother and in his letters to his dad in the last year of his life. They show a yearning to be understood by the two people who brought him into life. His written words show some growth over time, but the anger and addictions remain.

A new environment allowed Rob to grow beyond who he was in Taylor, but for all the miles Jimmy roamed, he never really left. He was still the punk who abused his brother, and no matter how far he ran, he couldn't escape that.

There was a time when Rob wanted no one to know about what happened to him. Having a number of people in his life who have reacted warmly and compassionately to his story shows him many of the assumptions he carried as a victim were false.

"Before I told anybody, I just thought people were going to be disgusted at me—that I was a part of something like that...I was worried about how people were going to look at me. It turns out they just wanted to get me help and get me steered in the right direction. It got easier to tell people about this fucked-up situation in my life. I've been able to just, you know, talk about it and talk about it...I try to delete the memories and disassociate from them, but it's not a big deal to talk about it now."

At the same time, there's no getting around the fact abuse shaped Rob's perception of himself. That perception is still evolving.

"It's made me push my limits." It also made him say things just to get a rise out of people, often to his detriment. One acquaintance describes it as throwing "conversational grenades." He's borne social ostracism at times, as well as formal disciplinary action, as a result of lobbing them. His words and actions, inappropriate though they sometimes are, have been a shield to protect Rob from closer scrutiny.

"It's made me overly shy. It's made me more of a loner...because talking to people, I'm afraid they'll see into me. At an earlier age, it was like even if I talked with them, they would know I was a part of this situation, this gross situation, and I was just afraid to talk to people, to expose myself."

He feared they would know he was different, without him even telling them directly that he'd been abused as a child.

"They would just know," and point, "like, 'There he is.'"

He's tried to overcome that.

Today, Rob doesn't hide the fact he has issues, but he hasn't felt the need, until now, to let everyone know what his issues are.

"I don't tell anybody that I work with or nothing, but they know that I go to the therapist and they know that I'm getting medication and that's as far as they need to know…I've tried to water the thing down to something they can understand, because they have problems in their life, too. Everybody, everybody that I work with—and I think I'm special because I had to overcome all these things? But the fact is about 90 percent of people I work with have had fucked-up situations that they've had to deal with, and I respect that…saying I had a rough childhood and it gave me ADD, and I'm taking meds for it, and it helps; that's about the extent of what I tell people."

Rob has not escaped a false perception of his physical appearance, so common in people who have been sexually abused.

"I guess my abuse made me feel ugly. I've always felt really ugly. That is mainly how I went through life, wondering what would a woman want with me?"

Looking back now that his self-image is more realistic, he realizes how many times he was simply oblivious to any hint of interest on the part of women. How many opportunities did he simply shrug at and walk away? He'll never know.

He's not so hard on himself anymore. He's ready to take a chance on someone again.

One Mother's Day before Jimmy passed away, Rob's present to Charlene was a new front door for her house. That same week, Charlene had Rob's name added to the deed in order to ensure Jimmy couldn't come back after her death and try to fight Rob for her one valuable asset.

"I was somehow afraid that Jimmy would come home, and if something would happen to me, Rob would have to split it with Jimmy…so I went to the deed office."

Changing the deed, Charlene learned, would also streamline the process for Rob to inherit her house someday.

"And I felt that he would have the discretion if he wanted to give his brother something, then that would be up to him, but it would legally be his."

Rob knows how big this gift is. Seated in his mother's living room, he acknowledges that.

"Your house is everything to you," he tells her.

Charlene gets tears in her eyes just thinking of it.

"It's the biggest gift I could ever give you because it's the biggest thing I've ever done in my life," she says.

Rob appreciates the trust his mother has shown in him by making these arrangements.

"She wanted to put my name on it, like, so that way it was mine and hers…but I want to do it the right way and make sure everything is laid out the way we are intending it, and that's what we did," with a real estate attorney to see that it was handled properly.

Charlene just felt so good she had something she could give him.

"And the other point is that he appreciates it."

Appreciating the son she has in Rob helps Charlene deal with the pain of the son she lost. It's almost as if one son got a double dose of bitter and one got a double dose of sweet. Charlene refers to both of her boys, when they were little, as her "sweet baby boy," but only one son, Rob, turned out to be a sweet man. For what else do you call a man who surfs eBay auctions to find his mother the perfect gift?

"She always talked about her grandma's button jar," Rob says, so he embarked on an odyssey to try to recreate the button jar Charlene pined for.

"All she ever wanted was that damn button jar." Rob laughs. He understands the desire for lost things, like the Lionel train set Jimmy hocked. The button jar was Charlene's train set.

"I went on to eBay," and discovered the "freakish" obsession of people who collect buttons.

"I just wanted something that looks like an old jar of buttons—a whole bunch of them," but instead found buttons of every color, shape, and grade. Eventually, he found exactly the type of button jar he'd been looking for.

"I finally bid on one," winning several pounds of buttons in a jar for $17.

Rob enjoyed the hunt for the buttons and enjoyed even more his mother's reaction to receiving them.

"It wasn't something you could just go out and buy at the mall, put the quarter in and pull the lever back," he says, which made it special for both of them.

Over the Fourth of July 2010, Charlene gave Rob another meaningful gift.

After Jimmy's memorial service, she'd kept Jimmy's ashes on the plant stand by her front door. She was not really sure what to do with them, so they sat there for almost nine months. She planned a trip to Virginia to visit her friend, Estella, and Rob planned to meet her there. He asked Charlene if she would bring Jimmy's ashes along. Rob told her he wanted to scatter his brother's ashes on the Blue Ridge Parkway. Charlene realized it was time for her to give the ashes to Rob to do with as he pleased.

"For once in his life…he will have control—total control—over Jimmy. I hope it will bring him further closure," Charlene tells me.

Rob put the ashes in the trunk of his Mustang for the ride home to North Carolina, and that's where the ashes will stay until he makes the trip to a scenic byway he has long wanted to travel. It's the same drive Jimmy said held spiritual significance for him. Now they will make that drive together, in their childhood dream car.

I have a hard time, when Rob tells me his plan, understanding where his compassion comes from. He still hasn't forgiven Jimmy, and he still believes his abuser belongs in hell.

If that's how he really feels, I wonder, why is he giving Jimmy's ashes a respectful send off?

"I'm not doing it for him," he says. "I'm doing it for me."

Such wisdom. Such strength. Such decency. Kindness should never be equated with weakness. Honor is not about rank.

It's no wonder I love Rob.

To some he'll always be the bank robber's brother.

But to me, he's everything his brother couldn't be.

Made in the USA
Charleston, SC
23 April 2011